Corporate and Organizational Identities

"Much food for thought for scholars and practitioners. A new framework about corporate and organizational identities. A collection of articles with new ideas about such diverse subjects as brand management, corporate communication, organizational culture, leadership, and change."

Chris Argyris, James Bryant Conant Professor of Education
and Organizational Behavior at Harvard Business School and
Director at the Monitor Group

"Clients, employees and shareholders need to have a clear understanding of what a firm stands for, what it does and what it tries to achieve. Identity management ought to be high on the modern corporate leader's list of priorities. I find this book highly relevant and very useful in dealing with this multifaceted strategic issue."

Paul Hermelin, CEO, Cap Gemini Ernst & Young

"This book demonstrates the broad reach of organizational identity, both as a theoretical perspective and as a management tool. Moingeon and Soenen have assembled a first rate group of authors, who bring insightful perspectives to bear on difficult conceptual and practical questions. As a bonus, the editors present their own thoughtful and well-reasoned framework. This is an important contribution to an emerging field of study."

David A. Whetten, Jack Wheatley Professor of Organizational Behavior,
Brigham Young University, Former President of the
Academy of Management

"Moingeon and Soenen have successfully addressed the challenge of integrating multiple approaches on identity management. The result is a framework which combines strategy, marketing, communication and organizational theory perspectives. It will have a strong appeal for both researchers and managers."

Bernard Ramanantsoa, Professor and Dean,
HEC School of Management, Paris

Modern organizations are confronted with a series of unprecedented changes such as globalization, as well as the rise of virtual organizations made possible by new communication technologies. A manager's universe is marked by increased complexity and uncertainty; the challenge for organizations and their leaders is to remain coherent whilst dealing with more specific demands from their stakeholders. In such a world, identity plays a critical role, providing both meaning and stability. Managing the multiple identities in organizations is probably the most challenging task that leaders face. This book offers an integrative model – the five-facet framework – that helps managers and scholars addressing these central concerns.

Although the issue of organizational identity has grown in importance in management theory and practice, until now there has been little integration amongst the various disciplines and practices, resulting in conflicting definitions, and very little cumulative research. *Corporate and Organizational Identities* provides a synthesis of insights drawn from leading names in disciplines as diverse as strategic management, organization theory, marketing, and communication, as well as the world of practice. Bertrand Moingeon and Guillaume Soenen have developed an invaluable integrative framework – the five-facet framework – that unites all the contributions, from Europe and the US, into a single conceptual structure.

The book will be an excellent resource for academics and practitioners alike, balancing empirical and theoretical insights, and presenting original case-study research drawn from field research in Europe and the US – from law firms, to public utility companies.

Bertrand Moingeon is Professor of Strategic Management and Associate Dean for Executive Education at HEC School of Management, Paris. He recently co-edited *Organizational Learning and Competitive Advantage*.

Guillaume Soenen is Research Associate at HEC School of Management; he also works as academic adviser at Cap Gemini Ernst and Young Corporate University.

Corporate and Organizational Identities

Integrating strategy, marketing, communication and organizational perspectives

Edited by

Bertrand Moingeon and Guillaume Soenen

London and New York

First published 2002
by Routledge
11 New Fetter Lane, London EC4P 4EE

Simultaneously published in the USA and Canada
by Routledge
29 West 35th Street, New York, NY 10001

Routledge is an imprint of the Taylor & Francis Group

© 2002 Bertrand Moingeon and Guillaume Soenen for selection and
editorial matter; individual contributors for their chapters

Typeset in Garamond by
BOOK NOW Ltd
Printed and bound in Great Britain by
MPG Books Ltd, Bodmin

British Library Cataloguing in Publication Data
A catalogue record for this book is available from the British Library

Library of Congress Cataloging in Publication Data
A catalog record for this book has been requested

ISBN 0–415–28204–7 (hbk)
ISBN 0–415–28205–5 (pbk)

Contents

Figures

Tables

Contributors

Edward Adams is the Howard E. Buhse Professor of Finance and Law at the University of Minnesota Law School. He specializes in commercial, bankruptcy, and corporate law. He has practiced law with Latham & Watkins in Chicago. He was Managing Editor of the *University of Chicago Law Review* and he is a former Associate Dean for Academic Affairs at the UMN Law School. He was honored with the Stanley V. Kinyon Teaching and Counseling Award in 1994 and 1996, and was a co-holder of the Julius E. Davis Chair in Law for 1999–2000.

Stuart Albert is Associate Professor in the Department of Strategic Management and Organization in the Curtis L. Carlson School of Management at the University of Minnesota. He has a Ph.D. in social psychology and has been a visiting professor at MIT. In addition to his interest in hybrid identity organizations, his current research focuses on problems of timing.

Monique Brun is Professor of Marketing at the Institut d'Administration des Entreprise (the Institute for Business Administration) at the University Jean Moulin (Lyon III) in Lyon, France. She is the director of the masters program in services marketing (DESS Marketing des Services). Her research has focused on international marketing and communication, and she has published widely on these topics.

Samia Chreim is Assistant Professor of Business Policy and Strategy at the University of Lethbridge, Canada. She holds a Ph.D. from the École des HEC, Montreal. Her research focuses on organizational identity and identification, and their interface with organizational change. Her work has been published in the *Strategic Management Journal*, *Human Relations*, and the *Academy of Management Best Paper Proceedings*.

Jan-Jelle van Hasselt is partner of Twynstra Gudde management consultants, specialized in project communications and strategic corporate positioning. He studied management sciences and law, and obtained in 2000 a Master's degree in corporate communication. Jan-Jelle has been involved in defining communications strategies for a broad range of projects and organizational changes. He is editor of the magazine *Communicatie* and co-author of various books on corporate communication, the Intranet and project management.

Bernard Kahane is Associate Professor of Strategy and in charge of the biotechnology track at the ISTM (Institut Supérieur de Technologie et Management), France. His research and consultancy works focus on R&D strategies, innovation systems, and research policies. He is dealing mainly with networks, loosely coupled organizations, and systems. He is currently visiting Faculty at the Recanati Center of the Tel Aviv University.

Jean-Noël Kapferer is Professor of Marketing at HEC School of Management, Paris. He holds a Ph.D. from Northwestern University (USA) and is internationally held as one of the best experts in brand management. He is the author of more than one hundred articles and two books on the topic: *Strategic Brand Management* and *Re-inventing the Brand*, both published by Kogan-Page.

Bertrand Moingeon is Professor of Strategic Management and Associate Dean for Executive Education at HEC School of Management, Paris. He holds a Ph.D. in sociology and was Visiting Research Scholar at the Harvard Business School. He has published some forty books and articles on organizational learning, strategic management, organizational identity, knowledge management, and has completed numerous consulting and training missions.

Michael G. Pratt (Ph.D., University of Michigan) is an Associate Professor of Business Administration at the University of Illinois. His research utilizes theories of identity/identification, symbolism, socialization, and sense-making in examining the individual–organizational relationship. He is currently exploring the relationship between identity and technology, especially among distributed groups. His work has recently appeared in the *Administrative Science Quarterly*, *Academy of Management Journal*, and *Academy of Management Review*.

Roland Reitter (Ph.D., Harvard Business School) is Professor of Strategic Management at HEC School of Management, Paris. He wrote the first book on identity in France in 1979, and he has been teaching and directing research on this topic ever since. He has been a scientific adviser for Accenture for many years. He has just published *Stratégie et Esprit de Finesse* (Economica, 2002).

Johan van Rekom is Assistant Professor in Marketing Research at the Department of Marketing Management at the Faculteit Bedrijfskunde, at the Erasmus University in Rotterdam, the Netherlands. His research focuses on organizational identity and on image, both of organizations and of their brands.

Cees B. M. van Riel is Professor of Corporate Communication at the Rotterdam School of Management of the Erasmus University, Rotterdam. He is the author of several books and articles about corporate identity, reputation management, and corporate branding. He is the Editor in Chief of the *Corporate Reputation Review* and Managing Director of the Reputation Institute together with Charles Fombrun of the New York University.

Kevin W. Rock is a Ph.D. candidate at the University of Illinois. His research uses theories of socialization, group behavior, identity, and identification to examine how individuals come to define themselves in terms of their professions, organizations, and organizational teams. He is currently studying these issues specifically among dispersed employees and within virtual teams.

Guillaume Soenen is Research Associate at HEC School of Management in Paris, France, where he teaches strategy implementation and the management of change. He works as academic adviser at Cap Gemini Ernst and Young Corporate University. His current research focuses on corporate and organizational identity, as well as knowledge management. He has published notably in the *European Journal of Marketing*, and he is actively involved in executive development.

Foreword

What makes great organizations "tick"? Why do some organizations enjoy enduring success while others stumble and fail? For years managers and researchers have struggled to find recipes for combining human and organizational ingredients to produce efficiency, productivity, profitability, and morale. The result has been a wide-ranging mix of theoretical frameworks at both the micro and macro levels, each of which points to those distinctive features of organizations without which performance could not result.

At the micro level, the stress is invariably put on the systemic interaction between the *structural* features of an organization and its *socio-cultural* features. Favorable outcomes result when managers create structures that induce employees to attach themselves to the organization. Strong attachments produce identification and commitment, stimulate creativity and productivity, and so contribute heavily to organizational performance.

At the macro level, the emphasis is generally placed on the *strategic positioning* of the organization in an *institutional field*. Favorable outcomes result when managers convince resourceholders such as consumers and investors to buy their products and invest in their shares. Strong endorsements by these stakeholders (and by powerful intermediaries like media journalists and financial analysts) enhance the organization's future prospects.

Both sets of theories clearly share a common interest in claiming that individual *perceptions and interpretations* are central to explaining patterns of organizational performance. Strategically, they justify managers' search for ways to strengthen employee identification with the company. They also legitimate managers' efforts to project attractive features of their organizations to external groups in order to generate favorable appraisals of their prospects.

In their 1996 best-selling book, *Built to Last*, authors Jim Collins and Jerry Porras demonstrated the importance of such perceptions and interpretations in their comparative study of some long-lived companies. They showed how IBM, Xerox, Kodak, and others succeeded in building enduring businesses where arch-rivals had failed because they were able to develop strong ideologies over the years that (1) were deeply embedded in their corporate cultures and (2) became widely regarded on the outside.

How insiders view the organization they work for is vital to understanding their behavior and attachments. In turn, how outsiders see the organization is vital in explaining the resources it can acquire. In both cases, the far-flung organizational literature urges us to examine closely how organizational identities are first produced and then reproduced from the interactions between companies and their stakeholders.

It is to this vibrant literature that the contributors to this volume add their diverse points of view. The editors employ an integrative model of "organizational identity" that recognizes its cognitive, social, functional, and strategic components to frame the book. They remind us that identity is about *cognitions* – it resides in the minds of individuals who participate in and around an organization. Identity is also *social* – it is through interactions with others that identity is manifested. Identity is more or less *functional* – it helps organize the sense-making experiences of individuals. Identity therefore has a *strategic* dimension – it is partly shaped by and reflected in managerial efforts to create shared meanings for employees and other stakeholders.

My own work with organizations has taught me how central a construct organization identity is in organizational life. Top managers routinely struggle to project their interpretations of the company on to employees, investors, and customers. They do it personally and symbolically, through speeches, press releases, conference calls with analysts, annual statements, advertisements, donations, and sponsorships. At the same time, employees, stakeholders, analysts, and journalists interpret managers' projections, from which they develop a more or less shared understanding of the company, and differing levels of attachment and motivation.

Nowhere is this more visible than in crisis situations. Take energy giant Royal Dutch Shell, one of the world's largest companies. In 1995, the company experienced significant social disruption due, on the one hand, to the contested disposal of an oil platform in the North Sea (the "Brent Spar"), and on the other, to its perceived role in supporting an illegitimate military regime in Nigeria. The result was a media frenzy that fuelled a public backlash against Shell's operations and reduced the company's market value. It also significantly damaged employees' sense of self, their pride in working for Shell, and the company's "reason for being." The considerable brouhaha generated would serve to catalyse widespread discussions about Shell's identity, both inside and outside the Group. Externally, Shell created roundtables of prominent opinion leaders from around the world to discuss the role a company such as Shell should play when it interfaces with governments, particularly in developing nations. Internally, employee focus groups were brought together throughout Shell to discuss identity issues: "Who are we?," "Why do we work for Shell?," "What does Shell stand for?"

The results were pervasive: a revised set of "Business Principles" was issued; a leadership training institute was created; dialogue with nongovernmental groups like Greenpeace was instituted; internal closed-circuit broadcasts were started ("Shell TV"). These changes were designed to shape a new identity for

Shell employees – a new way of thinking and communicating inside the company. Time will tell whether employees come to experience the company differently and so to act in new, identity-consistent ways.

Shell is not alone in these efforts. Leading companies today increasingly recognize that their reputations rest on the bedrock of their identity. To be well-regarded, they have to be distinctive, consistent, and authentic. This is precisely what the Reputation Institute that I direct is devoted to understanding. The contributors to this volume help us considerably by shedding much needed light on how organizational identities develop and how they are reflected and refracted both internally and externally. Read on.

Charles J. Fombrun
Professor of Management, Stern School (NYU)
Executive Director, The Reputation Institute
New York
April 2002

Acknowledgments

The editors would like to thank Cap Gemini Ernst and Young and the Research Division of the HEC School of Management, Paris, for their support in this research.

Introduction

Bertrand Moingeon and Guillaume Soenen

Modern organizations are confronted with a series of unprecedented changes, such as largescale mergers and acquisitions, globalization, as well as the rise of virtual organizations made possible by new communication technologies. Accordingly, a manager's universe is marked by increased complexity and uncertainty. The challenge for organizations and their leaders today is to remain coherent while dealing with the increasingly specific demands of its many different stakeholders. In such a world, identity plays a critical role because it provides meaning, stability, and distinctiveness. "Who are we?" is one of the most critical questions organizations and their executives need to address. Answering the identity question will bear on the positioning of the company, its structure, its culture, its communication strategy, and its human resource policies. In fact, it will inform much of what the company does. Executives are not, however, the only ones concerned with providing an answer: employees, clients, and various external audiences also have vested interests and will make certain that their voices are also heard. As a result, firms have multiple identities, and these identities have multiple facets. If well managed, they may be a source of competitive advantage, but left unattended, they may become liabilities.

Traditionally, there has been a division between a marketing and an organizational approach to identity management, that is, between an external and an internal focus. This dichotomy is no longer sustainable as organizational boundaries wane, and networks come to be the dominant organizational form. More and more, practitioners and researchers call for the integration of these two traditions and the inclusion of other disciplinary insights, notably those drawn from strategic management and communication research. This is because in practice, identity issues are transversal and concern many disciplines. In fact, identity issues will appear in managers' agendas across functions and across levels. Let us take a few examples. For instance, when a human resources director needs to fashion new management policies to help his organization achieve its strategic objectives, he must choose the right mix of financial and symbolic rewards to include in the incentive system. He must also set up a series of procedures for employee evaluations. Should he, for example, adopt a system that favors individual compensation or should he adopt instead a system with collective bonuses? There is no one best way, and the incentive system must be designed to take into account the organization's identity. For instance, the company may have historically been operating as an up-or-out system with fast-track careers and high employee turnover, or conversely, it may have been characterized by a system of internal promotions and low turnover. Confronted with such an identity diagnostic, the human resource director faces a choice: either choose a system that supports the current identity, or on the contrary, deliberately opt for a different system that will help the identity evolve. The choice depends on whether or not the existing identity supports the organization's strategic intent. Similarly, albeit different in appearance, when a communications director wants to integrate all her organization's communication activities under a common umbrella in order to strengthen their impact, she too must confront identity issues. Indeed, what should be the common "theme" in all the organization's manifestations? Should the corporate brand's identity be aligned with the organization's internal identity, or should it be different, more future oriented, in order to create a favorable perception of the organization in its markets? What importance should be accorded the identity that key stakeholders attribute to the organization? A third example concerns the case of a general manager initiating change programs. What are the change strategies most likely to be successful and are there certain types of change programs that are easier to implement than others, all things being equal? These managers too are confronted with identity issues. They must understand how employees experience their organization – what the organization represents for them – in order to foresee what is likely to be accepted, and on the other hand, what organizational features, if altered, will lead to an identity crisis triggering resistance to change. These three examples make it clear that identity is a strategic issue for organizations and, furthermore, that it is a multifaceted issue. This calls for an integrative approach.

The objective of this book is to provide such an approach. It offers a synthesis of insights drawn from disciplines as diverse as strategic management, organization theory, marketing and communication, as well as from the world of practice (corporate identity, brand management, etc.). To facilitate its diffusion, this synthesis is presented in the form of an integrative framework: the five-facet model of collective identities. Fourteen scholars from Europe, the US, and Canada have contributed to nine chapters that explore various aspects of collective identities using the five-facet model. The book covers the following topics:

- the five facets of organizational identities and how they form a dynamic system,
- how organizations can sustain hybrid identities (using the example of law firms),
- the challenge of employee identification within virtual organizations,
- strategies for managing identity dissonance (showing how this was achieved in one of Canada's "big six" banks),

- the power of narratives in building and sustaining collective identities and the central role a leader's personal promise and commitment plays in this process,
- the strategies and processes used for building a new identity at France Telecom,
- change strategies for identity management and how research findings can be transformed into practical actions (based on several real-life examples), and
- provocative ideas for building and managing corporate brands and their links with organizational identity.

The five-facet framework articulated in Chapter 1, and the subsequent illustrations in the other chapters, provide an integrative perspective. The book will be useful both for academics and for thoughtful practitioners. It includes a balance of theoretical and empirical chapters, and presents original empirical data drawn from research in a variety of settings as well as insights drawn from practice.

Content

The book contains three parts that deal, respectively, with (Part I) the dynamics of identities, (Part II) identities in action, and (Part III) managing identities. In Part I, the first chapter by Soenen and Moingeon articulates the five-facet model of collective identities, which serves as an anchor point and common thread for the rest of the book. Then, in Chapter 2, Albert and Adams apply the five-facet framework to the case of law firms. They illustrate the dynamic relationships that exist among the various identity facets in organizations with hybrid identities. In Chapter 3, Rock and Pratt focus on the dynamics of identification when employees are dispersed.

In the first chapter, "The five facets of collective identities: integrating corporate and organizational identity", Guillaume Soenen and Bertrand Moingeon introduce an integrative model that distinguishes five facets of collective identities:

- The *professed* identity refers to what a group or an organization professes about itself. It is the answer, the statement(s) or the claim(s) that organizational members use to define their (collective) identity.
- The *projected* identity refers to the elements an organization uses, in more or less controlled ways, to present itself to specific audiences. It notably consists of communications, behaviors and symbols. The key distinction between the *professed* and the *projected* identity is that the latter is mediated.
- The *experienced* identity refers to what organizational members experience, more or less consciously, with regard to their organization. It consists of members' collective representation of their organization.
- The *manifested* identity refers to a specific set of more or less tightly

coupled elements that have characterized the organization over a period of time. It may be conceived as an organization's "historical" identity.

- The *attributed* identity refers to the attributes that are ascribed to the organization by its various audiences. It differs from the *experienced* identity, which is self-attributed.

The five-facet model offers an analytical language for the study of identity phenomena and organizations, and it serves as a backbone for the rest of the book. The five identity facets form a dynamic system subject to both centripetal and centrifugal forces, in relation with both the wider environment and other organizational sub-systems. In this first chapter, prior studies are revisited to highlight some of these dynamics. In the subsequent chapters, authors from diverse academic horizons further explore the facets of organizational identities and their interactions. Some contributions focus on a single facet, while others deal with several and their relationships to each other.

In Chapter 2, "The hybrid identity of law firms," Stuart Albert and Edward Adams examine organizations with hybrid identities, that is, organizations that embody two or more identities at the same time. Law firms constitute an extreme case of a hybrid, as they contain identities that are perceived internally as inviolate (nothing about each can be compromised), incompatible (conflict is inevitable), and indispensable (no identity can be eliminated): law as a profession versus law as a business. Albert and Adams explore the question of how an organization with such hybrid identities can endure. What are the mechanisms of coherence and balance by which hybrids may sustain themselves? In the case of law firms, the authors show that a key to their sustainability lies in the time it takes to become a partner. In the first six to nine years of their careers, associates are primarily concerned with law as a profession. When they become partners, they become increasingly involved in law as a business. This long transition period allows them to manage the conflict between the two identities. Yet another impact of timing is that the conflicts brought about by the hybrid form are sometimes manifest, sometimes latent, that is, they wax and wane – if they were always present, law firms would probably disintegrate. In addition, structural mechanisms, such as compensation schemes not tied to outcome, help sustain the hybrid form. In conclusion, Albert and Adams show that within each identity facet, there are counterbalancing forces, that is, there are conflicts because the hybrid form generates conflicting demands, but there are mechanisms in place to correct imbalances. In addition, it is not only that each identity facet has counterbalancing forces and mechanisms within it, but the facets, taken as a whole, work together to create and sustain the hybrid form. Hence, this chapter provides a clear illustration of the proposition made in Chapter 1 that organizational identity facets form a dynamic system. Taken together, the facets of identity need not be in alignment. Indeed, as a general rule, law firms are managed as businesses, present themselves as professions, but are experienced internally as hybrids.

In Chapter 3, "Where do we go from here? Predicting identification among dispersed employees," Kevin Rock and Michael Pratt explore the issue of identification among dispersed workforces. In relation to the five-facet framework, identification refers to the process that links individuals to the *experienced* identity, and the authors argue this may be the key that helps connect individual conceptualizations of identity to that of the collective. The chapter begins with the acknowledgement that scholars and practitioners are ever more aware of the need for organizations to manage identification among their members. However, the authors remark that managing this aspect of the individual–organizational relationship has become complicated by the increased use of dispersion – the practice of sending employees out in mobile work arrangements (e.g., telecommuters). Rock and Pratt offer a fine-grained analysis of the interplay between the lack of member co-location and member organizational identification by examining employee dispersion patterns (EDPs) that take into consideration specific aspects of the dispersed worker's social context (e.g., working alone or in a team). They then suggest how organizations can best manage the identification of dispersed workers. Aside from altering dispersion patterns based on employees' degrees of identification, the authors offer three additional strategies to further manage the identification of dispersed workers: (i) target attitudes towards dispersion, (ii) target attitudes towards the organization, and (iii) replace physical co-location with psychological co-location. In conclusion, they discuss the implications of their research on the five-facet framework. Notably, a focus on identification and on the micro–macro bridge allows them to argue that identity in organizations is not only multi-faceted, but also multi-layered. They examine how dispersing individuals may change identity dynamics at the micro-level, and imply that these changes may ultimately reverberate to the macro-level.

The chapters in Part II focus on the relationship between identity and action. The three chapters in this second part report results from empirical research conducted in various countries. In Chapter 4, Chreim recounts the results of a qualitative study that tracked, over a thirteen-year period, the actions taken by a large Canadian bank in response to "identity dissonance." In Chapter 5, van Rekom reports the results of a quantitative study conducted in the Netherlands that explored the links, or absence of links, between how employees experience their organization, the sense they attach to their own actions and the comparisons they draw between their own organization and competitors. Finally, in Chapter 6, Kahane and Reitter consider the interaction between narration, action, and identity, notably in the case of AFM, the French muscular dystrophy association that promoted gene therapy in France.

In Chapter 4, "Reducing dissonance: closing the gap between projected and *attributed* identity," Samia Chreim explores the issue of "identity dissonance." Identity dissonance occurs when different facets of an organization's identity are inconsistent or even conflictual. Chreim posits that identity dissonance creates uncertainty about what the organization is and that organizational leaders make different attempts to reduce this uncertainty since it threatens their legitimacy as leaders. On the other hand, identity dissonance can also be avoided, but such avoidance requires the use of ambiguity in self-presentations (i.e., in the *professed* and *projected* identities). To explore these issues, Chreim details the results of a longitudinal study she conducted at the Royal Bank Financial Group, one of the largest federally-chartered financial institutions in Canada. She traced the evolution of top management's discourse and actions in situations characterized by a gap between the identity externally *attributed* to the bank (in opinion polls) and that *projected* by the bank (particularly in its annual reports). Using her analysis over a 13-year period, the author showed that management actively implemented different strategies to resolve identity dissonance. First, significant actions were taken to change the organization (its *manifested* identity) so that it would correspond to the *projected* identity. As competitors were also involved in parallel change efforts, however, these actions were sometimes, but not always, successful. Second, the *projected* identity was adjusted several times so as to remain consistent with the externally *attributed* identity. Third, some of management's statements of identity (*projected* identity) became immune to external confirmation through the use of abstract terms. To help the reader grasp these three alternative strategies, Chreim provides detailed examples for two identity features:

–   first, the "quality service to customer" theme, which illustrates a gap between the *professed* identity and the *attributed* identity, as well as the successful and unsuccessful attempts made to narrow the gap, and

–   second, the "leader" theme which illustrates the use of ambiguity in statements of identity (*projected* identity) to avoid identity dissonance.

In the conclusion, Chreim discusses abstraction as a flexible discursive resource and the limitations to its use.

In Chapter 5, "Manifestations in behavior versus perceptions of identity: convergence or not?," Johan van Rekom provides an empirical investigation of the relationship between organizational identity and action. From a managerial perspective, identity is thought to be important because it guides organizational members in their behavior and decision making. Identity can provide people with a clear sense of what their organization stands for and where it intends to go. Hence, the question of how identity affects organizational members' cognitions and actions is crucial. In order to explore these ideas empirically, van Rekom explores the degree to which members' actions (part of the *manifested* identity) relate to their perception of their own organization (the *experienced* identity). Do the members' perceptions of their organization correspond to what they believe they are doing? Two contradicting propositions are tested:

–   *Proposition 1*: how people experience their own organization is closely related to the sense they make of what they do.

–   *Proposition 2*: how organizational members experience their organization is closely related to the difference they perceive between their own organization and their peer organization(s).

In the first proposition, one assumes that the *experienced* identity is shaped through sense-making, whereas in the second proposition, it is assumed that the *experienced* identity is shaped through a process van Rekom refers to as "creative comparison." To test these propositions, the author conducted research in a housing corporation in the Netherlands with a combination of research techniques, notably interviews using the "laddering technique," and questionnaires. The research results provide evidence of a strong effect for perceived differences with other organizations on organizational identity and a weak, only partially significant, effect of what people acknowledge to be working on. Also discussed are the many more insights that resulted from the research. This chapter will be of particular interest to researchers as it illustrates how the different facets of identity can be operationalized.

In Chapter 6, "Narractive identity: navigating between 'reality' and 'Fiction'," Bernard Kahane and Roland Reitter explore the reciprocal links between narration, organized action, and identity, drawing on insights from psychoanalytical theory. Organizational members, in their search to escape chaos and ambiguity, and in order to perform collective and coordinated action, must create and exchange narratives. Organizations tell stories (narratives) about themselves. These stories are not fantasies: they are related to past and future organizational actions, to the factors that lie behind these actions, and are their cause and consequence. Since organizational narratives are built by and for action, Kahane and Reitter refer to them as "narractives." Through narractions, then, organizations define themselves, where they stand and what they want to achieve: narraction is central to identity. In terms of the five-facet framework, a narraction consists of a *professed* identity, which is actively *projected* and gradually reinforced or disconfirmed by the evolving *manifested* identity, and is *gradually attributed* to the organization. Through the notion of promise, the authors offer a way to understand how such a discourse about identity is created and how it slowly shapes reality. Keeping the promise appears to be a necessary condition for the *professed* identity to become a reality manifested in the organization's positioning, routines, capabilities, and achievements. In Chapter 2, Rock and Pratt propose that it is through identification processes that the link between identity at the micro and macro levels is established. In this chapter, Kahane and Reitter focus on the role leaders play in this process: the link between identity at the individual and collective level is established when an individual comes to the fore and puts himself at risk by making a personal promise whereby he ties his or her own fate to that of the organization. After reviewing historical examples of similar instances, such as Luther, Gandhi, and Steve Jobs at Apple, the authors report the results of research undertaken within AFM, the French muscular dystrophy association that promoted gene therapy in France.

Part III contains contributions on the management of identities. Brun's (Chapter 7) is a case study of France Télécom's identity change when the company transformed itself from a national monopoly to a multinational firm.

Van Riel and van Hasselt (Chapter 8) articulate four strategies that can be used to implement identity changes, and Kapferer (Chapter 9) explores the link between corporate brand and organizational identities.

In Chapter 7, "Creating a new identity for France Télécom: beyond a visual exercise?," Monique Brun investigates the management of the *projected* identity, especially visual identity. She argues that while firms often consider the implementation of a visual identity to be a mere graphic exercise, it is in fact linked to more strategic issues. She illustrates her argument through the case of France Télécom. The change in France Télécom's *projected* identity (new logo, new visual identity) in 1998 corresponded with a shift in its *manifested* identity: the company evolved from being a state-owned organization operating in the sector of fixed telecommunications to being an international group with markets in mobile communications and the Internet. Brun addresses the dynamics of identity by considering the relationships between the different facets of identity and the role of corporate communication. She shows that in the case of France Télécom, the identity change involved the creation of a new corporate brand and was a turning point for the group's evolution. This chapter contains a rich description of France Télécom's evolution over 30 years, detailing the reasons that motivated the change of identity, how this change was implemented and particularly, the role of the design agency, Landor. In conclusion, Brun reflects on the lessons that can be learned from this example. Notably, the case is illustrative of an aspect of identity management that she terms "the preparation of possible futures." Overall, this chapter dwells on two issues: the strategies for managing identity change and the relationship between organizational identity and corporate brands. These two issues are further developed in the last two chapters.

In Chapter 8, "Conversion of organizational identity research findings into actions," Cees van Riel and Jan-Jelle van Hasselt develop a framework destined to help managers transform research findings into action programs. It is designed to fill the gap between the academic focus on defining and measuring organizational identity and the practical focus of the business world on implementing a desired identity. The authors review some of the techniques, based on external surveys or on internal audits, that make it possible to identify the identity currently *attributed* to an organization by its publics. However, once the results are known, how can a firm *project* the identity it desires so as to change public perception? The authors describe four identity change strategies, each involving a different combination of the following "identity instruments": behavior, communication, and symbol. These strategies vary on two important aspects: first, some focus on rigidly planned change, whereas others focus on open change; second, some focus on planned instruction as a vehicle for group change, while others focus on explorative individual learning as a vehicle for group change. The four symbolically colorcoded strategies are: "Blue-print – project and result," "Green-print – learning," "Yellow-print – power and coalitions," and "White-print – chaos and energy." An identity strategy is based at its core on a "sustainable corporate story" that is a realistic and relevant description of the organization. Stories are useful because they are difficult to imitate and because they simplify the management of consistency in all corporate messages. Notably, they are a source of inspiration for all external and internal communication programs. The authors provide a detailed description of what each identity change strategy entails in practice in terms of behaviors, communications, and symbols. They then report on three short case studies to illustrate how these strategies were put into action within companies (the Dutch government, the Rabobank, and Nuon, an energy company). In conclusion, they discuss the practical consequences of this approach and suggest the types of studies that need to be implemented in the near future to elaborate on their findings. In terms of the five-facet framework, van Riel and van Hasselt's contribution addresses the following issue: how can an organization manage its *projected* identity in order to achieve a desired *attributed* identity? The authors provide an answer grounded in both research and practice. They decompose the *projected* identity into two components: first, the content of the *projected* identity that they propose be summarized in a Sustainable Corporate Story; second, the means actually used to express this identity, that is, various behaviors, communications, and symbols.

In Chapter 9, "Corporate brand and organizational identity," Jean-Noël Kapferer investigates the role of organizational identity in corporate brand management. The modern usage of brand identity no longer merely involves graphics or attractiveness, but rather, refers to a clear definition of what the brand wants to represent. Unlike for product or service brands, for corporate brands, this definition does not have an infinite degree of freedom. It is largely influenced by organizational values, culture, personality and know-how, and there are significant identity transfers between brands and corporations. Identity plays a key role in brand management. This is further reinforced by the fact that in modern competition, authenticity is a success factor: corporations need to promote their own truth, and truth cannot be found in market research, but in the organization's identity, both *experienced* and *manifested*. Kapferer starts by reviewing two conceptual revolutions: first, that from brand image to brand identity, and second, the shift from mere organizations to companies as brands. He then presents a methodology for defining the identity of corporate brands. This method highlights the central role organizational identity plays in brand management. He then develops several examples, notably a comparison between two French car manufacturers, Renault and Citroën. In the case of Renault, he shows how the *manifested* identity strongly influenced the brand identity. Similar identity transfers are also reported in the case of Peugeot. He also shows examples where identity transfers from the brand identity to the organization identity occur. Notably, he stresses that when a new or renewed corporate brand is forged, its identity should infuse everything the organization does and thus, should gradually influence the *experienced* and *manifested* organizational identity. Additional case studies such as Crédit Mutuel or Intermarché are provided to further illustrate the issue of identity transfer. In conclusion, the author argues that a balance should be found between two extreme positions: a corporate brand's identity is not destined to strictly portray the organization's identity – it is destined as much to create as it is to reflect reality. However, it should not be too different from the organization's *projected* identity, for fear that the brand will be perceived as fake and will be unable to deliver its promises.

Part I

The dynamics of identities

1 The five facets of collective identities

Integrating corporate and organizational identity

Guillaume Soenen and Bertrand Moingeon

Introduction

The concern for identity in management is not new. Balmer (1994) traced its origin back to the late 1950s when design consultancies in the US began to emerge. These consultancies aimed at managing companies' corporate identities, which at the time essentially meant logos and visual identification systems. In 1958, in a *Harvard Business Review* article, P. Martineau wrote about the "personality" of retail stores. Within academia, in the field of management, the "parenthood" of the concept of "organizational identity" is generally attributed to S. Albert and D. Whetten. Since the publication of their seminal article in 1985, research on identity and related subjects, such as organizational image and identification, have multiplied. In the past five years, this activity has been even more enthusiastic. In parallel, within business circles, issues relating to identity, such as corporate identity (which now encompasses more than just design), corporate image, reputation management, and corporate branding have come to the fore. Industry surveys have reported that identity now ranks high on business leaders' agendas.

One can distinguish between two historically separate traditions dealing with identity as it relates to organizations: a tradition in marketing, which is concerned with corporate identity, and a tradition in organizational theory, which focuses on organizational identity. The topic has also attracted attention from scholars in strategy (Gray and Smeltzer, 1985; Peteraf and Shanley, 1997; Barney *et al.*, 1998) and in business communication (Cheney, 1991; Rebel, 1997; Christensen and Cheney, 2000). Furthermore, there have been distinct national traditions, which have developed in relative isolation (Moingeon and Ramanantsoa, 1997; Moingeon, 1999). In the 1990s, these various traditions began to interact and slowly cross-fertilization among certain approaches began to occur. As a result, a multidisciplinary approach to identity has emerged (van Riel and Balmer, 1997; Schultz, Hatch, and Larsen, 2000), opening up many new fruitful alleys and greatly enhancing our understanding of collective identities, both *of* and *in* organizations. However, the modern landscape of identity scholarship is complex. Fragmentation and some confusion still prevail, even in the definition of core concepts. There are many good reasons – and a wide consensus exists – for portraying identity as an important concept, both for research and management practice. These include the search for new means of differentiation in markets for products and employees and the need for a coherent strategic direction in rapidly changing environments. They also include the challenges posed by globalization and the associated need for increased pluralism, and those caused by dispersed workforces and modern forms of employment that modify the patterns of employee identification, etc. One common thread connects these wide-ranging issues: the identity question, that is, who are we as an organization? Providing an answer will bear on the company's positioning, its structure, culture, communication strategy, and human resource policies. In fact, it will inform about much of what the company does. Executives are not the only ones concerned with answering the question because employees, clients, and various external audiences also seek to defend their interests and will therefore make certain that their voices are heard. Hence, most firms will have multiple identities. If well managed, they can be a source of competitive advantage, but left unattended, they may become liabilities.

Managing organizations' multiple identities calls for an integrated approach. However, multiple perspectives, competing epistemologies, multiple issues, distinct traditions – all contribute to rendering the task of providing an integrated synthesis difficult. Still, as identity-related issues become more and more tightly coupled, both academics and practitioners are calling for the adoption of a multidisciplinary stance. In this chapter, we offer an integrative framework: the five-facet model. The model is a synthesis of existing research on organizational and corporate identity and related topics. Our goal is to provide a unified analytical language with a reduced set of concepts for the study and management of identity phenomena as they relate to organizations.[1]

The rest of the chapter is structured as follows: in the first section, we briefly review the existing literature and examine previous attempts to establish an integrative approach to identity. We then articulate our own approach, the five-facet framework. We define the five facets of organizations' identities before explaining the theoretical foundations upon which the delineation of the five facets is based. Subsequently, we explore the dynamics of organizations" identities, notably by revisiting previous empirical works.

Identity scholarship

The concept of organizational and corporate identity has been researched by scholars and practitioners for a number of years (Martineau, 1958; Olins, 1978; Larçon and Reitter, 1979, 1984; Albert and Whetten, 1985; Abratt, 1989; Dowling, 1993; Balmer, 1995; van Riel, 1995; Whetten and Godfrey, 1998; Pratt and Foreman, 2000a; Balmer, 2001a). As noted earlier, research on identity originates in several disciplines, notably organizational behavior and organization theory, marketing, communication, and strategic management. However, despite the many contributions made to clarify the understanding of an organization's identity, confusion still prevails as to its exact nature. In their seminal article, Albert and Whetten wrote: "Historically, identity has been treated as a loosely coupled set of ideas, distinctions, puzzles, and concepts that are best considered as a framework or point of view" (1985: 264). Ten years later, in his review of the corporate identity literature, van Riel wrote: "One must, unfortunately, accept that at a conceptual level, there is no ambiguous, generally accepted definition of corporate identity" (1995: 72). Similar conclusions have also been reached in organizational theory literature. For instance, Pratt and Foreman (2000: 142) recently concluded that identity theory suffers from "identity confusion" and that this may potentially limit the growth and development of this perspective.[2]

Let us illustrate the significance of "confusion" with an example. Consider a central question: what is the "identity" of an organization and can it be managed? Some authors view identity as a set of more or less tangible manifestations that are, to varying degrees, controllable (Olins, 1989; van Riel and Balmer, 1997). This is characteristic of many practitioners who write about "corporate identity": they offer a prescriptive definition in which an organization's identity involves all of the enterprise's behavioral manifestations, visual cues, and corporate communications, that is, the "corporate identity mix," as defined by Birkigt and Stadler (1986). Although it is claimed that corporate identity has its roots deep within an organization's "soul" – sometimes referred to as the *corporate personality* (a concept that lacks a clear definition itself) – the emphasis is on the consistent management of all identity manifestations to achieve a distinct and favorable Corporate Image and Reputation (Abratt, 1989; Schmitt, Simonson, and Marcus, 1995). This is why such a perspective can be termed a "manifestation" perspective.

For other authors who tend to use the term "organizational identity," identity is the basis of a descriptive theory of the organization – a theory that, for instance, documents the factors influencing or impeding organizational adaptation (Larçon and Reitter, 1984; Dutton and Dukerich, 1991; Reger *et al.*, 1994). Among those who adopt such an approach, some argue that identity cannot be managed, whereas others claim that it can. For most of them, identity is a collective representation (see for example, Pratt and Foreman, 2000b). This echoes an earlier definition articulated by Dutton and Dukerich (1991). Such an approach can be referred to as a "representation" perspective.

So, is an organization's identity a collective representation or is it a set of manifestations? Things are actually even more complex than this. Reflecting upon multiple approaches to identity scholarship, Gioia (1998) suggested that the functionalist, interpretive, and postmodern perspectives be differentiated. Functionalists assume that identity is a social fact, while interpretivists stress that identity is not a given, but is socially constructed. Postmodernists question the very idea of identity, arguing that it is merely a linguistic manifestation, that is, identity is not only enabled, but also produced, by the use of language. Therefore, at the collective level, identity is at best a fiction, produced by power holders to serve their interests. Of these three perspectives, Gioia noted that the functionalist is the most developed, and he stressed that "entertaining different ways of thinking about identity in fact changes the character of identity itself" (1998: 26). This makes the task of integration difficult, even hazardous.

Previous literature reviews (Kennedy, 1977; Abratt, 1989; Balmer, 1995; van Riel, 1995; van Riel and Balmer, 1997) have notably concluded that (i) identity is complex and strategic in nature, (ii) the field is surrounded by semantic confusion and contradicting definitions, and (iii) there is little cross-disciplinary fertilization (that is, until very recently, there were very few cross-references among distinct research traditions[3]). Unfortunately, considering our objective to build an integrative model, these reviews are of limited help. Kennedy's review (1977) is more concerned with the concept of image than with that of identity. Abratt's (1989) is limited to the communication and marketing literature. On the positive side, it uses conceptual categorization, that is, it is based on the core concepts of corporate personality, corporate identity, and corporate image. This feature is also shared by Balmer's review (1995), which integrates several marketing subfields (e.g. PR, design, strategic marketing) as well as some strategy texts. Balmer does justice to the conceptual richness of the field and has identified up to seven "schools of thought," which fall broadly into two categories: those that focus on questions of strategy, culture, and communication, and those that deal with how design can help bring about change. However, this categorization makes it difficult to integrate the various contributions on identity into a coherent whole. The same can be said of van Riel's review (1995). Balmer and Soenen (1999) have attempted to provide an integrated perspective. Building on Abratt's (1989) work, they have developed the ACID test model. This model, primarily based on empirical research in consultancy practice, distinguishes between four types of identity: Actual, Communicated, Ideal and Desired (for recent development of this model, see Balmer, 2001b). It introduces the important idea that there are multiple identity types, however it lacks clear theoretical and epistemological underpinnings. Hatch and Schultz (2000) have noted that although the multidisciplinary nature of identity and image and reputation research create considerable conceptual confusion, they are also a rich source for theorizing. To solve the trade-off between simplified and overwhelming complexity, Hatch and Schultz adopted the method of relational differences based on Saussurian logic, which involves comparing and contrasting a term to other related terms. Applying this logic, they compared and contrasted identity to two related concepts – organizational image and culture. This approach enabled them to propose a relational definition of identity, which contributes to a better understanding of the concept:

> Identity is formed both from internal and external positions. Who we are cannot be completely separated from the perceptions others have of

us and that we have of others. Multiple images of identity refer to the same organization. Identity is a text that is read in relation to cultural context. Tacit understandings sit alongside overt expressions of identity [and] identity involves the instrumental use of emergent cultural symbols.

(Hatch and Schultz, 2000: 27)

Building on all these works discussed above, we propose an integrated model of organizations' identities.

The five facets of organizations' identities

Identity emanates from someone and is attributed by someone to someone else – in the case of collective identity, the "someone" is a group. The five-facet framework articulated below is based on the premise that fundamentally, collective identity can be thought of as an answer to the question: who is this group? Clearly, this question can be answered by many people, such as group leaders, group members, key audiences or an external researcher studying the group or organization. This question may seem trivial, but when examined carefully, its responses shed light on the fragmentation, the contradictory definitions, and the lack of cross-fertilization that has until now characterized this field of research. Adopting a multistakeholders perspective, one realizes that much previous work on organizational identity and corporate identity does not actually deal with separate realities, but is instead concerned with the multiple facets of a common underlying empirical phenomenon. Contradiction and fragmentation stem from this "common phenomenon"'s possession of at least five distinct facets (Figure 1.1).

> The *professed* identity refers to what a group or an organization professes about itself. It is the answer, the statement(s) or the claim(s) that organizational members use to define their (collective) identity.

> The *projected* identity refers to the elements an organization uses, in more or less controlled ways, to present itself to specific audiences. It notably consists of communications, behaviors, and symbols. The key distinction between the *professed* and the *projected* identity is that the latter is mediated.

> The *experienced* identity refers to what organizational members *experience*, more or less consciously, with regard to their organization. It consists of a collective representation held by members.

> The *manifested* identity refers to a specific set of more or less tightly coupled elements that have characterized the organization over a period of time. It may be conceived as an organization's "historical" identity.

> The *attributed* identity refers to the attributes that are ascribed to the organization by its various audiences. It differs from the experienced identity which is self-attributed.

Figure 1.1 The five facets of collective identities – definitions.

1 *The* professed *identity*

The *professed* identity refers to what a group or an organization professes about itself. It is in the realm of discourse and it constitutes a self-*attributed* identity. It is the answer, the statement(s) or the claim(s) that organizational members use to define their (collective) identity. Such an answer can be provided by group members themselves or can be solicited, for instance by an external researcher examining the organization's identity. Within an organization, every group – and not only senior management – will have a *professed* identity. However, the extent to which this *professed* identity is actually communicated to others – hence, becoming part of the *projected* identity – varies positively with the group's legitimacy, status, and power within the organization. As a statement of identity, the *professed* identity can be future-oriented, programmatic.

This facet of identity evokes Albert and Whetten's original definition of organizational identity as a claim. Indeed, in their 1985 article, Albert and Whetten talked about "identity statements," positing that a statement of organizational identity consists of three claims: "the criterion of claimed central character . . . the criterion of claimed distinctiveness . . . [and] the criterion of claimed temporal continuity" (265). Another proponent of this approach is Glynn, who stated that developing an organization's identity can be construed as a claim-making process about those organizational attributes that are "central, distinctive and enduring" (2000: 286). Often, however, scholars and practitioners alike are concerned about a *professed* identity only when it comes to be projected through various communication means toward specific audiences. We refer to this latter mediated identity as the *projected* identity.

2 *The* projected *identity*

The *projected* identity refers to the elements an organization uses, in more or less controlled ways, to present itself to specific audiences. It notably consists of communications, behaviors, and symbols. This category is broader than that of the *professed* identity: the key distinction between the *professed* and the *projected* identity is that the latter is mediated. The *projected* identity varies according to circumstances (one could talk of a circumstantial identity) and according to audiences (one could talk of a "façade" identity). The *projected* identity can be the direct expression of the *professed* identity. For example, a letter to shareholders printed in an annual report forms part of the *projected* identity and can be regarded as the direct expression of management's *professed* identity. However, other elements of the *projected* identity are rooted in the identity *experienced* by organizational members and in the organization's *manifested* identity.

Most people writing from a marketing background adopt conceptual-izations of identity that fall in this category (Margulies, 1977; Garbett, 1988; Ind, 1997; Wilson, 1997; Melewar, 2000). For example, van Riel and Balmer defined corporate identity as "the way in which an organization's identity is revealed through behavior, communications, as well as through symbolism to internal and external audiences" (1997: 341). German authors Birkigt and Stadler (1986) defined corporate identity in terms of "the planned and operational self-presentation of a company, both internal and external, based on an agreed company philosophy" (cited in van Riel, 1995: 32). Bernstein considered it to be "the outward manifestation of an inner set of beliefs, a company persona" (1984: 58). Christensen and Cheney (2000), who wrote from a semiotic perspective, can also be positioned in this category as they focus on "expression of identity." They emphasized that "the organization and its symbols are coexisting dimensions of the same process of signification" (Christensen and Cheney, 2000: 267). Therefore, the *projected* identity can not be reduced to logos, designs, names, and other malleable signifiers of the organization. Hence, the concept of "visual identity," which falls in this category, is only a subset of *projected* identity. Everything an organization does, consciously or not, tells of its identity.

3 *The* experienced *identity*

The *experienced* identity refers to what organizational members experience, more or less consciously, with regard to their organization. It constitutes a collective representation. This has been conceptualized, for instance, as shared cognitive beliefs, as collective cognitive maps or as collective unconscious structures. It can also be defined as a local form of social representation. The *experienced* identity can be viewed as more or less stable, unique or multiple, monolithic or fragmented, ideographic or holographic. It may, for instance, vary across time and across the roles a group plays.

This conceptualization of identity is frequently adopted by organizations' theorists. For instance, Dutton and Dukerich (1991: 520) defined organizational identity, with reference to Albert and Whetten's 1985 article, as "what organizational members believe to be its central, enduring and distinctive character." Although they refer to Albert and Whetten, they add to their definition the notion that identity is that in which members believe. Recently, there has been renewed debate about whether this is a proper characterization of identity. Still, this view remains prevalent. For example, Pratt and Foreman stated that

> Organizational identity comprises those characteristics of an organization that its members believe are central, distinctive and enduring. That is, organizational identity consists of those attributes that members feel are fundamental to (central) and uniquely descriptive of (distinctive) the organization and that persist within the organization over time (enduring).
>
> (2000b: 20)

Dutton, Dukerich, and Harquail (1994), Reger *et al.* (1994), and Golden-Biddle and Rao (1997) also adopt this perspective. Gioia, Schultz, and Corley wrote: "Essential to most theoretical treatments of organizational identity is a view, specified by Albert and Whetten (1985), defining identity as that which is central, enduring and distinctive about an organization's character" (2000: 63). Yet in what does the "that" reside? In claims made by the organization? In members' collective beliefs? In the various ways an organization becomes known and is experienced by its audiences? Or ultimately, is all this nothing but image, as identity lies in the eye of the beholder? Or, on the contrary, does identity have substance?

4 *The* manifested *identity*

Over time, an organization's identity becomes manifest in its routines, structure, performance level, and market positioning, as well as in symbolic manifestations, such as rites, myths, and taboos, that span the organization's internal and external boundaries. This can be referred to as the *manifested* identity, that is, a specific set of more or less tightly coupled elements that have characterized the organization over a period of time. Thus, it may be conceived as an organization's "historical" identity. It is, for instance, what a researcher interested in organizational growth and inertia would try to (re)construct. If identity is an answer, then for those adopting this conceptualization of identity, the question is: what has been characteristic of this organization in the past? What made it the way it is today?

Many French scholars have adopted a definition of identity that falls in this category. The conceptualization they adopt was first articulated by Larçon and Reitter, by defining identity as a "set of interdependent characteristics of the organization that give it specificity, stability, and coherence" (1979: 43). A similar definition is adopted notably by Moingeon and Ramanantsoa (1995: 253), who added that it is not the characteristics in themselves but their configuration, their pattern, that constitutes the specificity of an organization's identity. Early definitions of identity in marketing can also be positioned in this category, such as Downey's:

> Corporate identity is the sum of all the factors that define and project what an organization is, and where it is going – its unique history, business mix, management style, communication policies and practices, nomenclature, competencies, and market and competitive position.
>
> (1986: 7)

5 *The* attributed *identity*

The final type of identity that must be distinguished is the *attributed* identity. It refers to the attributes that are ascribed to the organization by its various audiences. Each audience, or public, will give a specific answer to the question: who is this group? In addition, a given audience can provide different types of answers, revealing, for instance, the organization's perceived identity (what the organization or group represents concretely for that audience) or its prescribed identity (what the audience would like the organization or group to be).

Attributed identities can be approached from different angles. External audiences' perceptions of an organization have traditionally been referred to as "corporate image." Increasingly, this is being replaced by the term "reputation" (Fombrun, 1996). Gioia, Schultz, and Corley (2000: 67) even proposed to distinguish between "transient impressions," which are relatively short-term, and reputation, which is a more stable and long-term collective judgment. Furthermore, when an organization is primarily known as a corporate brand, then it is also considered to have a "brand image" (Kapferer, 1992; McDonald, de Chernatony, and Harris, 2001). In the five-facet framework, we group these concepts under the *attributed* identity category. The use of one of these terms instead of the other depends on the nature of the attributes ascribed to the organization. If these attributes are transient, one refers to "transient impressions"; if they are more stable, then the term "reputation" is used; and if they apply to the corporate brand, then "brand image" is used. In addition, one could try to further distinguish between identity and image attributes. Whether one can empirically distinguish between the image a third party attributes to an organization and the identity this third party attributes to the organization echoes marketing scholars' preoccupation with using various forms of probing to elicit different types of mental structures from customers. We believe that the extent to which *attributed* identity and image differ depends notably on the proximity between the organization and the third party. The closer I am to an organization, the better I am able to draw a distinction between its public image and its actual identity.

Yet a different approach is to consider the *attributed* identity as it is perceived by organizational members. For instance, Dutton, Dukerich, and Harquail (1994) define organizational identity as an image. They distinguish two type of identities, in fact, two types of images: "The first image, what the member believes is distinctive, central, and enduring about the organization, is defined as perceived organizational identity. The second image, what a member believes outsiders think about the organization is called construed external image" (239). Instead of "construed external image," Smidts, Pruyn, and van Riel prefer the term "perceived external prestige," which "represents how an employee thinks outsiders view his or her organization (and thus him or herself as a member thereof)" (2001: 1052). In the five-facet framework, these concepts fall in the *experienced* identity category since they are self-attributed.

Theoretical foundations underlying the delineation of the five facets

Organizations often have multiple identities (Albert and Whetten, 1985; Pratt and Foreman, 2000b). The five-facet model's contribution is that not only do organizations have multiple identities, but that identities have different facets. In other words, each of an organization's multiple identities has five distinct facets. In this section, we explore some of the theoretical foundations that can help us to better understand the nature of these five facets and their interactions. We also explore how the content of organizations' identities can be characterized and we draw a distinction between identity attributes, identity criteria, and identity determinants.

Distinguishing between professed *and* experienced *identities*

The distinction between *professed* identity and *experienced* identity corresponds to the now classic distinction, first introduced by Argyris and Schön (1974), between "espoused theory" and "theory-in-use," and reused by Schein (1984) as "espoused values" versus "basic assumptions." The *professed* identity can have an impact on behavior, even outside the group which professes it, notably if it is mediated through communication (hence, becoming a *projected* identity). As philosopher Austin (1962) noted almost 40 years ago, speech (discourse) can be performative, by illocution or perlocution. This supports the view that the notion of *professed* identity is close to that of strategic vision and strategic intent (Prahalad and Bettis, 1986). It is overt, official, in the realm of discourse, partly planned and partly emergent. At the individual level, it is used to rationalize actions – it has a retroactive quality as it helps to make sense of the past (cf. Weick, 1995), but it is also programmatic as it helps to project oneself into the future.

The notion of *experienced* identity is close to certain conceptualizations of organizational culture as a set of core beliefs. In fact, identity is always constructed and enacted within a cultural context. Certain cultural artifacts typical of an organization, such as a very informal work environment associated with open-space offices, may very well be at the heart of the organizational identity experienced by its members. If we draw a parallel with the theory of social representation in social psychology (Moscovici, 1976), the *experienced* identity (of a group) can be defined as members' collective representation of the organization. In other words, the *experienced* identity is a "local" form of social representation.[4] Stemming from the group's experiences, this collective representation corresponds to what individuals actually and sincerely believe about their organization. The adjective "local" refers to the existence of a social representation of organizations in society, and an organization's *experienced* identity is a local version of this. Furthermore, one must add that this representation can be partly unconscious. As previously mentioned, identity as a collective representation must be distinguished from the *professed* identity, which is a form of ideological discourse. This distinction is not typically found in standard social psychology research on social representation. Here, it is necessary since an organization is an "orthodox system."[5] This means that the organization, as an object of representation, is also the subject of an ideological discourse destined to shape individuals' and collective representations. An advocate of social representation theory would probably argue that, as such, identity cannot be a social representation, but only an ideological system. However, building on Argyris and Schön's work (1974), we believe that despite the official discourse, groups of individuals within organizations still develop social representations. What the specificity of this orthodox system entails, though, is that the dynamics through which a social representation is elaborated may differ from those characterizing more traditional forms of representation in nonorthodox systems. Like any social representation, the *experienced* identity is only partly constructed locally, as it borrows from existing schemes in the society at large and similar settings. Therefore, what does "distinctive" mean? This is an important issue that has not received much attention thus far in the literature (cf. Sevon (1996) on whether organizational identities are distinctive or whether they are determined via imitation processes). Focusing on *experienced* identity and adopting a conceptualization of identity as a form of social representation would mean that the forces shaping organizations' identities no longer reside solely within the organization itself, but within broader societal fields (DiMaggio and Powell, 1983).

Distinguishing between the projected and the manifested identity

The basis for distinguishing between the *projected* identity and the *manifested* identity is the temporal dimension. This articulation is less classical than the first one (that is, the distinction between *professed* and *experienced* identity). Marketing literature defines corporate identity as a set of projections that must be controlled for strategic ends. As mentioned earlier, we propose to define these sets of identity projections as the *projected* identity. All identity manifestations are not controlled, or even controllable. For instance, institutional communication constitutes part of the *projected* identity that is controlled, while after-sales employee behavior, also part of the *projected* identity, is less easily controllable. One can note that there is a strong tendency in many organizations to regulate these behavioral manifestations – the checklist handed to each McDonald's employees is a famous example. The *manifested* identity, as previously mentioned, includes organizational routines, the organization's structure, its products and services, and cultural artifacts. It also encompasses manifestations outside the organization, such as its market positioning. However, contrary to the *projected* identity, which is defined with respect to a specific moment in time, the *manifested* identity refers to organizational characteristics that have been stable over time. Naturally, the *projected* identity may very well refer to the same historical features that are part of the *manifested* identity, but conceptually, these two identity facets are different.

Additional characteristics of collective identities

The classification of collective identities we have articulated recognizes five conceptually distinct categories. We do not claim that this is the only way possible to classify collective identities. Clearly, there are additional dimensions of collective identities that are not captured in the typology. Let us consider two of them.

First, collective identities can be "current" or "ideal": "Current organizational identity refers to beliefs about the existing character of the organization . . . . In contrast, ideal organizational identity encompasses future-oriented beliefs about what is desirable" (Reger *et al.*, 1994: 574). In fact, the current versus ideal orientation applies to several identity types with varying degrees. As previously mentioned, *professed* and *projected* identities can be future-oriented or ideal (Gioia and Thomas, 1996). According to Reger *et al.* (1994), *experienced* identities can contain elements that are future-oriented, and we believe that such is also the case with *attributed* identities (we have termed this as "prescribed identity"). On the contrary, by definition, *manifested* identities cannot be future-oriented.

Yet another way to characterize collective identities is to consider the dichotomy between "conscious" versus "latent" identities. That is, while some conceptualizations of identity may be consciously held, others may be latent. Pratt and Foreman referred to this as the issue of latency. To the question "where do identities 'reside'?", they suggested

> that identities may reside in groups of individuals, as well as in roles, symbols and other storage places of organizational "memory" (e.g., policies, rules, and procedures). Thus, latent identities may be dormant until organizational issues or other events trigger their awakening.
>
> (2000b: 20)

As with the current versus ideal dichotomy, we believe the issue of latency applies not only to the *experienced* identity, but also to other identity types. For instance, at a given moment in time, *attributed* identities contain elements that are conscious or overt, while others remain in the background, latent.

Characterizing the content of collective identities: attributes, criteria, and determinants

The specification of identity types can be regarded as a preliminary step when doing research on organizations' identities, or even when attempting to manage them. The next task consists in describing the content of identity. This entails a two-step process. The first involves listing all the aspects, features or characteristics (of an organization) that must be considered when establishing an organization's identity: these are the identity attributes. Second, the criteria of inclusion of a given attribute in the identity definition must be established: these are the identity criteria.

Defining a list of an organization's characteristics or features that can potentially be constitutive of its identity – the identity attributes – depends on the facet of identity one considers. For the *experienced* identity, it is relatively straightforward: it is the perceptions of organizational members. There is actually no need to further specify the list of acceptable identity features. For the *manifested* identity, it is more complicated: on which elements should a researcher focus? The organization's structure, its product range, its routines, the composition of its Board? The list is practically endless. Mucchielli (1999) proposed a list of possible identity features based on broad categories:

- Ecological referents: characteristics of the eco-system.
- Physical referents: possessions, potentialities, physical appearance.
- Historical referents: origins, key events, historical legacy (such as rites and rituals).
- Cultural referents: cultural system (ideology, values, modes of expression), cognitive system, mentality.
- Social-psychological referents: social references (status, age), affiliations.

For an organization's identity, such a list might include nationality, core competencies, key activities, zone of operation, structure, degree of unionization, strategic alliances, governance form, type of growth, visual identity, reputation, leadership style, corporate culture, etc. The composition of the list varies from one academic discipline to the other. Marketing scholars tend to put the emphasis on identity attributes that can be perceived by external audiences, whereas organization theorists privilege attributes derived from psychological identity theory. Finally, strategists, notably in France, favor attributes that allow them to define organizational identity from the perspective of organizational actors' experiences (e.g., leadership, governance structure, professional qualities required for climbing the corporate ladder). Yet one may question the use of such lists, and instead, argue that the relevant features are better derived qualitatively in each specific research context.

Once the list of identity attributes is defined, the second step consists of clarifying the criteria for the inclusion of a feature in the identity definition. Albert and Whetten (1985) argued that to be part of the organization's identity, an organizational feature must be core, enduring, and distinctive. Larçon and Reitter (1979, 1984) had proposed a similar definition. While this characterization of identity has been long accepted, it has recently come under scrutiny (Gioa, Schultz, and Corley, 2000). As previously noted, it is likely that identity criteria are specific to each identity facet.

Finally, one must distinguish the list of identity attributes and the identity criteria from the determinants of identity, the factors that shape the construction of collective identities over time. These determinants influence the mechanisms of adaptation (Schein, 1985; Dutton and Dukerich, 1991) and attribution (Asforth and Mael, 1989) through which a collective identity emerges. The confusion between these notions stems from the fact that certain organizational features can be both identity attributes and determinants of identity. For instance, organizational structures can often constitute the distinctive, coherent, and stable element used to define an organization's identity (cf. Larçon and Reitter, 1979) – here structures are an *identity attribute*. In parallel, the structures an organization implements will often be a determining factor in orienting the development of a collective identity. For instance, adopting a virtual structure with dispersed work groups will shape the development of the organization's identities – here, structures are an *identity determinant*.

Organizations' identities as a dynamic system

In this section, we adopt a systemic perspective and develop the idea that the various facets, or types of collective identities, form a dynamic system. This means that the five identity types co-exist and influence each other. Naturally, the identity system, as we may call it, is an open system, in relation with both the external environment at large and other organizational sub-systems. However, in this section, we tend to focus primarily on internal system dynamics. The dynamics of identities vary according to the entity considered: the identities of a large multiunit organization exhibit different dynamics from those of a single group. In what follows, we tend to refer more to large and complex organizations.

System's dynamics

In Figure 1.2, we have indicated a number identity dynamics: solid arrows indicate strong (or automatic) influences, while dashed arrows indicate weak (or potential) influences. For example, the *projected* identity can be an expression of the *professed* identity (1), but it is also influenced by the *experienced* identity (2) and the *manifested* identity (10). The *experienced* identity and the *manifested* identity influence each other mutually (3). The *experienced* identity can also be shaped by the *projected* identity (4). The *attributed* identity is influenced by the *projected* identity (5), but also directly by the *manifested* identity (6), while changes in the *attributed* identity may trigger changes in the *experienced* identity (7). In addition, the *professed* identity and the *experienced* identity may influence each other (8), while over time, the *projected* identity may alter the *manifested* identity (9). We put the *experienced* identity in the center of the model because we posit that it plays a central role in identity dynamics.

Like any system, an organization's identity system is subjected to centrifugal as well as centripetal forces. These forces can originate either from within or outside of the organization. Centrifugal forces refer to events, sequence of events and processes that increase the gap between the facets, and thus, threaten the system's integrity. For instance, changes in competitors' communication strategy and positioning may force an organization to change its *projected* identity. Such an "adaptation" may well occur while the other facets of the organization's identities remain unchanged. On the contrary,

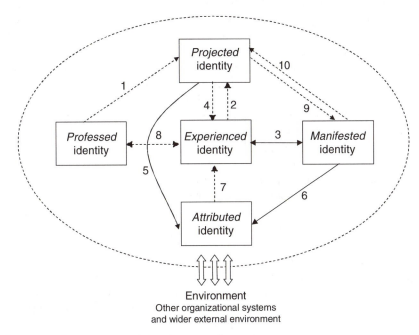

Figure 1.2 The dynamics of the identities of organizations.

centripetal forces refer to events, sequence of events or processes that contribute to maintaining the system's integrity by bringing identity facets into alignment. The "mirror effect" described by Dutton and Dukerich (1991), which we further explore below, is an example of a centripetal force. Empirical evidence for some of these mechanisms is provided in the following paragraphs, but a complete exploration of these dynamics is beyond the scope of this chapter.

Past research reinterpreted

Dutton and Dukerich's study (1991) illustrates several of these dynamics. These authors studied the New York Port Authority, a public organization in charge of transportation within the state of New York. Their study describes the organization's reaction when confronted with a sudden increase in the number of homeless people using the Port Authority's bus terminals and train stations as refuges. This rapid increase led to preoccupations about safety and public health for both commuters and employees. Using an inductive approach, the authors showed that prior to the crisis, the organizational identity (we would call this the *experienced* identity) was mirrored in the press and in the public (what we have called the *attributed* identity). Following the crisis, the image sent back by this metaphorical mirror no longer matched the *experienced* identity (nor did it match with the identity and reputation desired by members, or with that prescribed by the general public for such institutions). Indeed, the press depicted the organization as cold, remote from its users and citizens, solely motivated by profits, indifferent to the community's well-being. This gap created an identity dissonance – a state in which uncertainty about identity prevails (Elsbach and Kramer, 1996) – that generated a quick reaction from the organization (since reducing uncertainty about the definition of the self is a core human motivation (see Hogg and Terry, 2000)). Initially, the Port Authority had considered that the homeless problem fell outside its realm of responsibility and was instead a problem that the New York police force needed to handle. Prior to the crisis, the organization did not include the homeless issue in its "corporate mission," but following the public's and employees' negative reactions, it modified this mission to include the issue. In our framework, we would have interpreted this as a change in both the *professed* and the *projected* identity. Indeed, a change in an organization's corporate mission is indicative of a change in management's *professed* identity. Furthermore, since the change in mission was made public and was widely communicated, it led to a change in the *projected* identity. It was by vigorously affirming what they thought was (and ought to be) their organization's identity (based on their experience of it) that employees brought a change in the *professed* and *projected* identity. Hence, the arrows in Figure 1.2 can be explained in the following manner:

(7) => refers to the impact of a change in the *attributed* identity on the *experienced* identity, then
(8) => refers to the impact of a felt *experienced–attributed* gap on the *professed* identity and,
(2) => refers to the impact of an identity dissonance (a felt *experienced–attributed* gap) on the *projected* identity.

Furthermore, the *manifested* identity was also likely to have been altered since various organizational processes were implemented to facilitate the accomplishment of the new professed objective (9). We can assume that the *experienced* identity was also affected in return (3). Perhaps it simply reverted back to what it was before the crisis, but most likely, the homeless scandal did affect it profoundly, and made salient those features that had hitherto been latent. This example shows the kind of dynamics that a modification in the *attributed* identity can trigger. In their study of French saving banks, Moingeon and Ramanantsoa (1995) reached similar conclusions. This phenomenon has been referred to as the "mirror effect," and it constitutes a good illustration of the dynamics of organizational identity systems.

Gioia and Thomas' study (1996) offers another example. These authors related the strategic change initiated by a US university, and notably, how the desired image "to be among the top ten US universities" was used to fuel a largescale change effort. This desired image, which we would call the *professed* identity (of the top management team), was in this case very much future-oriented. It consisted of the identity that management wished for certain publics to attribute to the organization in the future. It was *systematically projected* toward both internal and external audiences. It functioned simultaneously as a "guiding philosophy" in senior management's decision-making processes and as an "organizing principle" for all communications with the rest of the organization (hence, (1) the arrow between *professed* identity and *projected* identity in Figure 1.2). Among other things, the authors concluded that during strategic change processes, identity and image, and notably the desired future image, are key to the sense-making process. What we retain from this research is that identity changes can be actively managed. Whereas the "mirror effect" described by Dutton and Dukerich (1991) had its origin beyond the scope of management's discretion, here, the identity change was actually initiated by top management.

Reger *et al.* (1994) showed that Total Quality Management programs often fail because the *experienced* identity acts as a cognitive frame that often creates resistance to change. They stress the necessity to generate a sufficiently wide gap between the current perceived situation and the desired future state so that change can be motivated. However, this gap must not be too wide, otherwise it creates paralysis. While the conceptual framework is slightly different (the identity–image dyad), the results are consistent with those on corporate missions and, more generally, on strategic change. This study points to the close connection between the *experienced* identity, the *projected* identity and the *manifested* identity (hence, the corresponding arrows (2), (3), (4), and (9) in Figure 1.2). Reinterpreted within our framework, this study and Gioia and Thomas' (1996) also reveal some of the conditions under which collective discourse can be performative, that is, carry behavioral consequences in itself. This idea of an "optimum gap" between desired and actual identity associated with the notion of performative discourse is probably a fruitful way to frame research on strategic change. It allows researchers to look at an old question through new lenses: under which conditions can a managerial vision rally individuals as opposed to creating only skepticism?

These studies are but three examples: there are many more in the literature. In addition, a large body of knowledge relating to organizational dynamics (which we do not detail here), could be used to enrich, to give "flesh" to, the five-facet framework. For instance, based on existing theory in social psychology and organization theory, it seems logical to posit a strong systemic relationship between *experienced* and *manifested* identity (3). Attempts to change the *manifested* identity cannot succeed if the role of the *experienced* identity is not acknowledged, and vice versa (hence, the two-way arrows (3) between *experienced* and *manifested* in Figure 1.2). How I experience my organization's identity is grounded in my everyday encounters with historically-established structures, routines, and symbols. In parallel, the modifications I am willing to accept to those same structures, routines, and symbols are conditioned by my perceptions of the organization's identity.

These three studies share something in common: all bear on the generative tension between identity as representation versus identity as manifestation. One may ask if these two conceptualizations are not bound to become increasingly blurred. When the boundaries of organizations were clearly delineated, it was easy to distinguish between the identity attributed from within the organization (the *professed* or *experienced* identity) and that attributed from outside the organization (the *attributed* identity or corporate image). Nowadays, these borders can no longer to be taken for granted as more and more organizations become "virtual" and use outsourcing, downscaling, lean manufacturing, and network organizing principles. The universality of the marketing doctrine means that every organization, irrespective of its size, makes systematic use of image and impression management (Pfeffer, 1981; Fombrun, 1996) to position itself strategically. According to Alvesson (1993), the systematic use of image is a detriment to substance. Increasingly, the battle for positioning, for the "share of mind" takes place on symbolic battle-fields, in the realm of imagery. One must sell much more than just a product or a service, but an "experience," if not an adventure. Does this race for "a share of dreams" lead to internal dysfunctions within organizations? Notably, what happens when the identity *projected* externally can no longer be reconciled with the identity *experienced* inside the organization? What are ideal relationships between a corporation's brand identity, *attributed* identity, and *experienced* identity? Is there not a risk that wide gaps add to the cynicism that is increasingly the hallmark of the psychological and legal contract between employers and employees?

Conclusion

In this chapter, we have argued that organizations not only have multiple identities, but that collective identities have multiple facets. By distinguishing five facets of collective identities, we have sought to provide an analytical language for the study of organizations and identity phenomena. Adopting a systemic approach, we propose that organizations' identities be viewed as dynamic and open systems. As such, they are subjected to both centripetal and centrifugal forces originating from the inside as well as from the outside of organizations. In reinterpreting past research within the five-facet framework, we have highlighted some of these dynamics. However, this is but one step in the journey toward a complete process theory of organizations' identities.

Despite its integrative nature, it is likely, however, that all conceptualizations and treatments of identity cannot be reconciled within the five-facet framework (nor probably within any single unified model). Clearly, not all epistemological methods lend themselves to such an approach. We recognize this very important limit. None the less, we believe that the framework has important merits, the first being the continuance of efforts initiated over the past few years in the development of an integrated multidisciplinary approach to identity.

The model has implications for both research and practice. From a research perspective, it particularly draws our attention to the necessity to specify identity types, identity attributes, and identity criteria. From the perspective of practice, it highlights the interdependencies that exist between identity management seen from marketing and human resource perspectives. Moreover, it confirms the strategic importance of identity-related issues for general management and the need for leaders to treat them accordingly.

In the chapters that follow, authors from diverse academic horizons explore further the facets of organizational identities and their dynamics. Some contributions focus on a single facet, while others deal with several facets and their relationships. Together, these works constitute a collective effort in the building of a cumulative knowledge-base on collective identity phenomena.

Notes

1 Besides the contributors to this edited volume – Edward Adams, Stuart Albert, Monique Brun, Samia Chreim, Jan-Jelle van Hasselt, Jean-Noël Kapferer, Bernard Kahane, Michal Pratt, Johan van Rekom, Rolland Reitter, Cees van Riel, Kevin Rock – we are also indebted to Craig Carroll, Dennis Gioia, and Bernard Ramanantsoa. We would also like to thanks Blake Ashforth, John Balmer, David Bromley, Grahame Dowling, Edmund Gray, Margaret Peteraf, Denise Rousseau, Mark Shanley, and David Whetten for their help in discussing our ideas. Certainly, the ideas expressed in this chapter remain the sole responsibility of the authors.
2 Cf. van Rekom (1997) for an illustration of how confusion at the conceptual level is echoed at the measurement/operational level.
3 The special issue of the *European Journal of Marketing on Corporate Identity* (1999, 31 (5/6)) can be regarded as a turning point in the development of the multi-disciplinary approach to identity.
4 A full exploration of this idea is beyond the scope of this chapter.
5 In social representation theory, a system is orthodox if it subject to a structured ideological discourse. Social representation that in fact represents naive knowledge cannot exist in such conditions.

References

Abratt, R. (1989) "A new approach to the corporate image management process," *Journal of Marketing Management*, 5(1): 63–76.
Albert, S. and Whetten, D. A. (1985) "Organizational identity," in L. L. Cummings and B. M. Staw (eds) *Research in organizational behavior, volume 7*, Greenwich, CT: JAI Press, 263–95.
Alvesson, M. (1993) *Cultural perspectives on organizations*, Cambridge: Cambridge University Press.
Argyris, C. and Schön, D. (1974) *Theory in practice*, San Franciso, CA: Jossey-Bass.
Ashforth, B. E. and Mael, F. A. (1996) "Organizational identity and strategy as a context for the individual," in J. A. C. Baum and J. E. Dutton (eds) *Advances in Strategic Management*, vol. 13, Greenwich, CT: JAI Press, 19–64.

Austin, J. L. (1962) *How to do things with words*, Oxford: Oxford University Press.

Balmer, J. M. T. (1994) "The BBC's corporate identity: myth, paradox and reality," *Journal of General Management*, 19(3): 33–47.

Balmer, J. M. T. (1995) "Corporate branding and connoisseurship," *Journal of General Management*, 21(1): 22–46.

Balmer, J. M. T. (2001a) "Corporate identity, corporate branding and corporate marketing – seeing through the fog," *European Journal of Marketing*, 35(3/4): 248–91.

Balmer, J. M. T. (2001b) "From the Pentagon: a new identity framework," *Corporate Reputation Review*, 4(1): 11–22.

Balmer, J. M. T. and Soenen, G. B. (1999) "The ACID test of corporate identity management," *European Journal of Marketing*, 15: 69–92.

Barney, J. *et al.* (1998) "A strategy conversation on the topic of organizational identity," in D. A. Whetten and P. C. Godfrey (eds) *Identity in organizations: building theory through conversations*, Thousand Oaks, CA: Sage, 99–168.

Bernstein, D. (1984) *Company image and reality*, Eastbourne: Reinhart and Winston.

Birkigt, K. and Stadler, M. (1986) *Corporate identity, grundlagen, funktionen und beispielen*, Landsberg an Lech: Verlag, Moderne Industrie.

Cheney, G. (1991) *Rhetoric in an organizational society: managing multiple identities*, Columbia, SC: University of South Carolina Press.

Cheney, G. and Christensen, L. T. (2000) "Identity at issue: linkages between 'internal' and 'external' organizational communication," in F. M. Jablin and L. L. Putnam (eds) *The new handbook of organizational communication: advances in theory, research, and methods*, Thousand Oaks, CA: Sage, 231–69.

Christensen, L. T. and Cheney, G. E. (2000) "Self-absorption and self-seduction in the corporate identity game," in M. Schultz, M. J. Hatch and M. H. Larsen (eds) *The expressive organization*, Oxford: Oxford University Press.

DiMaggio, P. and Powell, W. (1983) "The iron cage revisited: institutional isomorphism and collective rationality in organizational fields," *American Sociological Review*, 48: 147–60.

Dowling, G. R. (1993) "Developing your image into a corporate asset," *Long Range Planning*, 26(2): 101–9.

Downey, S. M. (1986/1987) "The relationship between corporate culture and corporate identity," *Public Relations Quarterly*, Winter: 7–12.

Dutton, J. E. and Dukerich, J. M. (1991) "Keeping an eye on the mirror: image and identity in organizational adaptation," *Academy of Management Journal*, 34: 517–54.

Dutton, J. E., Dukerich, J. M., and Harquail, C. V. (1994) "Organizational images and member identification," *Administrative Science Quarterly*, 39: 239–63.

Elsbach, K. D. and Kramer, R. M. (1996) "Members' responses to organizational threats: encountering and countering the *Business Week* rankings," *Administrative Science Quarterly*, 41: 442–76.

Fombrun, C. (1996) *Reputation: realizing value from the corporate image*, Boston, MA: Harvard Business School Press.

Garbett, T. F. (1988) *How to build a corporate identity and project its image*, Lexington, MA: Lexington Books.

Gioia, D. A. (1998) "From individual identity to organizational identity," in D. A. Whetten and P. C. Godfrey (eds) *Identity in organizations – building theory through conversation*, Thousand Oaks, CA: Sage, 17–31.

Gioia, D. A. and Thomas, J. B. (1996) "Identity, image and issue interpretation: sensemaking during strategic change in academia," *Administrative Science Quarterly*, 41: 370–403.

Gioia, D. A., Schultz, M., and Corley, K. G. (2000) "Organizational identity, image, and adaptive instability," *Academy of Management Review*, 25(1): 63–81.

Glynn, M. A. (2000) "When cymbals become symbols: conflict over organizational identity within a symphony orchestra," *Organization Science*, 11(3): 285–98.

Golden-Biddle, K. and Rao, H. (1997) "Breaches in the boardroom: organizational identity and conflicts of commitment in a nonprofit organization," *Organization Science*, 8(6): 593–611.

Gray, E. R. and Smeltzer, L. R. (1985) "SRM forum: corporate image – an integral part of strategy," *Sloan Management Review*, 26(4): 73–8.

Hatch, M. J. and Schultz, M. (2000) "Scaling the Tower of Babel: relational differences between identity, image, and culture in organizations," in M. Schultz, M. J. Hatch, and M. H. Larsen (eds) *The expressive organization*, Oxford: Oxford University Press.

Hogg, M. A. and Terry, D. J. (2000) "Social identity and self-categorization processes in organizational contexts," *Academy of Management Review*, 25: 121–40.

Ind, N. (1997) *The corporate brand*, Oxford: Macmillan.

Kapferer, J.-N. (1992) *Strategic brand management*, London: Kogan Page.

Kennedy, S. H. (1977) "Nurturing corporate images – total communication or ego trip?," *European Journal of Marketing*, 11: 120–64.

Larçon, L. and Reitter, R. (1979) *Structure de pouvoir et identité de l'entreprise*, Paris: Nathan.

Larçon, L. and Reitter, R. (1984) "Corporate imagery and corporate identity," in M. Kets de Vries (ed.) *The irrational executive*, Madison, CT: International Universities Press.

McDonald, M. H. B., de Chernatony, L., and Harris, F. (2001) "Corporate marketing and the service brands – moving beyond the fast moving consumer goods model," *European Journal of Marketing*, 35(3/4): 335–52.

Margulies, W. P. (1977) "Make the most of your corporate identity," *Harvard Business Review*, 55(4): 66–74.

Martineau, P. (1958) "The personality of the retail store," *Harvard Business Review*, 36(1): 47–55.

Melewar, T. C. (2000) "The role of corporate identity in merger and acquisition activity," *Journal of General Management*, 26(2): 17–32.

Moingeon, B. (1999) "From corporate culture to corporate identity," *Corporate Reputation Review*, 2(4): 352–60.

Moingeon, B. and Ramanantsoa, B. (1995) "An identity study of firm mergers: the case of a French savings bank," in H. E. Klein (ed.) *Case method research and application, volume VII*, Needham, MA: WACRA, 253–60.

Moingeon, B. and Ramanantsoa, B. (1997) "Understanding corporate identity: the French school of thought," *European Journal of Marketing*, 31(5/6): 383–95.

Moscovici, S. (1976) *Social influence and social change*, New York: Academic Press.

Mucchielli, A. (1999) *L'identité*, 4th edition, Paris: PUF.

Olins, W. (1978) *The corporate personality: an inquiry into the nature of corporate identity*, London: Thames & Hudson.

Olins, W. (1989) *Corporate identity: making business strategy visible through design*, London: Thames & Hudson.

Peteraf, M. and Shanley, M. (1997) "Getting to know you: a theory of strategic group identity," *Strategic Management Journal*, 18: 165–86.

Pfeffer, J. (1981) "Management as symbolic action: the creation and maintenance of organizational paradigms," in L. L. Cummings and B. M. Staw (eds) *Research in organizational behavior, volume 3*, Greenwich, CT: JAI Press, 1–52.

Prahalad, C. K. and Bettis, R. A. (1986) "The dominant logic: a new linkage between strategy and performance," *Strategic Management Journal*, 7: 485–501.

Pratt, M. G. and Foreman, P. O. (2000a) "The beauty and the barriers to organizational theories of identity," *Academy of Management Review*, 25(1): 141–3.

Pratt, M. G. and Foreman, P. O. (2000b) "Classifying managerial responses to multiple organizational identities," *Academy of Management Review*, 25(1): 18–42.

Rebel, H. (1997) "Towards a methaphorical theory of public relations," in D. Moss, T. MacManus, and D. Verac (eds) *Public Relations Research: An International Perspective*, 199–224.

Reger, R., Gustafson, L., Demarie, S., and Mullane, J. (1994) "Reframing the organization: why implementing total quality is easier said than done," *Academy of Management Review*, 19: 565–84.

Schein, E. (1984) "Coming to a new awareness of corporate culture," *Sloan Management Review*, 25: 3–16.

Schein, E. (1985) *Organizational culture and leadership*, San Francisco, CA: Jossey-Bass.

Schmitt, B., Simonson, A., and Marcus, J. (1995) "Managing corporate image and identity," *Long Range Planning*, 28(5): 82–92.

Schultz, M., Hatch, M. J., and Larsen, M. H. (2000) *The expressive organization*, Oxford: Oxford University Press.

Sevon, G. (1996) "Organizational imitation in identity transformation," in B. Czarniawska and G. Sevon (eds) *Translating organizational change*, Berlin: Walter de Gruyter.

Smidts, A., Pruyn, A. H. and van Riel, C. B. M. (2001) "The impact of employee communication and perceived external prestige on organizational identification," *Academy of Management Journal*, 49(15): 1051–62.

van Rekom, J. (1997) "Deriving an operational measure of CI," *European Journal of Marketing*, 31(5/6): 410–22.

van Riel, C. M. B. (1995) *Corporate communications*, London: Prentice Hall.

van Riel, C. M. B. and Balmer, J. M. T. (1997) "Corporate identity: the concept, its measurement and management," *European Journal of Marketing*, 31(5/6): 340–55.

Weick, K. (1995) *Sense-making in organizations*, Thousand Oaks, CA: Sage.

Whetten, D. A. and Godfrey, P. C. (eds) (1998) *Identity in organizations: building theory through conversations*, Thousand Oaks, CA: Sage.

Wilson, A. (1997) "The culture of the branch team and its impact on service delivery and corporate identity," *International Journal of Bank Marketing*, 15(5): 163–8.

2 The hybrid identity of law firms

Stuart Albert and Edward Adams

Introduction

An organization that has a hybrid identity is one that embodies two or more identities at the same time. What is core, distinctive and at least relatively enduring about the organization is that it is both an X *and* a Y. A classic example is the university. As Albert and Whetten (1985) pointed out, a university is (or is like) both a religion and a business at the same time. How these diverse elements are merged, integrated, or kept separate is what gives the organization its unique hybrid status. Of course, not all hybrid organizations claim or have a hybrid *identity*. The latter requires that the hybrid character of the organization represent its distinctive and relatively enduring core.

Hybrid identity organizations have existed for a long time. Universities, law firms, health care organizations, professional sports are examples. Many of these organizations appear to be sustainable hybrids, that is, despite the internal contradictions built into the hybrid form, these organizations survive and sometimes prosper. However internally conflicted, organizations that embrace two or more identities have staying power. The principal form of the hybrid with which we will be concerned are those made up of identities that are perceived internally as inviolate (nothing about each can be compromised), incompatible (conflict is inevitable), and indispensable (no identity can be eliminated).

The test that something is *inviolate* is that even a small change will be resisted "in principle." For example, to adopt anything that could be construed as sympathetic to pacifist values is to cease to be a military organization; or, to reject any aspect of the sacred is to cease to be a church. An indication that one is dealing with an element that is part of the inviolate core of an organization is the length of time and the passion devoted to dealing with what from another perspective would be a very small matter. The test that identities are *incompatible* is the depth of conflict that surfaces over questions of resource allocation, future direction, etc., which depend on being able to answer the focal question: Who are we and who do we want to be? The test that an identity element is held to be *indispensable* is the degree of outrage that follows an attempt to eliminate it: that is, we would no longer be a church, business, hospital, etc., if we no longer did that (embraced that value, offered that service, etc.).[1]

The intent of this chapter is to examine how the identity of an organization that is made up of identities that are each defended as inviolate, experienced as incompatible, and yet found to be indispensable, can be sustained. Indeed, the question is how an organization so constituted can endure. To say that a hybrid identity organization has a sustainable form means its contradictory identities have found some quasi-stable form of mutual accommodation or coherence. The task is to specify how they have done so in a way that does not simply translate the problem into one of quantification, namely, that the solution consists of some *degree* of compromise among the elements. In short, the purpose of this chapter is to examine mechanisms of coherence and balance by which hybrid identity organizations sustain themselves. We organize our presentation around the central features of the five-facet framework (Soenen and Moingeon, 2002).

The case example we use to study the sustainable hybrid form is that of a (US) law firm, which is both of a profession dedicated to serving the law and that of a business with an eye toward the bottom line (Adams and Albert, 1999). Since the nineteenth century, there has been a gradual shift from a professional identity to one that places an increasing emphasis on business. The resulting hybrid form of the law firm has given rise to a host of internal conflicts and dilemmas. Indeed, Adams and Albert have proposed that principles of law are themselves ideal instruments for managing law firms as hybrids.

In this chapter, we use Soenen and Moingeon's five-facet framework as a way to shed light on these issues. The framework is particularly useful in revealing the complex ways in which the firm sustains its hybrid identity through a set of counterbalancing claims and obligations. What on the surface should fly apart, does not. We consider each of the facets of the Soenen and Moingeon framework separately.

The *professed* identity

The *professed* identity of an organization is the answer organizational members provide to and for themselves when asked for their identity (Soenen and Moingeon, 2002). Lawyers normally identify themselves as members of a profession and the law firm as the organizational vehicle that allows them to practice their profession. As a result, the identity of a law firm is heavily influenced by its lawyers' individual identities as members of a profession.

Many prominent elements of practice continue to infuse law practice with the qualities of a profession. Chief among these are the lawyer's duties to her clients and to her profession. While these duties support the *professed* identity of law as a profession, lawyers have other, and sometimes conflicting, obligations: that is, they must act to further the interests of other partners in the firm and, ultimately, must act to pursue their own self-interests.

A lawyer's duty to her clients requires zealous representation.[2] Lawyers will evaluate competing courses of action based on what is most likely to benefit their clients. Presumably, this duty requires lawyers to put their clients' interests, financial or otherwise, before their own. As such, the duty to one's client is consistent with the concept of law as a profession. Lawyers do maintain some control over the selection and termination of clients. This is consistent with the idea of zealous representation in that lawyers can seek out those clients who they can best represent. Such freedom of choice allows lawyers to provide for the professional needs of representation while balancing business needs to select clients who will support their practices.

As an integral member of the larger legal system, lawyers owe a duty to the system, as well as to each other and to society. This duty can be thought of broadly as a lawyer's duty to her profession. Lawyers frequently interact with other lawyers, whether on a collegial or adversarial basis, as well as with judges, clerks, and other professionals within the system. Such interactions are conducted with the expectation that lawyers, while maintaining zealous representation of their clients, will work to resolve disputes or conduct transactions in an honest and forthright manner. The duty to the legal system is important to maintaining a neutral legal process. It ensures that all viewpoints are represented in the system. As with the duty to the client, the lawyer's duty to other legal actors and the legal system is consistent with the idea of law as a profession.

The societal element of the lawyer's duty to her profession is manifest in the expectation that lawyers perform pro bono work.[3] State bar associations, to varying degrees, require lawyers to perform pro bono work annually (Rhode, 1999: 2415). Further, many large law firms credit their attorneys for pro bono work just as if the hours had been billed to a paying client (Tabak, 1996: 931). While consistent with law as a profession, pro bono requirements also display aspects of law as a business. Requiring pro bono work of all lawyers in a given state or market removes that aspect of the legal business from competition. Law as a business benefits from such standardization because it aids in making predictable for whom and for what one should compete.

The fact that many, if not most, law firms operate as partnerships creates a distinct set of duties for lawyers that follow from applicable partnership laws.[4] Lawyers have an obligation to act in a way that benefits their partners. Specifically, lawyers have a duty to contribute to their partnerships financially. This financial obligation, unlike a lawyer's duty to her clients and to the profession, raises the specter of a hybrid organization. Further, that law firms are organized as partnerships and not as corporations, whether public or private, limits the number of constituencies to which the firm and its lawyers owe a duty. Corporations owe a legal duty to their shareholders, and in some instances to nonshareholder stakeholders. If law firms were organized as corporations rather than partnerships, the added complexity of stockholders would complicate the hybrid form and perhaps seriously compromise it as the profit motive would play an even more significant role in decision-making.

We conjecture that structuring law firms as partnerships rather than as corporations is one way of making the hybrid form sustainable despite the obligations imposed by partnership laws that inject law practice with the elements of a profit-making enterprise. Managing a corporate hybrid would be a much more complex and difficult undertaking.

Lawyers' involvement in pro bono projects notwithstanding, their pursuit of the practice of law is undoubtedly an effort to make a living. Thus, the final duty the lawyer possesses is a duty to herself. The lawyer's practice is inextricably linked to her own financial security. The potential conflict raised by serving clients while also providing for oneself again implicates the hybrid nature of law firms in a way not dissimilar to the practice of medicine.

The duties to zealously represent clients and to be responsible to the legal system are largely consistent with the *professed* identity of the organization, that of a profession. Conversely, the second two duties, those to the partnerships in which lawyers typically operate and the duty lawyers owe to themselves, hybridize law firm identity by bringing business concerns to the fore. This dilemma is inherent in the *professed* identity of the organization. To claim that one's firm is a legal organization and not a business is not to absolve oneself from having to confront the predicaments that are inherent in the legal organization and legal representation.

The architecture of many law firms attests to their professional identity. The library, the ubiquitous dark paneling, and the overall quietness convey the scholarly nature of the firm. Reading and writing are core activities. Even the specialized and arcane language used by attorneys serves to reinforce the firm's professional identity to its clients, and a sense of identity is important if for no other reason that it implies a code of ethics and communal sanctions for those who overstep the bounds.

The legal hybrid is sustained through an intricate system of checks and balances. Professional duties often conflict with business duties. As a business, a firm must be economically successful, but to attract and retain clients over the long run, it must adhere to and internally reinforce professional values. Ideally, it tries to find ways of doing both. Pro bono work, for example, promotes firms' professional identity while providing the firms with a marketing device. Specialization and certification allow firms to promote professional niches while continuing to compete in a world of increasingly commodified legal services.

The *experienced* identity

The *experienced* identity of an organization is the "local" form of social representation. It consists of a common knowledge collectively constructed about what the organization is for its members. "This has been conceptualized . . . as shared cognitive beliefs, as collective cognitive maps, or as collective unconscious structures" (Soenen and Moingeon, 2002: 9). As experienced, a law firm is filled with conflicts that stem from its hybrid form. Norms that emphasize attracting new businesses, the internal distribution of profit, and the methods lawyers use to bill clients for services may come into conflict with the duties attorneys have to their clients and to the system as a whole.

Employment as an attorney with a large law firm is typically premised on a six to nine-year period of service as an associate, followed by ascension to the rank of partner. Partners are the owners of the firm, with their earnings tied to the firm's profitability. Firms are typically structured as pyramids, with associates generating billings in excess of their salaries and associated overhead. For example, a firm may pay an associate $80,000 or $100,000 per year and bill the associate's time to clients at $100 or $150 per hour. If the associate bills 2000 hours per year, she would generate upwards of $200,000 in fees. After expenses, there might be $50,000 per associate for the partners to share. When a partnership does this with four or five associates per partner, it creates a tremendous leverage opportunity.

An associate's suitability for elevation to partner is typically dependent on his potential for attracting and retaining clients. After a few years of practice, the associate notices a shift in emphasis from just doing the work to actually building a book of clients, a business. A young lawyer starts out learning the law but knows most of what it takes to be effective after five or six years of practice.[5] From that point on, however, the existing partners will increasingly look to the senior associate to generate new business for the firm. The focus shifts very clearly from learning the law as a profession to becoming proficient at the business of law. If the time until partnership were shortened, the profitability of the firm would decrease. If that were to occur, there would be increasing economic pressures which would move the law firm into acting more like a pure business. Yet if the time to become partner were lengthened in the present environment, there would be some question about whether an associate would or could persevere. If a reward is made too distant it is unclear whether anyone will seek it. Thus, the amount of time necessary to become a partner, which is difficult to alter, along with the ratio of associates to partners, is part of what creates a sustainable hybrid form.

While associates will often receive a base salary that is uniform for all lawyers in a given year, partner compensation is typically based on a division of the firm's profits. Oftentimes, this division of profits yields an equal share for all partners with a given number of years of service. Thus, two partners with equal tenure who generate vastly disparate levels of revenue might receive equal shares of the revenue at the end of the year.[6] Such a scheme is clearly consistent with the *professed* identity of law practice as a profession. Even in firms where a partner's share of the profits might be more directly tied to the specific business that the partner generates, it is virtually unheard of for a partner's compensation to be based directly on the success or failure of her client's case or transaction. Certainly, an incompetent attorney might encounter difficulty attracting paying clients, not to mention remaining employed. However, it is unlikely that a partner would receive less in compensation for losing a case in a given year.

Such an egalitarian method of dividing profits promotes the professional identity of the law firm over the business identity. What also helps is that salary issues are usually decided by a small committee, allowing most of the members of the firm to concentrate of the practice of law. Since compensation is independent of outcome, the system promotes the idea of the attorney as an officer of the court. The attorney's task is to uphold the law and, if it turns out that her client is on the losing end of the legal argument, that is fine. The attorney's job is to zealously represent the client. That makes her a servant of the profession and of the legal principles, and not a businessperson. The system also provides some measure of checks and balances. While partners are compensated for generating business, they are not directly compensated for the number of cases they win or lose. Every partner has a stake in the financial success that each partner generates. Avoiding a linkage between client success and compensation ensures that a given client will not be deprived of representation solely on the basis of a weak case and, thus, a partner's slim odds of compensation. This element, in particular, speaks to the sustainability of the law firm structure.

Like the method of dividing the partnership's profits, billing practices also implicate the hybrid nature of the law firm structure. A firm bills either on an hourly basis or on a contingency basis, whereby the attorney is entitled to a predetermined percentage of the proceeds of the case. A firm would be more inclined to accept a contingency fee where the likelihood of prevailing is higher. Thus, there is a case-by-case determination and the compensation scheme may be variously consistent with the professional identity or the business identity or with some combination of both. If an attorney bills by time (rather than some other basis, such as the value of the transaction to the client, for example), then in a sense, the firm is being paid to be inefficient. On the other hand, being able to bill by the hour means that one can represent someone who might not win, which is consistent with the professional identity of the firm. If billing is based on the completion of a deal, then there may be a conflict in that an attorney may wrongly advise the client to do the deal in order to get paid. However, in practice, many firms discount the number of hours an associate bills to a client. A partner may ask: what did a client really get out of that transaction, and reduce the number of hours billed to it accordingly. A partner will want an associate to bill as many hours as possible, but not to his client, who may object. On the other hand, a partner will want his associate to bill as many hours as possible to other clients since that represents more revenue for the firm, profit that will be divided by the partners. Thus, the partner is saying to his or her associate, don't bill my client. The partnership is saying, of course, you must bill your client. If there were no restrictions on billing, the client would suffer. If there were no incentive to bill, the firm as an economic entity would be impossible. Thus, the firm's flexibility in structuring payment terms promotes the sustainability of the hybrid form.

The free initial consultation is an important ancillary of these billing methods. Most attorneys will provide clients with an initial consultation during which the client can explain the issue and the attorney can provide some insight about the likelihood of success. This consultation is typically free of charge to the client. Notwithstanding the general rule that compensation is not directly tied to success, partners, as owners of the firm, still want to see the firm be financially successful. This is particularly at issue in client selection where a contingency fee is involved. The free initial consultation allows the attorney to assess the expected value of the representation. Further, the attorney can "pitch" the client, letting him know what experience she has in similar cases or transactions and letting the client decide if she is the right attorney for him. The initial consultation extends the flexibility of billing methods by allowing the attorney to be cognizant of business concerns, namely, the likelihood of prevailing, and letting the client evaluate the professional aspects of the attorney's practice. In this way, the initial consultation fits within the hybrid elements of billing practices.

The norms of law firm operation, the emphasis on leveraging associates to generate profits for the partnership, the distribution of those profits, and the standards for billing clients all compel actors within the law firm to confront the hybrid nature of the organization. First, and perhaps most obviously, the shift in the mid-level to senior associate's focus from learning the law to generating business creates conflict. While learning and serving the client were previously foremost in the associate's duties, the looming partnership decision encourages him to think more about the business aspects of practice. Some attorneys might seek to preserve the professional identity of practice in the face of such economic imperatives by performing pro bono work. Structural mechanisms such as compensation schemes may be useful in managing multiple identities (Pratt and Foreman, 2000).

The attorney's duty to her client, as embodied in the requirement for zealous representation, presents another conflict between the firm's professional and business identities. Professional standards require zealous representation. In seeking financial success for a client and herself, however, an attorney might become "superzealous." Professional standards, however, inhibit such misconduct in most cases. Thus, an attorney's advocacy on behalf of her client that follows from business interests is constrained by the legal community's professional standards.

As with zealous representation, the attorney's duty to the legal system as a whole can sometimes create a conflict between business and professional ambitions. Following from their professional duty to the legal system, attorneys have a duty to inform a court of authority contrary to their position.[7] Thus, an attorney might be required to disclose a precedent that is detrimental to her own client's case. Further, an attorney would be obligated to report if her client were about to commit a crime. Clearly, both of these duties create conflict between the duty to the profession and the duty to the client. Where the duty to the client implicates business interests, such as wanting to see the client prevail, the conflict aligns with the hybrid nature of law firms.

Like their duties to the client and the system, the third duty that lawyers have, that to their partners, may also create conflict. A partner's desire to take on a particular client may be constrained by the partnership's efforts to project a certain professional image. For example, one partner may see a lucrative relationship in representing a tobacco company while the firm as a whole is committed to refraining from representing big tobacco. Further, one partner may be ultimately responsible for a particular client engagement, a so-called "billing partner." She obviously has an incentive to keep billing rates low in order to please the client while the other partners want to see rates maximized so as to maximize their own take at the end of the year. In sum, both of these conflicts represent the delicate balance between serving the client's interests while simultaneously attending to those of one's colleagues.

Finally, a lawyer's duty to herself may also require her to confront a conflict between the firm's professional and business identities. As an associate, the emphasis is clearly on billing a lot of hours. As a partner, however, an attorney might be more focused on doing quality work. Somewhat perversely, hourly billing creates some incentive to work inefficiently. Yet, when an attorney ascends to the rank of partner, her interest in retaining client business creates an incentive to do good work. Clearly, racking up billable hours comports more with law as a business while emphasizing the work product is more consistent with the practice of law as a profession. As with the attorney's duty to the partnership, personal values about representing certain clients also may create conflict. An attorney may be uncomfortable defending an accused sexual harasser but will need to sidestep her personal ethics in order to fulfill a duty to the partnership to generate revenue. Organizations have a desired future image, consisting of a visionary perception the organization would like external others and internal members to have of the organization sometime in the future (Gioia and Thomas, 1996). A balance between short-term and long-term effects must be achieved. Firms obviously contemplate such conflict since every major firm employs some system for managing conflicts of interest, ensuring that a firm's advocacy will not be compromised by the fact that it simultaneously represents adverse parties or has done so in the past.

As is evident, lawyers often experience a conflicted identity within the law firm, one that implicates elements of hybrid organizations. Norms related to firm structure and client billing often force attorneys to confront the hybrid nature of the organization. Why such conflict does not force an exodus from the profession or demand change within the organization is the focus of the next section.

The *manifested* identity

The *manifested* identity refers to the way identity is manifest in the organization's routines, structure, performance, marketing position, etc. (Soenen and Moingeon, 2002). Were the conflicts in law firms between business and profession continuous and severe, it is unlikely that the hybrid form would be sustainable. The nature of law practice, however, is that hybridization is at times manifest and at other times latent. The annual cycles of law firms and their attorneys, and a firm's own finite life cycle provide a context in which to examine the waxing and waning of the hybrid induced conflicts. (See Albert (1995) for a general framework on the study of timing.)

The focus on dividing partnership profits, and the coincident emphasis on the firm as a business, typically takes place at the end of the fiscal year. Although partners undoubtedly have an eye on partnership profits throughout the year, the emphasis is strongest at the close of the fiscal year. Thus, while the question of how profits are to be divided brings the conflict between profession and business to the fore, it is most acute only once each year. Further, because firms must plan for hiring, capital investments, and new businesses on a multi-year basis, it is likely that some partners may not need to confront the issue of profitability annually. Similarly, partners may labor on a case or transaction for years, thus uncoupling the time when the legal issues that determine whether a case is won or not and the time when the profit motive is most salient. If winning or losing a case were synchronized for all attorneys with the yearly economic cycle of the firm, there would likely be more "intermingling" of the two value systems.

Associates will likely begin to experience the conflict between profession and business as they approach the partnership decision, sometime after their sixth year of practice. As discussed previously, the focus for associates shifts from learning and doing to attracting clients. To be sure, a seventh or eighth-year associate will be making a nice salary but, without the prospect of attracting clients, his chances for remaining with the firm are slim. Law firms are very "up or out" in nature. Associate turnover, as one would expect, is significant, particularly at large, more highly leveraged firms.[8] As such, an associate who does not make partner may move on to a smaller firm, where there is less emphasis on rain-making, or to an in-house position with a corporation. This structure, however, still provides five to eight years during which the associate only gradually experiences the conflict between profession and business. Associates might experience practice as wholly professional in nature up until the point that attracting clients becomes key. As such, the conflict is neither continuous nor severe enough for the associate to question his role in the law firm.

A final issue of timing in the balance between business and profession involves a partner's decision to leave the firm. Although partners generally share in the profits generated by all clients, each client is typically thought of as "belonging" to a particular partner, usually the attorney who brought in the business and has overseen most of the client's work. When a partner chooses to leave the partnership, the nature of her relationship with a client requires her to confront the conflict between business and profession. Professional guidelines require departing partners to notify clients and partners to allow them to discuss the possibility of the client remaining with the firm. The client has an interest in continuity of representation, either in the form of the departing partner's familiarity and expertise, or the firm's infrastructure, such as associates who have worked on the client and associated files and documents. Conversely, the departing partner has an interest in retaining the client's lucrative billings. The conflict between professional interests, as represented by what is best for the client, and business, embodied in the partner's pecuniary concerns, once again implicates hybridization. The fact that such a divestiture occurs only periodically contributes a temporal element to the conflict.

The unique timing aspects of the conflicts detailed above help to sustain the hybrid nature of the organization. Similarly, the firm structure may provide unique benefits to attorneys that make it advantageous to stay with the firm, even in the face of the conflict in identities. For example, a lawyer with a particular area of expertise may receive business from one of the firm's existing clients despite the fact that the client was initially lured to the firm for other expertise. The diversity of skills across the firm's attorneys helps all of them attract and retain clients. In summary, while a law firm's attorneys will experience conflict between the business and professional aspects of the organization, the conflict will often be mitigated by timing or other issue, such as incentive systems, that make the hybrid structure sustainable. Organizations may manage multiple identities by "attending" to or evoking the identity most salient to the immediate context (Pratt and Foreman, 2000).

The *projected* and *attributed* identities

A *projected* identity refers to those identity manifestations that are (more or less) consciously manipulated and presented to certain publics or audiences, while the *attributed* identity is the way the firm is seen by various publics (Soenen and Moingeon, 2002). The differing identities that law firms project, both internally and externally, and the additional identities that external audiences attribute to the firms, complete the five facets of the hybrid organization. Law firms tailor their images to varying communities. Further, a firm's choice to specialize in a particular area helps to narrow its *projected* identity. Internally, a law firm's *projected* identity may conflict with the identity perceptions of its attorneys. Finally, the identity that the public attributes to law firms may invoke the conflict between profession and business. The ability to present the firm differently to different publics and to have outsiders see the firm differently permits a degree of flexibility. A firm is not one thing to all parties. Being "multivoiced" allows a firm to be heard in a variety of different ways that reinforces its hybrid identity.

Law firms' attempts to project an image to a specific community was represented historically by the existence of firms of a distinctly Jewish or WASP identity. Though such identification along ethnic or religious lines has waned over time, many firms still attempt to cater to a specific ethnic or racial community. Thus, a firm of predominantly Hispanic lawyers may attract predominantly Hispanic clients and a firm whose partnership ranks include African-Americans might market itself to African-American businesspeople. Such identification helps firms attract clients on the basis of shared experiences or values that may contribute to overlooking other conflicts, such as those between financial and professional obligations.

Many law firms specialize. For example, one firm might specialize in health-care, another in bankruptcy. Similarly, some firms might devote their practices exclusively to one side of an issue, such as representing defendants in civil or criminal trials or advocating on behalf of management, to the exclusion of unions, in the practice of labor law. Interestingly enough, such specialization is often specialization in balancing rights, obligations, and duties. Managing the hybrid form is therefore part of the content of the law firm's work that may give it special expertise in creating a sustainable hybrid.

The tendency for firms to specialize, or at least to possess some practice areas with disproportionately large numbers of partners and associates, can however, create internal conflict. Some attorneys may feel the firm's partners do not value their expertise because of the smaller share of revenue that their department produces. Similarly, partners in a more lucrative area may resent the equal share of profits that partners in a less lucrative area draw at the end of the year. Where partners feel the firm's identity is unmanageably inconsistent with their own, they may split off from the firm and create their own, one more consistent with the identity they wish to project. Were it not for this "safety valve," the hybrid form might self-destruct.

Market forces in today's legal environment also appear to promote special-ization. As legal services become more of a commodity, law firms must project an identity of specialization to maintain their client bases and, oftentimes, to justify their high billing rates. Furthermore, the Internet represents a major shift toward accessibility for all audiences to legal information and forms that were once the sole province of lawyers and their firms. Thus, lawyers increas-ingly seek certification in various specialties in order to market themselves as qualified to perform specific legal work.

Members of both the general public and the narrower legal community attribute various identities to lawyers and their firms. Lawyers may be per-ceived as mercenaries or "hired guns," willing to parse words interminably if it benefits their clients,[9] or as defenders of the Constitution, of fair process, and hence, the common good. As a potential client, one wants the former, as a member of society, the latter. That both desires can be present in the same individual legitimize the hybrid form. Indeed, being able to claim that every-one deserves a defense, regardless of what they are accused of, means that the law firm is filled with people who are accustomed to see and argue both sides of an issue at the same time and that they are skilled negotiators, able to resolve the resulting disputes. It is difficult to imagine a better recruitment tool for a hybrid, namely, to attract those people who are able to see the value and to argue for multiple sides of an issue. Furthermore, attorneys learn not to take an issue or argument personally. While this form of disengagement raises a threat to a lawyer's integrity, being always ready to argue for what she does not believe, or being trained to see both sides of an issue, is a potent resource for sustaining the hybrid form.

The difference between a firm's *projected* and *attributed* identities is most apparent in lawyers' conscious manipulation of client perceptions. Pro bono requirements, as already discussed, are one example. Firms may tout their pro bono records to prospective clients and attorneys alike. What may go unsaid, however, is that such pro bono work is required of all firms under applicable state guidelines. Similarly, firms may promote their policy of giving lawyers billing credit for pro bono hours without disclosing the fact that lawyers have little time to perform pro bono work because of client demands. Clients may receive only the impression that their attorneys are committed to their best interests. In truth, however, all attorneys, partners, and associates alike, must contribute to the financial health of the firm. Thus, while projecting an image of professional commitment to the client, attorneys must always be mindful of their business responsibilities. Clients likewise attribute an identity of professional responsibility to their attorneys in spite of obvious business goals.

Conclusion: a necessary incompatibility

A theme that has been sounded in many ways as we considered the five-facet framework is that there are complex counterbalancing forces within each facet that make the hybrid form both inevitable (because conflicts among different demands exist) and sustainable (because mechanisms are in place to correct imbalances). For example, we pointed out that a lawyer must simultaneously or sequentially balance her obligation to her clients, her partners, her profession, and to society (*professed* identity). No single obligation can dominate without penalty. Every new attorney experiences a shift from learning the law to learning the business of law (*experienced* identity). Moreover, there is usually also a temporal separation between when profits must be divided and when a case settles or a transaction is closed. This gap in time mitigates against the experience of constant and severe conflicts.

However, it is not merely that each identity facet has counterbalancing forces and mechanisms within it, but that the facets taken as a whole work together to create and sustain the hybrid form because they are not aligned – or at least not permanently aligned – with one another. What makes the hybrid viable is that the five facets exhibit what may be termed *a necessary incompatibility*. It is the functions and virtues of incompatibility that sustain the hybrid form.

What attorneys and their firms claim about their identity (*professed* identity) need not fit with how that identity is manifest in internal routines and procedures (*manifested* identity). A lawyer's professional identity, her duty to her client and to the legal profession cannot easily be reconciled with internal procedures that focus on recording a large number of billable hours: a greater number of billable hours does not necessarily translate into a more successful legal argument. Yet it is sometimes fortunate that the need for billable hours and the need for zealous representation are not the same. If they were, an attorney might spend an exorbitant amount of time on a case that could not be won simply because she believed that her client's rights were violated. Doing so would ultimately bankrupt the firm. On the other hand, an exorbitant number of billable hours would drive away future clients "with the law on their side." It is necessary that the need for zealous representation be balanced by the need for a sufficient number of billable hours.

Conflicts that are experienced (*experienced* identity) do not necessarily find their expression when an attorney is asked about her work identity (*professed* identity). Such conflicts may be regarded as "insider" knowledge, dirty linen that one does not air in public. To the extent that such conflicts are seen as unavoidable, and provided that they are not too severe, living with them can even become a source of self-esteem, a barrier overcome in pursuit of more noble objectives.

There is also value in being able to project an identity that is different from the one that one experiences. A *projected* or *professed* identity may be a useful form of self-persuasion and self-criticism, or like the clown who smiles outwards as he cries inwardly, simply another demonstration of the art of advocacy under trying conditions, the essential condition under which the lawyer practices his craft.

The identity that is *manifest* in internal routines and procedures may not fit with how the identity of the organization is *experienced*. Some routines may not be taken seriously; procedures or norms can be circumvented. Indeed, one of the distinguishing features of any ritual is that it can be empty of true emotional involvement. Pro bono work can be done in a half-hearted manner and no one will be the wiser. That a firm's identity can be *experienced* differently from those aspects of identity that are manifest in routines, procedures, and rituals means both that experience is richer than routines, procedures, and ritual (*manifested* identity), and that individuals are capable of living differently from what the environment seems to prescribe. The ability to choose how one will respond to environmental conditions is the hallmark of human freedom.

The perception that attorneys are "hired guns" or mercenaries (*attributed* identity) is also paradoxically what recommends the legal profession as an ally and advocate when the client finds himself embattled or wrongly accused. Yet few would choose an attorney who publicly views his own profession poorly: one would not trust such an attorney to represent one's own interests. Hence, one expects and values a "gap" between a *projected* and an *attributed* identity – provided, of course, that the gap is not too large.

Thus, taken together, those facets of identity that are *professed, experienced, manifested, projected,* and *attributed* need not be in alignment. Indeed, there are advantages associated with their nonalignment. That being the case, it is not surprising that, as a general rule, law firms are managed as businesses, present themselves as professions, but are experienced internally as hybrids. In a sense, that is at the heart of our argument. No one would want to manage a law firm as a hybrid. The result would be endless, impossible-to-resolve conflicts. Nor would one want to present the firm to clients as a hybrid: the client would not appreciate knowing the degree of internal conflict that is present in any true hybrid.

Part of the reason that nonalignment is possible, and more particularly, that the law firm can be internally managed as a business, is due to what we might call the institutionalization of virtue, the fact that the law firm operates in an environment that demands and can enforce certain standards of virtuous conduct. A law firm does not have the managerial burden of complete and thorough self-policing. A lawyer, for example, is an officer of the court and must turn over exculpatory evidence to one's opponents: she must file certain kinds of reports, etc. In practice, a firm would search for some privileged basis to retain documents that might be damaging to its side. Of course, there must be a basis for asserting privilege, but the grounds on which it can be asserted are quite broad. However, any law firm that does not act according to the law loses its reputation and, hence, places its survival in doubt. As a result, law firms tend to have a zero tolerance for breaches of the law. Moreover, a law firm is in an environment that is focused on detecting and punishing infractions of the law. All of this makes it possible to focus on managing the firm as a business: virtue, to overstate the case, has been institutionalized. Thus, the deeper one investigates this issue, the more one finds that one principle, procedure, or force is balanced by another, that all facets of identity need not be in alignment.

Inconsistency, nonalignment, or incompatibility among the different facets of identity are, from our perspective, useful and perhaps even necessary *resources* in managing the hybrid form. Being out of alignment and thus having the potential to work in opposite directions is one of the ways a firm's multifaceted identity sustains the hybrid form. The key, however, is *movement* among *potentially* counterbalancing forces, not a fixed equilibrium among them. We suggest that in an enduring hybrid form such as the law firm, each facet of identity is capable of changing in response to changes in other facets. When one mechanism is blocked, another can perform the same function. For example, when client selection fails because one has *projected* an identity that dissuades the most lucrative prospects from becoming clients, one can adjust (within limits) the billable hours of the clients that one can attract until the firm is repositioned in the market place. Redundancy of function helps insure survivability.

A final comment. For a hybrid to remain a vital form, the differences on which it is based must be preserved rather than eliminated. An important consequence of the fact that identity has many facets is that each facet can be strengthened and defended independently of the others. Only when potentially contradictory aspects of identity are preserved are they available to play a counterbalancing role when needed. Each aspect of a hybrid therefore requires some form of defense for its extreme or pure form. The mechanisms for doing so can be subtle. For example, consider the profit motive. One may condemn a windfall profit, while secretly admiring the bold imagination or tenacity that secured it, or secretly admire, while condemning, the sheer audacity of a business enterprise that succeeds by skirting the edge of the law. Such is the romanticized appeal of pirates. We admire their swagger, their lives of adventure, however sordid. If only our more noble lives were the subject of such tales. We not only praise the artist who starves for his art (the lawyer who defends only those he knows to be innocent), we may also secretly pity him. It is this ambivalence towards extremes that defends them, that insulates them from unbridled attack. It is not merely that a pure type (the law firm as business) may be counterbalanced by another pure type (the law firm as defender of a system of justice), but that our attitudes towards the pure types themselves exhibit a certain degree of internal complexity: we are hybrid in our attitudes and not just in our organizational forms. (Moreover, if our attitudes and not just our organizational structures are organized according to the five facets that Soenen and Moingeon have identified and described, that may explain why some attitudes are difficult to change: they exhibit the resilience of the hybrid form. We relate to the different facets of the attitude in ways that make the attitude very difficult to change.)

Nothing is sustained in a changing environment without interior complexity. Open any mechanical watch and note the complexity of the mechanisms by which it sustains its metronomic precision in the face of changes in position, atmospheric pressure, and temperature. We cannot know whether we have located the most important mechanisms of balance and counterbalance associated with the hybrid law firm, or whether they work exactly as indicated, but what is clear is how useful it is to have a framework that helps uncover the requisite degree of complexity of the hybrid form that is the key to its survival. That the different facets of hybrid identity may not always be consistent may not be a liability, but an advantage. As Ralph Waldo Emerson wrote, "A foolish consistency is the hobgoblin of little minds" (1968: 152).

This chapter has focused on a species of rich description. Not that measurement and analysis of causal structure are unimportant. Simply, that if one begins with a clear "fact," namely, that hybrid identity organizations exist and have existed for a long time, then the task is to understand how that is possible. The five-facet framework provides an excellent starting point for understanding the mechanisms that contribute to the stability of the hybrid form. Like its biological equivalent, the hybrid I^4 form (an organization whose Identity is formed from identities that are Inviolate, Incompatible, and Indispensable) is hardy: it can weather a changing environment by managing the complex dynamics that arise among the different facets of its identity.

Notes

1 I would like to thank David Whetten and Paul Godfrey for their contribution to formulating the criteria of inviolate, incompatible, and indispensable elements.
2 American Bar Association (2000) *Model Rules of Professional Conduct*, 2000 Edition, Chicago: American Bar Association. Rule 1.3, page 15.
3 American Bar Association (2000) *Model Rules of Professional Conduct*, 2000 Edition. Chicago: American Bar Association. Rule 6.1, page 88.
4 The literature on law firm organization, however, is not without suggestions to allow incorporation. See, e.g., Adams, E. S. and Matheson, J. H. (1998) "Law firms

on the big board?: a proposal for nonlawyer investment in law firms," *California Law Review*, 86(1): 1–40.

5   The 80–20 rule of thumb is applicable here. A lawyer likely spends 80 percent of her time on 20 percent of her clients, a fact that makes much of the work repetitive by nature.

6   Some say super-attorney David Boies is said to have left his prestigious New York law firm for this reason. See With, Daniel Orkent (2000) "Get me Boies!" *Time*, 25 Dec. : 107.

7   American Bar Association (2000) *Model Rules of Professional Conduct*, 2000 Edition, Chicago: American Bar Association. Rule 3.4, page 67.

8   As high as 38 percent after the third year, according to a recent National Association for Law Placement study. See Dilucchio, D. (2000) "Lawyer compensation: beyond a seller's market," *Metropolitan Corporate Counsel*, 8(11): 34.

9   Consider President Clinton's "depends what the meaning of the word 'is' is." See Simpson, G. R. (1998) "Impeachment of the President: the charges, the evidence, and the President's defense," *Wall Street Journal*, 21 Dec.: A8. Similarly, Vice President Gore referred to "no controlling legal authority" in defense of his campaign finance activities. See Broder, David S. (1998) "Fine-tuned lawyering," *Washington Post*, 1 Dec.: A25.

References

Adams, E. and Albert, S. (1999) "Law redesigns law. Legal principles as principles of law firm organization," *Rutger's Law Review*, 5: 1133 –206.

Albert, S. (1995) "Towards a theory of timing: an archival study of timing decisions in the Persian Gulf War," in L. L. Cummings and B. M. Staw (eds), *Research in organizational behavior, volume 17*, Greenwich, CT: JAI Press.

Albert, S. and Whetten, D. (1985) "Organizational identity," in L. L. Cummings and B. M. Staw (eds), *Research in organizational behavior, volume 7*, Greenwich, CT: JAI Press, 263–95.

Emerson, R. W. (1968) *The selected writings of Ralph Waldo Emerson*, New York: The Modern Library.

Gioia, D. A. and Thomas, J. B. (1996) "Image, identity and issue interpretation: sense-making during strategic change in academia," *Administrative Science Quarterly*, 41: 370–403.

Pratt, M. G. and Foreman, P. O. (2000) "Classifying managerial responses to multiple organizational identities," *Academy of Management Journal*, 25(1): 18–42.

Rhode, D. L. (1999) "Cultures of commitment: pro bono for lawyers and law students," *Fordham Law Journal*, 67(2): 2415.

Soenen, G. and Moingeon, B. (2002) "The five facets of collective identities: integrating corporate and organizational identity," in B. Moingeon and G. Soenen (eds) *Corporate and organizational identities – integrating strategy, marketing, communication, and organizational perspectives*, London: Routledge.

Tabak, R. J. (1996) "Integration of pro bono into law firm practice," *Georgetown Journal of Legal Ethics*, 9(1): 931.

3 Where do we go from here?

Predicting identification among dispersed employees

Kevin W. Rock and Michael G. Pratt

Introduction

One of the most critical issues in management today is creating a sense of identification among one's workforce (Cheney, 1991). However, several barriers exist that prevent members from developing perceptions of "oneness" with their organization (Ashforth and Mael, 1989). To begin, organizations are becoming increasingly diverse (e.g., through changes in employee demographics and globalization). Research suggests that this diversity may lead to employees viewing themselves less as members of organizations, and more as members of nonwork groups, such as those based on nationality, gender, age, and race. At the same time, the nature of organizations is changing. As organizations become "flatter" and empower their workers, traditional "hierarchical" means of creating a sense of membership among workers may no longer be effective. The dilemma for organizations is this: organizations face a lack of control at the same time workers are being given more opportunities to invest their loyalty elsewhere.

Exacerbating this dilemma is the increasing use of dispersed workers, such as telecommuters, mobile sales workers, and the like. If workers continue to spend increasing amounts of time outside of the physical boundaries of the company, how can managers foster a sense of identification among their organizational members? These trends have led identification researchers to posit that a key managerial challenge is to ensure that members identify with the organization, rather than to some other outside group (Pratt, 2000a).

Unfortunately, theory and research in identification (as well as most theories of organizational behavior) have been built in contexts where members are assumed to be co-located. Does managing identification for dispersed workers create any new challenges for managers? We argue that it does. Hence, the purpose of this chapter is to examine how the dispersion of organizational members influences identification with the organization.

Using extant research in identification as our point of departure, we highlight in the first section, *Identification and the challenges of dispersion*, some critical issues in the management of identification. We also briefly review the literature on dispersed work, and introduce the concept of *employee dispersion patterns* (EDPs) as a more precise way to understand workers that are distributed. In the second section, *EDPs and identification*, we then discuss some of the unique challenges in maintaining identification among employees with various distribution patterns. Finally, in the third section, *Where do we go from here?*, we review managerial practices that can be used for managing dispersed identification. We conclude the chapter by considering opportunities for future research and discussing the implications of our approach for this book's five-facet model of collective identities (Soenen and Moingeon, 2002).

Identification and the challenges of dispersion

Point of departure – Identification

Identification occurs when members of a group or organization come to see their membership as self-defining (Pratt, 1998). Fostering identification among employees has been posited to lead to numerous benefits for members and for organizations. To illustrate, individuals who strongly identify with their organizations can fulfill a variety of needs, including safety, uncertainty reduction, a sense of belonging and self-esteem (Deux *et al.*, 1999; Hogg and Mullin, 1999; Pratt, 1998). Organizations with highly identified workers can also benefit from lower levels of turnover and increases in employee motivation, job satisfaction, and compliance (Ashforth and Humphrey, 1993; Cheney, 1983; Dutton, Dukerich, and Harquail, 1994; Mael and Ashforth, 1995).

In some ways, fostering identification is easy. Early laboratory research in social identity theory suggests that simply placing someone in a group is likely to foster identification with that group (see "minimal group paradigm," (Tajfel, 1970; Tajfel *et al.*, 1971)). However, three major findings from identity research suggest that identification with an organization may instead be more complex in nature.

Individuals have multiple identities

Nearly all theories of identity presume that individuals have multiple self-conceptualizations (Pratt and Foreman, 2000). Social identity theory, for example, suggests that individuals have as many social identities as they have group memberships (Tajfel and Turner, 1979). Hence, John may have an identity based on his work in a project team at IBM, but may also have an identity based on his participation in a soccer club. Similarly, identity theory suggests that individuals have as many identities as they have roles (Stryker, 1987; Stryker and Serpe, 1982). Hence, Mary can have an identity as both a CEO and as a mother – two distinct roles that she maintains (see Hogg, Terry, and White (1995) for a comparison of these two theories).

The importance of social context in determining salience of multiple identities

Research suggests that individuals do not express their multiple identities simultaneously; rather, at any one time, certain identities are salient and others are not. It is these salient identities that are most likely to influence behavior (Stryker, 1987). Social context is one factor that influences salience: different social situations serve as lenses by which different identities are brought into focus, thereby shaping individual attitudes and behaviors.

Self-categorization theory (SCT), for example, suggests that social context plays a role in whether one adopts a "personal" or a "social" identity. These two basic types of identities differ in terms of their levels of inclusiveness (Pratt, in press; Turner, 1999; Turner *et al.*, 1987). Personal identities are the least inclusive and are based on idiosyncratic characteristics (e.g., one's personal preferences). Social identities, by contrast, can range from identities based on membership in small groups to more inclusive identities, such as ones based on being a member of a broad social category, such as gender. The level of inclusiveness at which one identifies depends on which identity serves as the category that most meaningfully organizes the world into things that are similar and things that are different (see Hogg, Terry, and White, 1995; Turner, 1985; Turner *et al.*, 1987). Specifically, the salience of a particular identity depends on the composition of people that surround an individual in a particular situation.

To illustrate, while not the only precursor to identification, SCT research suggests that one is more likely to identify at the level of a social group if members of an out-group (e.g., one's competitors or rivals) are salient in one's social context. Thus, if I am in a room full of identity researchers and accountants, I am more likely to draw upon my identity as an identity researcher than if the room was full of only identity researchers. If surrounded by all identity researchers, I may have to draw upon a more personal identity (e.g., as a lover of ballet) to meaningfully categorize myself in the social field. Therefore, characteristics of the social context influence (a) whether I adopt a personal or social identity, and (b), if I adopt a social identity, which social identity I adopt.

Identity theory similarly suggests that context matters in determining salience. For example, I would be *more* likely to enact a parental role when surrounded by my spouse and kids than when I am with my co-workers. Identity theory, however, further argues that salience is influenced by one's commitment to a role (Stryker, 1968, 1987). Commitment is determined here by the costs (both relational and emotional) associated with abandoning a particular role in a specific social network (Stryker, 1968, 1987). Identities that induce more commitment are more likely to be made chronically salient (Hogg, Terry, and White, 1995), therefore impacting role behavior to a greater degree. This suggests that individuals with chronic identities will be more steadfast in keeping those identities, rather than changing identities based on new social contexts. For example, if an organizational identity is chronically salient for me, I am more likely to enact that identity in non-organizational settings (e.g., act like a CEO at home). Therefore, while social context influences identity salience, it is not the sole predictor of which identity an individual enacts. From identity theory and SCT, then, we assume that the salience of an identity is influenced by commitment to that identity (how chronic the identity is), as well as by the particular configuration of individuals in one's social field.

Identification is emotional and ongoing

Just because an identity is salient it does not mean that an individual always has a positive emotional reaction towards it. Initial definitions of social identity, for example, note that these identities have an "evaluative component" to them (Tajfel and Turner, 1979). However, much research in identification has neglected this component (Harquail, 1998). Only recently has research suggested that identification can be infused with emotions, and can be of three types: positive, negative, and ambivalent (Dukerich, Kramer, and Parks, 1998; Elsbach, 1999; Pratt, 1998). Hence, individuals can love (positive identification), hate (disidentification), or feel conflicted towards (ambivalent identification) organizations with which they identify. Moreover, these feelings can range from weak to strong, from detached to strong attachment, and likewise, from mild dislike to utter and complete contempt.

Furthermore, members' cognitive and emotional reactions towards an organization can change over time. Just as identity salience can change depending on the context one finds oneself in, so too can one's emotional evaluation of a particular identity (Pratt, 2000b). Thus, a critical issue in managing member identification is not simply about attaining a sense of strong, positive identification. Rather, organizations must also be concerned about *maintaining* such identification. Unfortunately, there is scant research on how identification is managed over time and across contexts. This chapter will propose a model that takes into account both the temporal and contextual aspects of organizational identification change and management.

Given these three previous assumptions about identification, it becomes clearer why identification may be problematic when workers are not physically located within corporate headquarters. As members are dispersed, their social contexts change, which increases the potential for non-organizational identities to become salient. As a result, members' emotional evaluation of their relationship with the organization may enter a state of flux. However, differences in how and where members are dispersed may differentially affect these factors and therefore influence members' relationships with their organizations. Thus, we introduce the concept of EDPs to further investigate how dispersion might impact members' identification.

Employee Dispersion Patterns (EDPs) – identifying three types

Several authors have suggested that alternative work arrangements are emerging that involve organizations sending out individuals or teams of employees to work at home, or in the "field" with customers or other organizational constituents (Barnatt, 1995; Fritz, Narasimhan, and Rhee, 1998). Organizations are believed to be gravitating towards these types of arrangements because they seek to: (1) give employees different types of working options; (2) reduce capital costs by setting up multiple work sites; or (3) extend the organization by sending individuals to solve problems, sell products, or represent the company in some other environment (Gray *et al.*, 1993; Nilles, 1998).

Different work arrangements have traditionally been treated in the literature as variations of telecommuting, defined by one author as a "flexible way of working . . . remotely from an employer, or from a traditional place of work" (Gray, Hodson, and Gordon, 1993). In this largely functional, applied literature, telecommuting has involved not only individuals working at home, but also satellite offices (Doswell, 1992; Nilles, 1994), neighborhood work centers (Nilles, 1994; Olson, 1987), and persons who work while mobile (Pinsonneault and Boisvert, 2001).

Empirical research in this area is not conclusive, with researchers often coming to contradictory conclusions. Some researchers found that telecommuting has positive outcomes such as increased loyalty (Caudron, 1992), satisfaction (Chapman *et al.*, 1995), productivity (Baruch and Nicholson, 1997; Caudron, 1992; Huws, 1993; Olson, 1988), and lower absenteeism (Fitzer, 1997; Gordon and Kelly, 1986; Greengard, 1995; Nilles, 1994). Others, however, have found connections to decreased organizational commitment (Kinsman, 1987), increased feelings of isolation (Chapman *et al.*, 1995; Huws, 1993; Solomon and Templer, 1993), and reduced intraorganizational communication (Ramsower, 1985; Richter and Meshulam, 1993).

We build on research in telecommuting and other alternative work arrangements in three distinct ways. First, we broaden the scope of inquiry to include any organizational member who spends a majority of his or her time physically located outside of the organization. Second, we look not only at the outcome of being physically separate from the organization, but also at the process by which this happens. We favor the term "dispersion" over others (e.g., distributed, telecommuters, teleworkers) because we are interested in the *process* of organizations sending out their members. Third, unlike previous research that has largely focused on the increased utilization of technology during dispersion (Fitzer, 1997; Pinsonneault and Boisvert, 2001), we are interested in how these work arrangements influence members' connections with the organization (i.e., their identification). Specifically, we are interested in how the process of dispersing members influences their level and type of identification with the organization.

To elucidate this process, we examine some of the environments into which members are being dispersed. Drawing from research in identity and identification, we know that social context matters, so we examine different contextual conditions. We also know that just being in a group can cue a social identity. Thus, first, we examine whether individuals are removed from the organization to work alone or to work as a member of a team. By "team," we imply a stable cadre of employees that work interdependently for a significant period of time in a single location (co-located, not virtual), be it inside or outside of the organization. Second, we know that a member is likely to identify with his or her organization when competing organizations are noticeable (Pratt 2000a). Thus, we also examine whether one is dispersed into a team of fellow organizational members ("organizational team") or whether one is working in a new, dispersed context as part of a team consisting primarily of out-group members ("non-organizational team").

These two social context conditions suggest three types of dispersion patterns: individuals dispersed by themselves, individuals dispersed into organizational teams, and individuals dispersed into non-organizational teams.[1] Each of these three "types" of dispersion patterns has been found in practice. To illustrate, individuals who are dispersed alone, rather than in a team, would include telecommuters or teleworkers, and mobile salespeople. Employees who are dispersed as part of an organizational team would include consulting teams working with clients, or an entourage that is representing the organization in a merger, joint venture, or other co-operative agreement. Finally, an individual who is dispersed to work in a non-organizational team may include a consultant sent to work with a team of clients, or an organizational representative working on a committee consisting of members in similar roles across organizational contexts (e.g., working on an expert panel of members from various organizations). These dispersion types should be viewed as "ideal types" – certainly there are some that seem to fall between categorizations. However, we propose these as a starting point for theorizing about identification and dispersion.[2]

EDPs and identification

Having mapped out three different types of EDPs, we now turn our attention to how these EDPs might influence member identification. While treatments of alternate work arrangements have suggested that the fundamental differences among various types of dispersion need to be examined (Fritz, Narasimhan, and Rhee, 1998; Guimaraes and Dallow, 1999; Williams, 1982), very little research has studied how different types of dispersion affect an individual's connection with his or her organization. Our underlying argument to this point is that different EDPs embody different social contexts – and since social context influences identification, different EDPs will result in different identification patterns.

We add another layer of complexity, however, to this rather straightforward argument by assuming that (a) members may already identify with an organization prior to dispersion, and (b) these members may differ in their level and type of identification. While previous research has examined identification dynamics among certain types of distributed groups (e.g., Wiesenfeld, Raghuram, and Garud, 2001), most extant research has focused on the presence or absence of positive identification. However, we have noted that identification should not be seen as a positive, dichotomous variable. There are at least three types of identification (positive, negative, and ambivalent), all of which can vary by degree (e.g., strong or weak). Taking just these two dimensions, we see that many orientations are theoretically possible (e.g., strong positive, weak negative, etc.). We narrow our focus by choosing three that are most likely to exist in organizational contexts.

To begin, we will examine individuals with both strong and weak levels of positive identification with the organization. This provides an analysis of a range of positive identification, rather than taking just a slice, or assuming all employees with a positive orientation identify similarly. We also look at individuals with more negative attitudes towards the organization. While we believe that individuals who strongly disidentify with their organizations are likely to quit, individuals with weaker levels of disidentification may remain. Finally, we do discuss ambivalent identification, but not as a starting point for identification. Rather, we view ambivalence as a relatively transient state that must be resolved (e.g., Pratt 2000b).[3]

In sum, we argue that employees' type and level of identification prior to dispersion will be changed by the act of dispersion. In addition, we argue that different types of dispersion patterns will moderate this change in identification. These arguments are summarized in Figure 3.1.

We further unpack Figure 3.1 by examining the expected changes in identification of strong identifiers, weak identifiers, and weak disidentifiers who are dispersed in three types of EDPs: (1) a single individual working alone; (2) an individual working in an organizational team; and (3) an individual working in a non-organizational team. We conclude by discussing the managerial issues raised by this analysis.

Figure 3.2 is organized to read from the right to the left. Each different prior identification is situated as a column, corresponding with the "starting" identification place on the bottom axis of the graph. In total, we examine nine scenarios that combine prior identification with a specific EDP. The arrows (if present) represent the directional changes in identification we predict given the prior identification and the corresponding EDP.

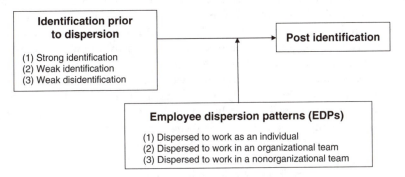

Figure 3.1 A model of employee dispersion patterns (EDPs) and organizational identification.

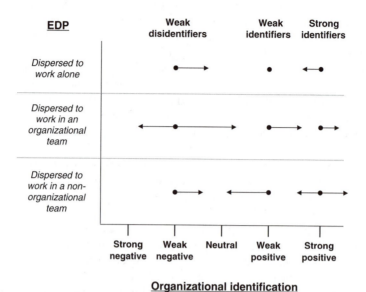

Figure 3.2 The effect of employee dispersion patterns (EDPs) on organizational identification.

Strong identifiers and EDPs

Individual working alone

We argue that sending a single highly identified worker to work alone outside of the physical confines of the workplace is likely to decrease that member's strong, positive identification. Building from our earlier review, taking this individual outside of the organization is likely to lower the salience of that identity, and thus, lower his or her level of identification. Identity theory supports this in suggesting that moving members to a non-organizational context is likely to elicit increased salience of non-organizational identities (e.g., parental role identity if employee is working at home).

However, despite these social context cues, it is unlikely that members' strong identification would entirely vanish. Identity theory also argues that salience is not simply a function of social context, but also of a member's level of commitment to that identity. Since we assume that individuals with strong organizational identification are also committed to their organizational identity, we expect that employees in this condition will continue to draw upon their organizationally-based identities, although perhaps not as often. Thus, positive identification will likely remain, even if in a slightly weakened form.

Individual working within an organizational team

In contrast to the previous EDP, sending an individual employee to work within an organizational team is likely to increase the salience of his or her identity as an organizational member, thus maintaining or even strengthening his or her strong organizational identification. Here, non-organizational out-groups are very prominent, thus creating the conditions for interorganizational comparisons, and consequently for social identification based on organizational membership. Moreover, this social context is likely to make organizational roles salient, as team members come to define their functions within the team based on their organizational roles. As these conditions heighten the salience of one's organizational identity, members may come to view their team as an "extension" of the organization.

Individual working within a non-organizational team

This last EDP poses the most difficulty for making identification predictions. On the one hand, holding a strong identification may mean that one's organizational identity is chronically salient, and therefore, may not be highly influenced by this new context. Moreover, if the team refers to a member in terms of his or her organizational membership, the social context might maintain or strengthen one's organizational identification.

On the other hand, being in a new team also offers a new group membership that may serve as a powerful category for identification. This would be especially true if one's new team is competing with "out-group" teams from one's home organization or from the "visiting" organization. In addition, in this new, non-organizational team, there may be other meaningful categories that help a member make sense of his or her social context. For example, he or she might be one of three accountants working with three human resource specialists. Here, one's professional identity may be more salient than one's organizational identity. This suggests that organizational identification may weaken.

Taken as a whole, we predict that individuals in this last EDP may feel ambivalence, or the feeling of being pulled in opposite directions (Merton, 1976; Pratt and Doucet, 2000; Sincoff, 1990). If ambivalence is not resolved, members are likely to either experience behavioral paralysis or vacillation, both of which could lead to poor performance. However, ambivalence can be resolved by increasing or decreasing the strength of one's identification (see Pratt and Doucet, 2000). Given our arguments above, we suggest that if the employees' non-organizational team works in isolation, and if there are not other meaningful social categories that would divide the team (e.g., different professions), then it is likely that strong identifiers will retain their strong identification with the home organization. However, if the non-organizational team is interacting with salient "out-groups," or if there were other meaningful categorizations (e.g., professional) within the team, we would suggest, following Social Identity Theory (SIT), that one's identification with the organization might weaken.

Weak identifiers and EDPs

In contrast to strong identifiers, employees in this condition are not as emotionally invested in their organizational membership. In SIT terms, one's social identity based on organizational membership is evaluated positively, but not strongly. In terms of identity theory, one's organizational role is not as chronically salient as other role identities.

Individual working alone

As depicted in Figure 3.2, we propose that dispersing employees alone, in order to work alone, is likely to maintain their already weak levels of identification with the organization. Given that organizational identity is not highly salient initially, removing them from a social context that reminds them of these roles (e.g., the physical presence of co-workers) is not likely to increase the salience of these roles. Similarly, as is the case with strong identifiers, working alone is not likely to make organizationally relevant out-groups salient, and thus is not likely to trigger an increase in organizational identification due to social comparisons.

Individual working within an organizational team

By contrast, we argue that dispersing members with weak identifications within organizational teams is likely to make employees' roles and member-ship highly salient. Thus, we would expect that employees in this condition would likely increase their organizational identification given the prominence of a new, non-organizational out-group. As a result, we can view this condition as a type of organizational "intervention" for increasing identification among weak identifiers.

Individual working within a non-organizational team

Dispersing a weak identifier alone into a non-organizational team is likely to lead to a further weakening of his or her identification. While there may be some push to identify with the organization since that may be one of the only meaningful differences that helps categorize one's self in relation to the social context, several conditions mitigate the likelihood of this happening. To begin, the employee's initial commitment to their organizational identity is weak. Thus, it is likely that a more chronically salient identity may be invoked when factors, such as the absence of organizationally relevant symbols and the presence of co-workers, do not serve to strengthen the salience of one's identity based on organizational membership. Moreover, the social context of a new team will be an even more powerful "draw" for weak identifiers than for strong identifiers, especially if membership in this new team enhances the employ-ees' self-esteem, or reduces social uncertainty. Thus, we believe that in this condition, the potential for weak identifiers to separate even further from the organization is high, making the adoption of non-organizational identities and consequent "defection" a strong possibility.

Weak disidentifiers and EDPs

As noted, organizational disidentifiers are those that view themselves as separate from the organization (Elsbach and Bhattacharya, 2001) and have a negative evaluation of their social identities based on organizational membership (Pratt, 2000b). At a weak level of disidentification, these employees are likely to be somewhat discontented with the organization, but are not so negative towards it as to psychologically or physically leave it completely. That is, their evaluations of the identity are negative, but the identity is not chronically salient. In view of their attitudes, organizations may be most willing to disperse these individuals, so as not to hurt the morale of those who remain. However, these employees may prove not to be the best "ambassadors" for the company. Hence, dispersing weak identifiers raises several interesting challenges.

Individual working alone

Unlike in the case of those with positive identification, dispersing a weak disidentifier alone, in order to work alone, may have a positive impact on identification. If an employee's evaluation of his or her organizational role and membership is negative, then changing the social context such that the organization is less salient should cause the employee to think of the organization less often, thereby decreasing the amount of time spent feeling negatively towards it. In other words, dispersing the individual alone is likely to decrease the importance of an identity based on organizational membership, thus decreasing the experience of disidentification.

It may be the case that disidentifying employees may even appreciate being removed from their organizational context, especially if the source of their disidentification is due to another member(s) in the organization (e.g., their supervisor). If this is the case, then dispersing employees alone may not only decrease their negative evaluation of the organization, it may even slightly increase their positive evaluation.

Individual working within an organizational team

This second EDP is reported to strengthen identification in both weak and strong identifiers. For weak disidentifiers, however, the increase in organizational identity salience – inherent in this EDP – is likely to lead either to some degree of positive identification or to higher levels of disidentification. On the one hand, making one's identity based on organizational membership salient makes it difficult to separate one's self from this categorization. Employees with highly salient identities that bear a negative evaluation may attempt to alter their perceptions of their in-group membership in order to maintain their own self-esteem (see "social creativity" (Tajfel and Turner, 1979)). This reaction is especially likely if the employee perceives barriers to exiting this organizational team to be high (i.e., low "mobility" between groups). This situation could therefore lead members to experience some positive identification. On the other hand, making a nonsalient, negative identity more prominent may make one's disidentification more chronic. The employee may resent conditions whereby this organizational category is thrust into higher importance thereby strengthening disidentification.

Individual working within a non-organizational team

Similar to weak identifiers, dispersing weak disidentifiers into a non-organizational team is likely to lead to defection on the part of the employee. The relatively low salience of their organizationally relevant identity, combined with their low evaluation of it, makes it unlikely that this category will be used to meaningfully interpret the environment. Rather, these employees are likely to use other categories, especially non-organizational categories, to best differentiate similarities and differences in their social context.

Sending an individual into this EDP is also less likely to reap the positive benefits of dispersion that the organization might accrue if it were simply sending the weak disidentifying employee out by him- or herself. In this third EDP, employees not only have a chance to physically and emotionally distance themselves from an unsatisfying context, but a substitute identity is ready-made for them, that of the new, non-organizational team, or the new organization. Thus, while the arrow in Figure 3.2 suggests that the strength of disidentification may be weakened, this may not be ideal for organizations. A tradeoff exists for these organizations: dispersion may cause disidentifiers to relax their hatred towards the organization, but at the price of possibly having them defect to other organizations, or having them share negative public statements with organizational and non-organizational members.

Managerial issues and EDPs

Our arguments, summarized in Figures 3.1 and 3.2, predict how members with three different types and levels of organizational identification – strong identification, weak identification, and weak disidentification – will differentially respond to one of three types of dispersion: alone, into an organizational team, and into a non-organizational team. Organizations that wish to manage their members' identification may wish to carefully choose which type of individual gets placed in which type of EDP.

Strong identifiers

For strong identifiers, the best scenario with the least amount of risk is to send them out within the confines of an organizational team. If an individual is already identifying strongly with the organization, the organization likely does not want to remove the "connection" that maintains that relationship. By keeping these members in organizational teams, members can retain their categorization as organizational in-group members while allowing out-group comparisons to be made even more salient. This outcome may also be attained if a strong identifier is placed in a non-organizational team. However, this dispersion pattern carries with it significantly more risk: instead of an increase, the presence of new social categories could lead instead to a decrease in identification.

The worst managerial decision concerning strong identifiers is dispersing them alone in order to work alone. Here, strong identifiers may feel abandoned and will lack the social context cues that reinforce their strong identification. However, a potential trade-off exists for the organization. Organizations may wish to disperse these individuals to work alone knowing that identification will not entirely wane, but that employee productivity (Baruch and Nicholson, 1997) and/or satisfaction (Chapman *et al.*, 1995) may improve.

Weak identifiers

As with strong identifiers, dispersing individuals into organizational teams also seems to be the best decision. Shared organizational membership may be the characteristic that these team members use to define themselves in this new situation.

Unlike strong identifiers, dispersing weak identifiers alone will not likely change their identification. The worst dispersion decision for these employees would be to send them out into non-organizational teams. As noted, this scenario will likely lead to the defection of an individual as he or she adopts a new, non-organizational team identity.

Weak disidentifiers

Deciding how to disperse weak disidentifiers is perhaps the most challenging and the most daunting of the dispersion decisions. At one level, any intervention may be beneficial, as dispersion is likely to cause a decrease in the salience of the disliked organizationally-based identity, and thus, a decrease in the time spent negatively evaluating the organization. However, upon closer examination, it seems that some solutions are riskier for the organization than others.

The only condition that may engender positive identification appears to be the dispersion of these individuals as part of an organizational team. However, this strategy is risky, as another outcome associated with this EDP is a move towards higher disidentification. A safer bet is to attempt to simply tone down their level of disidentification towards a more neutral point by dispersing them alone in order to work alone.

A similar "toning down" of disidentification will also occur if the individual is dispersed to work in a non-organizational team. However, this condition carries with it some potentially negative outcomes for the organization. As noted, not only may this scenario lead to the defection of an employee to an non-organizational team, but it may also result in the member "bad mouthing" the organization, or even revealing sensitive information to outside organizational sources.

Where do we go from here? Managerial practices

The previous section outlined dispersion as a possible identification management intervention – an organizational practice designed to change individual identification. However, choosing the type of dispersal pattern for members is just one possible identification management strategy that an organization can employ. In this section, we offer three additional strategies that organizations can use to further manage the identification of dispersed workers: targeting attitudes towards dispersion, targeting attitudes towards the organization, and replacing physical co-location with psychological co-location.

Target: attitudes towards dispersion

In our discussion, we have raised the notion that members – especially those that strongly identify with the organization – may see some types of dispersion as abandonment. The following tactics may serve to buffer employees against those feelings.

Assessing person–dispersion fit

The argument behind person–dispersion fit is that individual attitudes and behavior are not just a result of the individual or the environment, but from the interaction of the two (see "person–environment fit" (Edwards, 1996)). Consequently, it may be possible to preselect individuals that will not perceive abandonment in conjunction with their new dispersed environment.

To facilitate this selection process, the organization can offer members a realistic job preview of dispersed environments. This preview will allow both members and organizations to better predict responses to dispersion. This process may uncover whether or not a member is well suited for dispersion. If he or she is not, both the organization and employee could decide whether it is best for the member to undergo additional predispersion training, or simply to remain working within the physical confines of the organization.

Changing cultural assumptions about dispersion

This suggestion for the organization is likely the most difficult and the most extensive: creating an organizational culture that values dispersion. If an organization can change its negative (or missing) collective values – and ultimately change its underlying assumptions (Schein 1985) – about dispersion, then employees may see dispersion not as abandonment, but rather, as an opportunity or reward. By fulfilling a valued function for the organization, attitudes of members towards dispersion are likely to be bolstered.

Target: attitudes towards the organization

Another possibility for organizations is to improve attitudes towards the organization – especially for weak identifiers and weak disidentifiers. In this way, organizations are bringing individuals psychologically closer to the organization so that identification prior to dispersion is stronger.

Pre-dispersion socialization

Research has shown that institutionalized socialization can lead to identification with the organization, or the adoption of an organizational role orientation (Ashforth and Saks, 1996; Jones, 1986). What this implies is that prior to dispersion, individuals should be *resocialized* (assuming they are not newcomers) via these tactics before they are dispersed. This resocialization can serve to increase overall identification towards the organization, thereby buffering them from other possible work-related identities.

In a related vein, research has also shown that successfully combining sensebreaking and sensegiving socialization techniques – whereby organizations both create and satisfy the need for meaning among members – may produce strong identification with the organization (see Pratt, 2000b). These techniques also serve to preserve the identification of members when they are dispersed, by providing a belief system that helps them maintain a positive outlook when faced with organizational outsiders and detractors (i.e., ideological encapsulation).

Positive team role models

Another possibility for individuals that are working in team EDPs is to include positive team role models along with the "target" dispersed worker. To illustrate, Pratt (2000b) suggests that having positive "mentors" when working in distributed groups can facilitate the formation of strong identification with the organization. He argues that such mentors heighten the salience of positive aspects of organizational categories among dispersed members. The use of these positive team role models is likely to be especially important for weak identifiers and disidentifiers, where the potential for diminishing identification – or even for defection – is high.

Replace physical co-location with psychological co-location

This last set of tactics involves the creation of a dispersed environment that allows individuals to still feel "close" to the organization, even when dispersed.

Using organizational symbols to "extend" the organization

A symbol is a "sign which denotes something greater than itself" (Morgan, Frost, and Pondy, 1983). Pratt and Rafaeli (1997) suggest that physical symbols, especially those that are portable and functional, may be used to signal strong identification among a distributed workforce. These symbols, such as business cards and laptops embossed with the corporate logo, may be used in lieu of the traditional organizational markers (e.g., architectural design of corporate offices) that remind workers that one's work roles should be the most salient. As such, we argue that physical symbols may be used to "extend" the organization beyond its physical boundaries by changing members' physical (as opposed to social) context, thus making the dispersed worker feel less psychologically distant.

Enriching communication media

To further the effectiveness of symbol use, organizations may wish to use rich media – media high in expressivity and interactivity – to communicate with dispersed workers. Rich media, such as face-to-face communication, differs from lean media in its ability to transmit social context cues (Daft and Lengel, 1986). However, given that face-to-face interactions may be difficult for dispersed members, organizations can enrich lean media, such as e-mail or telephone communication, via additional media training (see "channel expansion theory" (Carlson and Zmud, 1999)). As with symbols, using "enriched" media can create a sense of psychological co-location to replace the lack of physical co-location (Pratt, Fuller, and Northcraft, 2000).

Conclusion

We believe that it is important for scholars and practitioners to examine the interplay of how organizations disperse their workers and manage changes in members' identification. Our goal was to provide a foundation from which to build research in this area by taking into consideration: (a) different types of member identification; (b) different types of possible dispersion patterns; and (c) different outcomes that can occur as organizations attempt to manage the identification of dispersed employees.

Our focus also suggests interventions can occur at the individual, team, and organizational level. We suggest that work continues at each of these levels. Work at the individual level should explore how personality and other individual differences may influence members' attitudes towards dispersion. For example, how might introverts respond differently to dispersion than extroverts? Are some individuals more likely to see dispersion as a reward (thus potentially increasing their positive identification) than others? Work at the team level can focus on factors such as team composition and the impact of team cohesion. It is likely that dispersing individuals into a team of disidentifiers will result in different identification outcomes than dispersing individuals into a team of strong identifiers. At the organizational level, research should continue to examine dispersed organizational culture and identity by investigating how these form and are maintained in dispersed environments.

Our chapter complicates and enhances the identity framework posed in this book through our focus on identification. Identification may be the key that helps link individual conceptualizations of identity with that of the collective (Pratt, in press). As such, we enrich the model by reaching across levels of analysis. We also raise some fundamental questions about the various facets of identity posited in this volume (Soenen and Moingeon, 2002):

- We suggest that continued work be conducted on the interrelationships among identity dynamics across levels of analysis (e.g., Kahane and Reitter, this volume). Research questions may seek to address, for example, how physically dispersing employees influences members' collective cognitive maps of their organization (i.e., their *experienced* identity).
- We suggest that a distributed organization may rely on technologically-mediated communication. How does an organization's communication technology come to *manifest* and change *experienced* identity over time?
- We note that when weak identifiers and weak disidentifiers are dispersed into non-organizational teams, defection to those non-organizational teams can occur. How might this potential defection influence how these non-organizational teams *attribute* characteristics to the organization?
- Finally, we note that dispersing individuals outside of an organization changes their social context, and thus, their attitudes towards and perceptions of the organization. How, then, can an organization best manage its *projected* identity towards dispersed workers so that the nature of the *professed* organizational identity can be maintained? What tools (e.g., symbols, technology, training) can the organization use to further this goal?

In summary, identity in organizations is not only multifaceted, but also multi-layered. We examine how dispersing individuals may change identity dynamics at the micro-level, and suggest that these changes may ultimately reverberate to the macro-level.

Notes

1 It is important to note that our attention here is on employees dispersed into contexts outside of their "home" organization, in environments where other, new, identities may become prominent. While we assume that an employee dispersed alone may work in isolation (e.g., in one's house), our other dispersion examples and arguments are based strictly upon teams being in organizational contexts away from the focal employee's "home" organization (e.g., a client's organization).
2 The aim of this chapter is not to claim that these are the only – or the only relevant – EDPs. There are definitely more EDPs that exist and need to be studied. One

example would be individuals that are dispersed to different areas or divisions of the same organization. This EDP would have identity implications separate and distinct from what we have provided here – a starting point for the study of identification and EDPs.

3 Pratt's (2000b) analysis of Amway distributors talked about ambivalent identification as a more permanent state. However, individuals in Amway were both distributed and often part-time. Thus, individuals were better able to deal with their ambivalence by avoiding contact with the organization; an option that is not available in many full-time employment situations.

References

Ashforth, B. E. and Humphrey, R. H. (1993) "Emotional labor in service roles: the influence of identity," *Academy of Management Review*, 18: 88–115.

Ashforth, B. E. and Mael, F. (1989) "Social identity theory and the organization," *Academy of Management Review*, 14: 20–39.

Ashforth, B. E. and Saks, A. M. (1996) "Socialization tactics: longitudinal effects on newcomer adjustment," *Academy of Management Journal*, 39: 149–78.

Barnatt, C. (1995) "Office space, cyberspace and virtual organization," *Journal of General Management*, 20: 78–91.

Baruch, Y. and Nicholson, N. (1997) "Home, sweet work: requirements for effective home working," *Journal of General Management,* 23: 15–30.

Carlson, J. R. and Zmud, R. W. (1999) "Channel expansion theory and the experiential nature of media richness perceptions," *Academy of Management Journal*, 42: 153–70.

Caudron, S. (1992) "Working at home pays off," *Personnel Journal*, November: 40–9.

Chapman, A. J., Sheehy, N. P., Heywood, S., Dooley, B., and Collins, S. C. (1995) "The organizational implications of teleworking," in C. L. Cooper and I. T. Robertson (eds) *International review of industrial and organizational psychology, volume 10*, Chichester: John Wiley & Sons, 229–48.

Cheney, G. (1983) "The rhetoric of identification and the study of organizational communication," *Quarterly Journal of Speech*, 69: 143–58.

Cheney, G. (1991) *Rhetoric in an organizational society: managing multiple identities*, Columbia, SC: University of South Carolina Press.

Daft, R. L. and Lengel, R. H. (1986) "Organizational information requirements, media richness, and structural design," *Management Science*, 32: 554–71.

Deux, K., Reid, A., Mizrahi, K., and Cotting, D. (1999) "Connecting the person to the social: the functions of social identification," in T. Tyler, R. M. Kramer, and O. P. John (eds) *The psychology of the social self*, Mahwah, NJ: Lawrence Erlbaum Associates, 91–113.

Doswell, A. (1992) "Home alone? – teleworking," *Management Services*, 36 (10): 18–21.

Dukerich, J. M., Kramer, R. M., and Parks, J. M. (1998) "The dark side of organizational identification," in D. A. Whetten and P. C. Godfrey (eds), *Identity in organizations: building theory through conversations*, Thousand Oaks, CA: Sage.

Dutton, J. E., Dukerich, J. M., and Harquail, C. V. (1994) "Organizational images and member identification," *Administrative Science Quarterly*, 39: 239–63.

Edwards, J. R. (1996) "An examination of competing versions of the person–environment fit approach to stress," *Academy of Management Journal*, 39: 292–339.

Elsbach, K. D. (1999) "An expanded model of organizational identification," In R. I.

Sutton and B. M. Staw (eds) *Research in organizational behavior, volume 21*, Stanford, CA: JAI Press, 163–99.

Elsbach, K. D. and Bhattacharya, C. B. (2001) "Defining who you are by what you're not," *Organization Science*, 12: 393–413.

Fitzer, M. M. (1997) "Managing from afar: performance and rewards in a telecommuting environment," *Compensation and Benefits Review*, 29: 65–73.

Fritz, M. B. W., Narasimhan, S., and Rhee, H.-S. (1998) "Communication and coordination in the virtual office," *Journal of Management Information Systems*, 14: 7–28.

Gordon, G. E. and Kelly, M. M. (1986) *Telecommuting: how to make it work for you and your company*, Englewood Cliffs, NJ: Prentice Hall.

Gray, M., Hodson, N., and Gordon, G. (1993) *Teleworking explained*, New York: John Wiley & Sons.

Greengard, S. (1995) "All the comforts of home," *Personnel Journal*, 73: 66–79.

Guimaraes, T. and Dallow, P. K. (1999) "Empirically testing the benefits, problems, and success factors for telecommuting programmes," *European Journal of Information Systems*, 8: 40–54.

Harquail, C. V. (1998) "Organizational identification and the 'whole person': integrating affect, behavior, and cognition," In D. A. Whetten and P. Godfrey (eds) *Identity in organizations: developing theory through conversations*, Thousand Oaks, CA: Sage, 223–31.

Hogg, M. A. and Mullin, B. A. (1999) "Joining groups to reduce uncertainty: subjective uncertainty reduction and group identification," in D. Abrams and M. A. Hogg (eds) *Social identity and social cognition*, Oxford: Blackwell, 249–79.

Hogg, M. A., Terry, D. J., and White, K. M. (1995) "A tale of two theories: a critical comparison of identity theory with social identity theory," *Social Psychology Quarterly*, 58: 255–69.

Huws, U. (1993) *Teleworking in Britain (report no. 18)*, London: The Employment Department Research Series.

Jones, G. R. (1986) "Socialization tactics, self-efficacy, and newcomers' adjustments to organizations," *Academy of Management Journal*, 29: 262–79.

Kinsman, F. (1987) *The telecommuters*, Chichester: John Wiley & Sons.

Mael, F. A. and Ashforth, B. E. (1995) "Loyal from day one: biodata, organizational identification, and turnover among newcomers," *Personnel Psychology*, 48: 309–33.

Merton, R. (1976) *Sociological ambivalence and other essays*, New York: Free Press.

Morgan, G., Frost, P., and Pondy, L. R. (1983) "Organizational symbolism," in L. R. Pondy, P. Frost, G. Morgan, and T. Dandridge (eds) *Organizational symbolism*, Greenwich, CT: JAI Press, 3–35.

Nilles, J. M. (1994) *Making telecommuting happen*, New York: Van Nostrand Reinhold.

Nilles, J. M. (1998) *Managing telework: strategies for managing the virtual workforce*, New York: John Wiley & Sons.

Olson, M. H. (1987) "Telework: practical experience and future prospects," in R. E. Kraut (ed.) *Technology and the transformation of white collar work*, Hillsdale, NJ: Lawrence Erlbaum Associates.

Olson, M. H. (1988) "Organizational barriers to telecommuting," in W. B. Korte, B. Steinle, and S. Robinson (eds) *Telework: present situation and future development of a new form of work organization*, Amsterdam: North-Holland.

Pinsonneault, A. and Boisvert, M. (2001) "The impacts of telecommuting on organizations and individuals: a review of the literature," in N. J. Johnson (ed.)

Telecommuting and virtual offices: issues and opportunities, Hershey, PA: Idea Group Publishing, 163–85.

Pratt, M. G. (1998) "To be or not to be: central questions in organizational identification," in D. A. Whetten and P. Godfrey (eds) *Identity in organizations: developing theory through conversations*, Thousand Oaks, CA: Sage, 171–207.

Pratt, M. G. (2000a) "Social identity dynamics in modern organizations: an organization psychology/organizational behavior perspective," in M. Hogg and D. J. Terry (eds), *Social identity processes in organizational contexts*, Brighton: Psychology Press.

Pratt, M. G. (2000b) "The good, the bad, and the ambivalent: managing identification among Amway distributors," *Administrative Science Quarterly*, 45: 456–93.

Pratt, M. G. (in press) "Disentangling collective identity," in J. T. Polzer, E. Mannix, and M. A. Neale (eds) *Research on managing groups and teams, volume V*, Stamford, CT: JAI Press.

Pratt, M. G. and Doucet, L. (2000) "Ambivalent feelings in organizational relationships," in S. Fineman (ed.) *Emotions in organizations, volume II*, London: Sage, 204–26.

Pratt, M. G. and Foreman, P. O. (2000) "Classifying managerial responses to multiple organizational identities," *Academy of Management Review*, 25 (1): 18–42.

Pratt, M. G., Fuller, M., and Northcraft, G. B. (2000) "Media selection and identification in distributed groups: the potential cost of 'rich' media," in T. L. Griffith, E. Mannix, and M. A. Neale (eds) *Research on managing groups and team, volume III*, Stamford, CT: JAI Press, 231–54.

Pratt, M. and Rafaeli, A. (1997) "Organizational chess as a symbol of multilayered social identities," *Academy of Management Journal*, 40 (4): 862–99.

Ramsower, R. M. (1985) *Telecommuting: the organizational and behavioral effects of working at home*, Ann Arbor, MI: UMI Research Press.

Richter, J. and Meshulam, I. (1993) "Telework at home: the home and the organization perspective," *Human Systems Management*, 12: 193–203.

Schein, E. (1985) *Organizational culture and leadership*, San Francisco, CA: Jossey-Bass.

Sincoff, J. (1990) "The psychological characteristics of ambivalent people," *Clinical Psychological Review*, 10: 43–68.

Soenen, G. and Moingeon, B. (2002) "The five facets of collective identities: integrating corporate and organizational identity," in B. Moingeon and G. Soenen (eds) *Corporate and organizational identities – integrating strategy, marketing, communication and organizational perspectives*, London: Routledge.

Solomon, N. A. and Templer, A. J. (1993) "Development of non-traditional work sites: the challenge of telecommuting," *Journal of Management Development*, 12: 21–32.

Stryker, S. (1968) "Identity salience and role performance: the relevance of symbolic interaction theory for family research," *Journal of Marriage and the Family*, 30: 558–64.

Stryker, S. (1987) "Identity theory: developments and extensions," in K. Yardley and T. Honess (eds) *Self and identity: psychological perspectives*, New York: John Wiley & Sons, 89–103.

Stryker, S. and Serpe, R. T. (1982) "Commitment, identity salience, and role behavior: theory and research example," in W. Ickers and E. Knowles (eds) *Personality, roles and social behavior*, New York: Springer-Verlag, 199–219.

Tajfel, H. (1970) "Experiments in intergroup discrimination," *Scientific American*, 223: 96–102.

Tajfel, H., Flament, C., Billig, M., and Bundy, R. (1971) "Social categorization and intergroup behavior," *European Journal of Social Psychology*, 1: 149–78.

Tajfel, H. and Turner, J. C. (1979) "An integrative theory of intergroup conflict," in W. G. Austin and S. Worchel (eds) *The social psychology of group relations*, Monterey, CA: Brooks-Cole, 33–47.

Turner, J. C. (1985) "Social categorization and the self-concept: a social cognitive theory of group behavior," in E. J. Lawler (ed.) *Advances in group process: theory and research, volume 2*, Greenwich, CT: JAI Press, 77–121.

Turner, J. C. (1999) "Some current issues in research on social identity and self-categorization," in N. Ellemers, R. Spears, and B. Doosje (eds) *Social identity*, Malden, MA: Blackwell, 6–34.

Turner, J. C., Hogg, M. A., Oakes, P. J., Reicher, S. D., and Wetherell, M. S. (1987) *Rediscovering the social group: a self-categorization theory*, New York: Basil Blackwell.

Wiesenfeld, B., Raghuram, S., and Garud, R. (2001) "Organizational identification among virtual workers: the role of need for affiliation and perceived work-based social support," *Journal of Management*, 27: 213–29.

Williams, T. A. (1982) "A participative design for dispersed employees in turbulent environments," *Human Relations*, 35: 1043–58.

Part II

Identities in action

4 Reducing dissonance

Closing the gap between projected and attributed identity

Samia Chreim

Introduction

A statement of organizational identity provides an answer to the question: "Who are we?"; an answer that will indicate what is of distinctiveness, centrality, and temporal continuity for an organization (Albert and Whetten, 1985). Statements of identity are strongly influenced by the preferences of power-holders, who have the responsibility to answer the identity question. Typically, these powerholders are the top managers of the organization (Ashforth and Mael, 1996; Barney *et al.*, 1998; Gioia and Thomas, 1996; Scott and Lane, 2000) who have the authority to speak on its behalf. In general, top managers are in the best position to elaborate on the attributes that define an organization since they are the agents charged with the responsibility to define its course. Management's definition of the organization is communicated to different audiences; in Soenen and Moingeon's (2002) five-facet framework, this is the facet of identity described as *projected*.

Identity is constituted or actualized in discursive constructions (Brown, 1994; Cheney, 1991; Cheney and Christensen, 2000). Cheney and Vibbert indicate that "much of what one calls 'an identity' is composed of words" (1987: 176). Through discourse, top management presents the organization, and in doing so, helps construct and define organizational identity. Top management's statements of identity constitute a claim (Albert and Whetten, 1985; Ashforth and Mael, 1996), and this claim is credible and legitimate only to the extent that it can be confirmed by the views that both the internal (i.e., the *experienced* identity) and external stakeholders (i.e., the *attributed* identity) have of the organization. There are situations, however, where management's claims about identity may not be confirmed by the experience or attributions of other stakeholders; this leads to identity dissonance, a state in which different facets of the organization's identity are inconsistent (Elsbach and Kramer, 1996).

In this chapter, I argue that identity dissonance creates uncertainty about what the organization is and that organizations make different attempts to reduce this uncertainty. On the other hand, identity dissonance can be avoided, but such avoidance requires the use of ambiguity in self-presentations. These issues are empirically explored in this chapter, which is organized as follows: in the next section, I elaborate on the notion of identity dissonance, then provide a description of the research methods and present the data and analysis. I then follow with a discussion of the findings, and the chapter concludes with the implications drawn from the study.

Identity dissonance

Ideally, different facets of an organization's identity are aligned and consistent with each other. However, different internal or external factors may bring about divergences between these facets (Soenen and Moingeon 2002), creating an identity dissonance (Elsbach and Kramer, 1996). This is a state in which uncertainty about identity prevails. Since reducing uncertainty about the definition of the self is a core human motivation (Hogg and Terry, 2000), we can expect dissonance to trigger organizational responses aimed at establishing consistency in the different facets of identity.

To avoid dissonance, top management needs to heed a number of factors that constrain its projections of identity. One factor is the view of the organization held internally by members. Cheney and Christensen (2000) indicate that formal organizational presentation discourses that do not take into account internal participants' views of the organization fail to be convincing. Another factor is the organization's image held by the external public (Dutton and Dukerich, 1991; Scott and Lane, 2000). Identity is not completely internally generated, for the claim made by an entity about its identity needs to be confirmed by the external world (Levitt and Nass, 1994). This external image – referred to by Dutton, Dukerich, and Harquail (1994) as the "construed external image" – is seen as a reflection of the organization that top managers use to adjust their portrayal of the organization. It corresponds to managers' experience of the *attributed* identity (Soenen and Moingeon, 2002).

An inconsistency between the organizational identity *projected* by top management and the identity *attributed* to an organization by the external public, such as customers, would create a state of identity dissonance. This dissonance is likely to trigger responses by one of the groups to reduce the gap. Since it is incumbent on an organization's management to achieve organizational legitimacy, we can expect the organization's management to engage in tactics to reduce the inconsistencies. Failure to remove inconsistencies raises questions about management's credibility. Scott and Lane (2000) indicate that managers are motivated to present "accurate" images of the organization, especially when strong evidence can be easily obtained and compared with management's claim. In fact, consistent presentations to and by different audiences enhance each other and increase top management's credibility (Whetten and Godfrey, 1998).

It is possible for top management to avoid a situation whereby disparities may arise between the organizational identity it projects and the identity *attributed* by the public. Dissonance avoidance can be achieved through the use of ambiguous terms in identity statements. Cheney (1991) indicates that organizations use ambiguity to unite stakeholders under one corporate banner and to stretch the interpretation of how the organization can be defined. However, not all statements of identity are ambiguous, and therefore management may face situations where the identity it projects is inconsistent with the identity *attributed* by external parties. To reduce this dissonance, top management can engage in a number of responses or strategies. The first strategy consists of engaging in action aimed at modifying the *manifested* identity so that, in turn, the external parties revise their perception of the organization and eventually attribute to the organization an identity consistent with the one projected by top management. Second, top management may resort to persuading the external parties of the "truthfulness" of its claims of *projected* identity. Third, top managers can change their statements of identity so that the identity they project is consistent with the identity *attributed* by the external public. Whether these strategies are used separately or jointly, they are likely to result in the change of one facet or another of the organizational identity as attempts are made to bring about an alignment of these facets.

Giddens (1991) indicates that identity resides in the capacity to maintain a coherent but evolving account about the self, an account that continually integrates the pertinent events in the external world. How the *projected* identity created by managers in discourse evolves and integrates elements of the external environment can be best understood through a longitudinal study. Such a study would enable us to trace the evolution of organizational identity over time, as different strategies may be used to reduce gaps between the divergent *projected* and *attributed* facets. This chapter describes a longitudinal study of the identity *projected* by top managers in an organization. It traces the evolution of the organization's top management identity discourse in a situation in which the external perceptions of the organization were inconsistent with top management's definition of the organization. The study indicates that action is undertaken to change the attributes of the organization in the direction of the *projected* identity and that statements of *projected* identity undergo shifts and adjustments to remain consistent with the *attributed* identity. The study also provides evidence of top management's statements of identity that, through the use of abstract terms representing flexible discursive resources, succeed in becoming immune to external confirmation.

The empirical study

The subject of the study is the Royal Bank Financial Group (RB). The RB, founded in 1864, is one of the largest federally chartered financial institutions in Canada. It provides a broad range of financial services and has an extensive national and international network. It is a highly visible and successful organization that has vied for a superior position among its competitors on many levels. The RB and five other Canadian federally chartered financial institutions are known at large as "the Big Six" banks in Canada. For many years, the RB's top management considered the bank to be superior to the other organizations in the "Big Six" group in several respects, and this was reflected in the *projected* identity. However, this *projected* identity shifted over the years. The study traces the process of change in top management's statements of identity, and reports on the contextual factors associated with the shifts.

The study focused on organizational identity themes in top management statements. In discourse, the use of the same word and its synonyms is known as a theme (Huff, 1983). I considered an identity theme to be revealed by a word, label, or short phrase that is self-referential and that indicates centrality, distinctiveness, and persistence. These criteria, proposed by Albert and Whetten (1985), have been considered to be those that define organizational identity in previous empirical research (e.g., Dutton and Dukerich, 1991; Elsbach and Kramer, 1996).

Traces of management discourse on identity are usually found in written texts – such as annual reports (Albert and Whetten, 1985) – that are archived and that can be retrieved for later analysis (Taylor, 1993). Annual reports present the organization's central and distinctive attributes, its significant undertakings and changes during the year, its major objectives and the external factors that are heeded by top management. Emphasis was placed on statements of corporate profile that provide a summary of top management's definition of the organization, as well as on the message to shareholders, which is an excellent indicator of the important topics to which top managers attend (D'Aveni and Macmillan, 1990). Since these texts are produced annually, they constitute a reliable source of information on the evolution of top management's presentation of the organization's identity. According to Soenen and Moingeon (2002), the concept of *projected* identity encompasses all forms of identity projections. In this study, I focused on the annual reports which, given their strategic nature for a firm, may be regarded as a good illustration of the *projected* identity.

Identity themes were traced for a period of thirteen years, from 1985 to 1997, inclusive. Quotations from the annual report with reference to a given theme were coded with the theme title and were later retrieved using the ATLAS software that facilitates search, management, and analysis of qualitative data. Time-ordered displays were adopted to present the data (Miles and Huberman 1994). Each identity theme was considered to represent a track. A track is a substantive category for which a progression of events can be traced and recorded (van de Ven, 1992). A trajectory that traces the evolutionary process (Kimberly and Bouchikhi, 1995) was elaborated for each theme. Information on the contextual factors that are relevant to the trajectory were obtained from a variety of industry and company publications, including *Interest* magazine, the RB house organ.

In this chapter, the data from the annual reports are integrated with the analysis of the trajectory of each theme. Quotations from the annual reports are presented verbatim, and each quotation is preceded by a dash. Contextual factors that have an impact on the evolution of top management's discourse on identity are addressed in the analysis provided below. Due to space limitations, only a representative portion of the quotations for two identity themes is reported here. These themes are *quality service to customers* and *leader*. The quotations reported are revealing of the identity themes' evolution in top management's discourse. While the *quality service* theme illustrates a gap between *projected* and *attributed* identity, as well as the attempts made to narrow this gap, the *leader* theme illustrates the use of ambiguity in statements of identity that make it possible for dissonance to be avoided.

Quality service to customers

Providing a distinctive quality service to customers appears to be an organization-defining attribute in the RB's top management statements at the outset of the study period. Variations on the quality service theme appear under such expressions as "customer service" and "serving customers well."

Top management presents quality service to customers as one of the bank's main defining attributes throughout 1985 and 1986. This is clear from the presentation of customer service as a mission, a primary goal, a tradition, a constant, a strength, a reason for everything else the bank does (1985), and a distinctive RB trademark (1986). It is a theme in the organization's discourse that stands above other themes.

1985 – Serving customers well remains at the heart of RB's mission. It is the basic reason for everything else we do. Traditionally, attention to customer needs, the "personal touch," has been a strong point at the Royal. It remains a constant. All our efforts to preserve the bank's financial soundness, manage costs, improve productivity, devise and introduce new products, new service-delivery methods and new technology – as well as to make continuing investments in staff training – all are ultimately aimed at one primary goal: serving customers' needs well.
– (Consumer deposits) come to us, and stay with us, because of the quality and convenience of the service provided through our network of branches and Personal Touch Banking machines.

(Message to shareholders, Annual report)

1986 – The central goal of the Management team is to build on our track record for top-flight customer service. By serving customers well, we aim over time to substantially improve profitability.
– Expanding into such new service areas is vital to one of our central corporate goals: to be recognized by our customers as a consistent leader in the value of our products and customer service. Commitment to quality service is a distinctive Royal Bank trademark.

(Message to shareholders, Annual report)

In 1985, more than half the message to shareholders revolves around the quality service issue. Continuity in the supremacy of customer service is noted in the 1986 message to shareholders where customer service is said to be a matter of track record and distinctiveness at the bank, as well as of centrality to management. It should be noted that a 1985 Canada-wide customer survey indicated that the RB was perceived as the best run bank by seven out of ten of its main customers, whereas only "five or six customers in ten at the other major banks say their bank is best run" (*Interest*, November/December, 1985: 21). *Interest* reports that the survey indicated that the most important measure of quality service to customers is to be served by experienced and well-trained employees. "The Royal leads the major banks in this category" (*Interest*, November/December, 1985: 22).

In 1987, a similar study indicated that the RB "tied the National Bank and Canada Trust in corporate reputation attributes and finished second to them in service delivery and pricing attributes" (*Interest News*, December, 1987: 9). However, the study reports that the RB ranked ahead of CIBC, TD, BNS, and BMO, the other major Canadian banks. Interestingly, in the 1987 and 1988 messages to shareholders, serving customers well is still mentioned as a central goal but no more as a distinctive feature of the bank. Furthermore, in 1988, the message to shareholders refers to "improv(ing) service quality." In fact, the ratings do not show the RB to be ahead of the competition in terms of this attribute.

1987 – Central among our goals, as I said in this space last year, is to serve customers well, and by doing so, to substantially improve profitability.

(Message to shareholders, *Annual report*)

1988 – Our drive to improve service quality is designed to generate solid returns from heavy investment in branches, staff training, technology and investment banking subsidiaries.

(Message to shareholders, *Annual report*)

In 1990, quality service to customers remains a top priority for improvement:

1990 – For RB an absolutely top priority continues to be improvement in the quality of our service.

– There is no doubt that the quality of service will be the major competitive arena in the 1990s, more so than product innovation and pricing. The fight for customer loyalty and market share will become increasingly intense as more players enter the financial services sector on various fronts and customer expectations continue to grow.

– In the past two years, we have made genuine progress in our quality of service initiatives. Our formal customer surveys which are carried out regularly tell us our customers are more satisfied now than in the past. But we are not resting on our laurels. A senior bank officer has been made responsible for our service quality group, which brings definition and focus to service initiatives at every level.

(Message to shareholders, *Annual report*)

Creation of a new senior position to deal with the quality issue underscores the importance the bank places on improving quality, which is "an absolutely top priority." Quality service is the weapon that will enable the bank to win the battle for customer loyalty, a battle that must be fought on many fronts in the competitive arena. This is a quite different statement from 1985's "(consumers) come to us and stay with us." Thus, action is taken to achieve a desired and *projected* identity attribute.

An article reported in *Interest* magazine states that for two years in a row, 1991 and 1992, the RB led the other banks in quality of service (except in automated banking machines for 1992). This article, entitled "Royal Bank leads Big Six in customer service," reports the RB's Vice President of Retail Banking as saying that "tremendous initiatives" have been undertaken by staff across the country, and that these initiatives "are clearly having an impact." He further adds, "While our challenge is to truly differentiate ourselves, the competition is making noticeable progress, and just staying the leader will be in itself a formidable task" (*Interest*, January/February, 1993: 10). This is reflected in the message to shareholders for 1991 and 1992:

1991 – We made good progress in 1991 towards our objective of differentiating ourselves from our competitors by being the clear leader in service quality. In 1991, more was done than ever before to learn what our customers need, want, and expect from us. A great deal of effort was also devoted to developing the effective measuring and monitoring techniques that we believe are essential to winning the battle for customer loyalty.

(Message to shareholders, *Annual report*)

1992 – Solid progress was made towards our goal of being the leading provider of financial services measured in terms of service quality, customer satisfaction, and profitability.

– Extensive surveys and other measures of customer satisfaction tell us that we are doing as well as the best of our competitors, perhaps even a little better. These surveys also help us measure and monitor performance against specific quality targets.

(Message to shareholders, *Annual report*)

The emphasis on the objective of achieving a "clear" differentiation from the competition demonstrates the importance, for the RB, of being recognized as being distinct from the competition in service quality. Other banks had made advances in different measures of the quality service attribute; that is, other banks could have been superior on one or more of these measures. The RB qualifies its progress in 1991 as "good," in 1992 as "solid," possibly implying that the bank is moving towards narrowing the identity gap that had been created by its weakening position in quality service relative to competitors. Despite this, top management was unable to portray the bank as the "clear" leader in quality; it is "perhaps" better than the best of its competitors.

The November/December, 1993 issue of *Interest* magazine reports on two major 1993 customer satisfaction surveys indicating that while the RB held its own, major bank competitors were catching up. The Vice President for Quality and Service Planning is quoted as saying that although the bank is doing several good things, "our competitors are pushing hard and the bar is rising quickly." The article further points out that the RB is still as good or better than other banks, although its overall quality service position has weakened given that competitors have shown improvements at a high rate. In this same article, the Vice President of Retail Banking mentions that "Retail Banking's number one strategic priority is to differentiate ourselves from the competition by setting the standard for quality service. Currently among banks, there's no significant difference. Our goal is to have RB lead the industry" (*Interest*, November/December, 1993: 11). Interestingly, the 1993 message to shareholders provides only minimal references to quality service. In fact, from 1993 to 1997, references to quality service decrease substantially. In 1994, providing customers with value (service at a competitive price) is portrayed as a competitive advantage to win the battle against the competition:

1994 – Providing customers with value means providing a level of service that consistently meets or exceeds their expectations at a reasonable and competitive cost. Providing value is where the battle for competitive advantage is being fought in the financial services sector.
– Increased revenue generation from traditional and emerging businesses is our top priority. We will achieve this by continuing to improve service quality, diversifying and expanding our global businesses and developing our fee-generating business.

(Message to shareholders, *Annual report*)

The battle metaphor, which first appeared in 1990 when the RB did not seem to be making superior advances in quality service relative to its competitors, is reiterated. In 1994, the battle involves providing value; the price element ("a competitive price") – deemed less important than service quality in 1990 – is factored in. In addition, improving service quality is clearly portrayed in the second quotation in 1994 as a means to some other priority, and is placed at the same level as other procedures like diversification and expansion. The September/October, 1994 issue of *Interest* magazine features an article entitled "Customer satisfaction rises but competition heats from other banks." This article again reports on two national surveys that show that while the RB has improved in terms of customer satisfaction with respect to previous years, so have competitors. "Royal Bank is in the middle of the pack at virtually the same level as Toronto Dominion, Scotiabank and Bank of Montreal. While the RB's score rose slightly since last year, the three other banks have all improved since 1992" (*Interest*, September/October, 1994:16).

In 1995, the message to shareholders makes no reference to quality service. Responsiveness to customers lies in the reconfiguration of the delivery network (which includes decreasing the number of branches). In this year as well, customer satisfaction is said to be part of the corporate objectives, a notion that is reiterated in 1997:

1995 – As customer acceptance of alternative delivery channels such as telephone banking grows, we will continue to reduce the number of branches and reconfigure the network to be more responsive to our customers.
    – Higher levels of employee satisfaction and rewards tied to corporate goals should lead to enhanced customer satisfaction, improved cost management and higher profitability.

(Message to shareholders, *Annual report*)

1997 – For our customers, we are raising the targets for customer satisfaction and providing employees with the training, technology and time to devote care and attention to their clients.
    – In 1997, we added customer satisfaction and performance relative to the competition as further criteria for (employee compensation) payouts.

(Message to shareholders, *Annual report*)

In 1997, customers are one of the four groups of stakeholders mentioned in the message to shareholders and about whom the bank speaks in terms of objectives. We are told that the targets for customer satisfaction have been raised. Customer satisfaction is now the responsibility of employees as individuals ("their customers") and has been established as one of the employees' performance objectives.

In summary, when the study period opens, statements of identity draw attention to the RB's distinctive and top-flight customer service. As the bank's customer service ratings become less distinguishable from the competition's, quality service ceases to be depicted as distinctive and is portrayed instead as a goal, or a desired identity attribute. When the bank's efforts fail to achieve a high ranking in quality service and to regain the external confirmation of distinction, quality service is portrayed as an attribute leading to improved profitability and references to distinctiveness in this attribute are dropped.

While evolving external views of the organization had impeded the RB's top management from continuing to claim superiority and distinctiveness in terms of quality service, different dynamics apply to the portrayal of the bank as a leader.

Leader

The RB is consistently presented in top management discourse as a leader. The following sample of quotations coded with leader and taken from the message to shareholders or the corporate profile in the annual report provides evidence of the degree to which this theme permeates top management's portrayal of the bank:

1985 – The Royal Bank is a leader in the application of new technologies for efficient operational management and in making possible a variety of sophisticated new services.

1986 – . . . one of our central corporate goals: to be recognized by our customers as a consistent leader in the value of our products and customer service.

1987 – Dominion Securities Limited has a track record of excellence in service and profitability, based on top-caliber leadership and highly respected professional talent.

1988 – We intend, over time, to lead the Canadian financial services industry not only in terms of size and scope of business, but in terms of profitability as well.

1989 – Our overall objective in Canada is to be the leader, not just in banking, but in providing a broad range of bank-based financial services to all sectors of the market.
     – Our leadership in systems and technology, particularly at the client servicing level, is a competitive advantage that we intend to exploit.

1990 – And we are the leader in developing and implementing bank-related technology.
     – We are immensely proud of the leadership Royal Bankers demonstrate
     – not only in the marketplace but also in the community.

1992 – As we move forward, Royal Bank's business strategy will continue to be driven by four corporate objectives . . . : – be the leading Canadian financial institution best positioned globally, – be a leading employer committed to excellence.

1993 – Royal Trust has brought with it strength and leadership in such businesses as personal and institutional trust, securities custody and investment management.

1995 – Royal Bank's strength derives largely from our leading share of the domestic retail financial services market.

1996 – As Canada's premier, and one of its most profitable, global financial institutions dealing with one in three Canadians, we will continue building on our strengths. They include a leading market position in Canada in most of our businesses.

1997 – Royal Bank is Canada's largest financial institution as measured by market capitalization, revenues and net income. We have leading positions in most Canadian financial services markets.
     – We want to continue to provide top quartile returns to our shareholders by continuing to lead the industry in ROE, earnings growth and valuation.
     – (We have) leading-edge work/family/life, gender gap and diversity policies and programs . . .

(Annual reports)

That the leader theme is central is evidenced by the number of times this theme appears in the organizational presentation discourse, by the depiction of major achievements and objectives as instances of the bank's leadership position, and by the presentation of the bank's employees and acquisitions as leaders.

Achievements are presented as signs of the bank's leadership; they include the bank's size, scope and profitability (1988), providing a broad range of bank-based services (1989), system and technology (1985, 1989, 1990), market share position (1992, 1995, 1996), and ROE and HR practices (1997), to name a few. The leader theme also includes a variety of the bank's objectives. Thus, in 1986, 1988, 1989, 1991, and 1997, *projected* identity attributes are cast in terms of leadership. Moreover, the bank's partners or acquisitions are said to be leaders in their field: Dominion Securities Limited, acquired by the bank in 1987, is said to have "a track record of excellence in service and profitability, based on top-caliber leadership." Royal Trust, acquired by the bank in 1993, is portrayed as having "brought with it strength and leadership". Even "Royal bankers demonstrate (leadership) . . . in the marketplace (and) the community" (1990). Being in a leading position is a sign of distinctiveness. A leader stands out from the other members of the group and implies the bank's ability to perform better than its competitors. In 1991, for example, the RB indicates that "being the clear leader in service quality" allows the bank to differentiate itself from the competition.

It is noteworthy that portraying the RB as a "leader" confers upon it an abstract identity attribute that can be applied to a variety of the bank's aspects. Since no concise definition of "leadership" is provided in top management discourse, the ambiguity of the term allows high flexibility in its usage. Due to this ambiguity, external evidence disconfirming that the bank is a leader would be difficult to marshal.

Dissonance reduction and avoidance

The analysis of the *quality service* theme reveals that as the RB starts to lose its superior position among competitors in terms of distinctive quality service, the latter is framed as a goal to be achieved. As superior quality service can no more be portrayed as an actual self-defining identity attribute, it is cast instead as a desired attribute to be achieved through a number of measures taken at the bank. The bank's *attributed* identity (the way it is viewed by customers and the public as indicated in surveys) helps top managers to reflect upon the organization and to adjust the way they define and project the bank's identity. Continuing to define the RB as distinctive in terms of quality service would fail to receive confirmation from the public and would undermine management's credibility.

When distinctiveness in quality of customer service fades, not only are statements modified to reflect *attributed* identity, but extensive action is also engaged and mobilized to recapture the superior position. Burgelman and Grove (1996) indicate that companies experience a certain level of dissonance

generated by divergences between internal capabilities and external requirements, and between management's intentions and strategic action. To these
authors, such dissonance can be advantageous when top management uses the
conflicting information to learn about the changing realities of the environment and to bring closer alignment between the internal capabilities and the
environment. It is clear that the RB's top management used the dissonance to
better learn and understand customers' needs and expectations, and to
undertake action to address such external requirements. For instance, a senior
executive was appointed to overlook the quality endeavors at the bank,
increased effort was placed into learning about customer needs and wants, the
bank strove to exceed customer expectations and employees across the country
engaged in tremendous initiatives (*Interest* and *Annual report*, 1990–4). However, other institutions in the Canadian financial services industry were also
observing the external factors and were responding to them with actions
similar to the RB's. This created a difficult situation for any one institution to
achieve long-lasting distinctiveness.

For the RB, the loss of a clearly superior position in quality of service was of
major significance. As the earlier annual reports (1985 and 1986) indicate,
superior quality service was a mark of distinctiveness and continuity, both
important cornerstones of identity. So important is this attribute to the bank's
definition that even the smallest advantage in quality service ratings over its
competitors was celebrated in 1992. However, as the bank's continued efforts
to gain the lost position and rank failed to yield satisfactory results, top
management's discourse about quality service distinctiveness gradually faded.
Attention gradually shifted from the goal of being in a superior position in
quality service to that of customer satisfaction. The presentation of this identity attribute in top management's discourse was reframed and made more
compatible with the attributions assigned by external stakeholders. The
identity *projected* by management reveals the shifts that reflect the changes in
attributed identity. This is consistent with the dynamics of collective identity
posited in the five-facet framework (Soenen and Moingeon, 2002). The authors
argue that the relationship between the *attributed* and *projected* facets is
mediated by the *experienced* identity. In other words, only shifts in the
attributed identity leading to perceived dissonance by management trigger
modifications of the *projected* identity.

The analysis of the "leader" theme suggests that ambiguity in the *projected*
identity attributes may weaken the impact of shifting *attributed* identity on
the *projected* identity. Indeed, while presenting the RB as offering superior
customer service may not stand the test of external confirmation, portraying it
and its partners as leaders is more difficult to disconfirm. In fact, the term
"leader" is not concisely defined in top management discourse, and therefore
invalidating this statement would be difficult. The claim that the RB is a
leader in "systems and technology" (1989), for example, can be interpreted as
referring to superiority in timing, quality, scope, or some other aspect of the
application of this "technology," which itself is an ambiguous term. Therefore,

the use of the "leader" label in the bank's definition illustrates the advantages of ambiguity in identity statements. Eisenberg (1984) notes that managers using strategic ambiguity refrain from providing precise information so as to allow different constituents to apply the interpretations they desire to symbols used by management. Cheney and Christensen (2000) indicate that symbolic resources, like discourse, provide top management with flexibility in presenting the organization.

Leader is a floating symbol that gets associated with a variety of organizational aspects, depending on the context. Thus, when the context allows top management to claim some superiority in terms of technology, the "leader" label is associated with this aspect of the bank. When the bank cannot claim superiority in terms of quality service, the "leader" label is dissociated from this attribute and associated with other aspects of the bank, such as market share position (1995, 1996, and 1997). This allows top management to consistently portray the bank as a leader.

In exploring how top managers can achieve consistency in defining an organization despite changing contexts, researchers have suggested using abstract labels and attributes (Barney *et al.*, 1998; Gustafson and Reger, 1995). *Leader* provides this abstractness. While the bank aspect to which the leadership label is applied changes over time, the label itself remains constant, providing some consistency in top management's *projected* identity (Gioia, Schultz, and Corley, 2000). Since this is an ambiguous label that defies external confirmation while implying distinctiveness and providing persistence, it appears to be an excellent symbol to use in defining an organization. However, it is important to note that the more concrete and precise the contextualization of the "leader" label is in discourse, the more the statements of identity become subject to confirmation or disconfirmation. Portraying the bank as a leader in market share (1995) is a more specific definition of identity than simply portraying it as a "leader" in general. The former definition is more amenable to comparison with external evidence.

Implications and conclusion

This study indicates that external views of the organization that are not consistent with the statements of identity by management can trigger attempts to reduce the gap between the two. In the present case, the external view of the organization was provided by customer surveys. This *attributed* identity can be perceived as providing an "objective" depiction of the organization – a depiction that cannot be easily manipulated by management. In the case of the RB, top management responded to the dissonance by engaging in action aimed at restoring a distinctive external view and by reframing its statements of identity so as to reduce the gap between *attributed* identity and *projected* identity. Identity undergoes continual evolution as divergence between the different facets occurs and attempts are made to reduce the dissonance. In the evolution process, voices external to the organization take on authorial properties. As discourse at the top faces a counter discourse, an integrative text on the organization is produced (Reitter, 1991). Top management's power in defining the organization has its limits. As Cheney and Vibbert indicate, "As a representation, an identity is developed dialectically and over time by both the focal person (or group) and others" (Cheney and Vibbert, 1987: 176).

Nevertheless, top management can avoid the counter-discourses when it utilizes abstract, and therefore flexible discursive resources that are immune to external confirmation. However, what is gained in avoiding disconfirmation can be lost in the ability to create meaning for stakeholders. Over-reliance on abstract terms may well leave the organization with a hollow core, one that cannot be appropriated by stakeholders in their quest for meaning and identification with the organization. Top managers must carefully choose the terms with which they project an organization since both the maintenance of credibility and the ability to mobilize and provide meaning are equally important for organizations.

References

Albert, S. and Whetten, D. A. (1985) "Organizational identity," in L. L. Cummings and B. Staw (eds) *Research in organizational behavior, volume 7*, Greenwich, CT: JAI Press, 263–95.

Ashforth, B. E. and Mael, F. A. (1996) "Organizational identity and strategy as a context for the individual," in J. A. C. Baum and J. E. Dutton (eds) *Advances in Strategic Management*, vol. 13, Greenwich, CT: JAI Press, 19–64.

Barney, J. *et al.* (1998) "A strategy conversation on the topic of organizational identity," in D. A. Whetten and P. C. Godfrey (eds) *Identity in organizations: building theory through conversations*, Thousand Oaks, CA: Sage, 99–168.

Brown, D. D. (1994) "Discursive moments of identification," *Current Perspectives in Social Theory*, 14: 269–92.

Burgelman, R. A. and Grove, A. S. (1996) "Strategic dissonance," *California Management Review*, 38: 8–22.

Cheney, G. (1991) *Rhetoric in an organizational society: managing multiple identities*, Columbia, SC: University of South Carolina Press.

Cheney, G. and Christensen, L. T. (2000) "Identity at issue: linkages between 'internal' and 'external' organizational communication," in F. M. Jablin and L. L. Putnam (eds) *The new handbook of organizational communication: advances in theory, research, and methods*, Thousand Oaks, CA: Sage, 231–69.

Cheney, G. and Vibbert, S. L. (1987) "Corporate discourse: public relations and issue management," in F. M. Jablin, L. L. Putnam, K. H. Roberts, and L. W. Porter (eds) *Handbook of organizational communication: an interdisciplinary perspective*, Newbury Park, CA: Sage, 165–94.

D'Aveni, R. and Macmillan, I. C. (1990) "Crisis and the content of managerial communications: a study of the focus of attention of top managers in surviving and failing firms," *Administrative Sciences Quarterly*, 35: 634–57.

Dutton, J. E. and Dukerich, J. M. (1991) "Keeping an eye on the mirror: image and identity in organizational adaptation," *Academy of Management Journal*, 34: 517–54.

Dutton, J. E., Dukerich, J. M., and Harquail, C. V. (1994) "Organizational images and member identification," *Administrative Science Quarterly*, 39: 239–63.

Eisenberg, E. M. (1984) "Ambiguity as strategy in organizational communication," *Communication Monographs*, 51: 227–42.

Elsbach, K. D. and Kramer, R. M. (1996) "Members' responses to organizational threats: encountering and countering the *Business Week* rankings," *Administrative Science Quarterly*, 41: 442–76.

Giddens, A. (1991) *Modernity and self-identity*, Cambridge: Polity Press.

Gioia, D. A., Schultz, M., and Corley, K. G. (2000) "Organizational identity, image and adaptive instability," *Academy of Management Review*, 25: 63–81.

Gioia, D. A. and Thomas, J. B. (1996) "Identity, image, and issue interpretation: sense-making during strategic change in academia," *Administrative Science Quarterly*, 41: 370–403.

Gustafson, L. T. and Reger, R. K. (1995) "Using organizational identity to achieve stability and change in high velocity environments," *Academy of Management Best Paper Proceedings*.

Hogg, M. A. and Terry, D. J. (2000) "Social identity and self-categorization processes in organizational contexts," *Academy of Management Review*, 25: 121–40.

Huff, A. S. (1983) "A rhetorical examination of strategic change," in L. R. Pondy and associates (eds) *Organizational symbolism*, Greenwich, CT: JAI Press, 167–83.

Kimberly, J. R. and Bouchikhi, H. (1995) "The dynamics of organizational development and change: how the past shapes the present and constrains the future," *Organization Science*, 6: 9–18.

Levitt, B. and Nass, C. (1994) "Organizational narratives and the person–identity distinction," *Communication Yearbook*, 17: 236–46.

Miles, M. B. and Huberman, A. M. (1994) *Qualitative data analysis*, Thousand Oaks, CA: Sage.

Reitter, R. (1991) *Cultures d'entreprise*, Paris: Vuibert.

Royal Bank (1985–97) *Annual Report*, Canada.

Royal Bank (November/December, 1985) "What do customers want?," *Interest*, Canada, 20–3.

Royal Bank (December, 1987) "Royal ranked third overall among 'big seven'," *Interest News*, Canada, 9.

Royal Bank (January/February, 1993) "Royal Bank leads Big Six in customer service," *Interest*, Canada, 10.

Royal Bank (November/December, 1993) "Competition gaining on bank," *Interest*, Canada, 11.

Royal Bank (September/October, 1994) "Customer satisfaction rises but competition heats from other banks," *Interest*, Canada, 16.

Scott, S. G. and Lane, V. R. (2000) "A stakeholder approach to organizational identity," *Academy of Management Review*, 25: 43–62.

Soenen, G. and Moingeon, B. (2002) "The five-facets of collective identities: integrating corporate and organizational identity," in B. Moingeon and G. Soenen (eds) *Corporate and organizational identity – integrating strategy, marketing, communication, and organizational perspectives*, London: Routledge.

Taylor, J. R. (1993) "La dynamique de changement organisationnel: une théorie conversation/texte de la communication et ses implications," *Communication and Organisation*, 3: 51–93.

van de Ven, A. (1992) "Suggestions for studying strategy process: A research note," *Strategic Management Journal*, 13: 169–88.

Whetten, D. A. and Godfrey, P. C. (eds) (1998) *Identity in organizations: building theory through conversations*, Thousand Oaks, CA: Sage.

5 Manifestations in behavior versus perceptions of identity

Convergence or not?

Johan van Rekom

Introduction

Identity is associated with action. One reason why managers like to invoke an organization's identity is the promise it offers to guide its members in their behavior and decision-making. For instance, at Koch industries, a diversified firm in Wichita, Kansas, Koch's identity as a "Discovery Company" constantly challenges employees to discover new routines that contribute to profit growth (Barney, 1998). Identity can give people a clear sense of what their organization stands for and where it intends to go (Albert, Ashforth, and Dutton, 2000). As Gioia states: "I can think of no other concept that is so central to the human experience, or one that infuses so many interpretations and actions, than the notion of identity" (1998).

The link between identity and behavior is one of the appeals of recent theorizing on organizational identity. The question as to how identity affects the cognitions and actions of the members of an organization is crucial to authors who assume that organizational identity can be managed and changed (Rindova, 1998). However, in studies about identity, scholars who deal with different conceptualizations of identity have been working for a long time in their own separate ways. There is little interaction between the different streams of research (Baker and Balmer, 1997; Soenen and Moingeon, 2002). The dominant stream in theorizing about identity has mainly focused on perceptions of the organization by its members (Gioia and Thomas, 1996; Elsbach and Kramer, 1996; Gustafson and Reger, 1999; Pratt and Foreman, 2000). Most scholars see identity as something that is perceived by the members of an organization. They tend to emphasize the social construction of common cognitions among employees. Albert, Ashforth and Dutton (2000), for instance, define "a sense of identity" as "an internalized cognitive structure of what the organization stands for and where it intends to go." Soenen and Moingeon (2002) label this the "representation perspective": identity is viewed as a shared mental representation that individuals have about their organization. In contrast, others embrace what they call the "manifestation perspective," which Soenen and Moingeon define in terms of its manifestations, such as logos, corporate advertising, and employee behavior. Soenen and Moingeon find a major division between scholars who focus on identity as representation and scholars who focus on identity as a set of manifestations. They observe that the distinction between "representation" on the one hand and "set of manifestations" on the other, strongly distinguishes the various contributions to organizational identity. Soenen and Moingeon posit a strong systemic relationship between *experienced* identity, that is, how organization members experience their organization more or less consciously, and *manifested* identity, that is, how the organization manifests itself though what it does. This relationship has not received much attention, as there has been little interaction between these approaches. The manifestations that are pertinent to this study are the actions of the members of an organization, because it is the effect of identity on employee behavior that often motivates managers to articulate their organization's identity. Although of importance, the relationship between the identity of an organization and the actions of its members has hardly been addressed in research (cf. Gustafson and Reger, 1999; van Rekom and van Riel, 2000).

The challenge of this chapter is to bring together the two different approaches. The aim is to compare performed behavior, which is in the realm of *manifested* identity, with how people perceive the identity of their own organization, that is, its *experienced* identity (Soenen and Moingeon, 2002). The main question is to what degree the actions of members of an organization relate to how they perceive their own organization. Do the perceptions of members of an organization of their organization correspond to what they believe they are doing?

This chapter will first review studies examining the interaction between identity and action. The next section will discuss how perceptions of externally *attributed* identity influence the other perspectives on identity and then deal with how social comparison processes may influence the creative attribution of salient aspects of identity to the own organization. Next, these connections are examined by conducting qualitative interviews and a subsequent survey. The implications for how action and identity may be related will then be discussed.

The relationship between identity and action

There seem to be two important forces in determining how members of an organization perceive themselves. Hatch and Schultz state: "Who we are is reflected in what we are doing and how others interpret who we are and what we are doing" (1997). This section will first review arguments regarding the link between identity and action. It will then deal with the other factor, namely, the influence of perceived differences with peer organizations on how members of an organization view the identity of their own organization.

The connection between identity and action

Our identity and our actions seem to be closely linked. What we care about and do defines us for ourselves (Hatch and Schultz, 2000). The importance of an organization's identity for what that organization does is most obvious when decisions of a strategic nature have to be taken. The question "Who are we?" becomes important when organizations face choices of some consequence, particularly when discussions about goals and values become heated (Albert and Whetten, 1985). As Dutton and Dukerich state: "An organization's identity is one of the vehicles through which preconceptions determine appropriate action" (1991). People working at the New York Port Authority associated the organization's identity with ways of doing things that they identified as "typical of the Port Authority." They perceived their organization as highly professional, ethical, altruistic, having a high commitment to regional welfare, and as a "fixer," able to solve problems adequately. Dutton and Dukerich observe how the identity of the New York Port Authority serves as an important reference point for assessing the importance of issues. The seeming intractability of the issue of the homeless hanging around in their premises challenged their perception of their organization as a "fixer" and a "doer." This perception of their own identity highlighted the importance of this issue. Their view of the organization as being ethical and altruistic strongly guided them in what they did further. They did not only emphasize the importance of "looking humane" in their actions, but also focused on "being humane." Port Authority members experienced positive emotions when organizational actions were identity-consistent and negative emotions when such actions were inconsistent with identity (Dutton and Dukerich, 1991). The Port Authority case shows how identity provides a set of recipes and a way of using those which produce characteristic ways of doing things.

The link between identity and action is most emphatically articulated when the organization is confronted with issues of strategic importance, as was the case with the New York Port Authority. This link plays a more inconspicuous but not negligible role in the normal course of corporate life. In order to act, people need some sense of who they are and some sense of what they are trying to do. This sense may not be in the forefront of consciousness, but sense-making depends upon having some sense of identity (Huff, 1998). Identity influences action, and action also influences identity. Often, identity is created through the reinterpretation of actions taken earlier (Reger, 1998). Thus, the sense made of previous actions may influence and maybe even create a sense of identity. It is not only action, but also what people want to achieve with their actions which relates to identity. As Stimpert puts it: "The theory of what we should do follows pretty quickly from the theory of who we are" (1998). This implies that action and identity influence each other mutually. The sense that people make of what they are guides what they strive for. Vice versa, the sense that people make of what they do molds their perception of the organization's identity. This leads to the first proposition in this research:

> *Proposition 1*: How people experience their own organization is closely related to the sense they make of what they do.

The connection between identity and perceived external image

It would, however, be rash to conclude that the mutual influence of identity and actions on each other would lead to both of them converging all the time. If the members of an organization believe the world around them sees them differently, this may heavily influence the way they see themselves (Gioia and Thomas, 1996). Feedback from outsiders concerning the impression we make on them prompts us to look at our own sense of self and to assess the similarity of the two views. If the discrepancy is pronounced and of consequence, it can suggest the need to reevaluate and change aspects of one's identity (Gioia, Schultz, and Corley, 2000). The study by Dutton and Dukerich (1991) demonstrates such a discrepancy. Here action served to restore the existing identity. Fombrun and Rindova (2000) describe a comparable case concerning the Shell oil company. Shell suffered a massive attack from the media and a consumer boycott in Germany when they wanted to dispose of the Brent Spar oil platform. This experience led the company to systematically examine stakeholder expectations, review its own core purpose, and then change organizational practices so as to achieve consistency with stakeholder expectations. This internal trajectory led to a new way of doing things, consistent with the new internal perception of the organization (Fombrun and Rindova, 2000). In this sense, the Shell case is comparable to that of the New York Port Authority: the long-term effect of media attacks on the identity of an organization created an alignment of *manifested* and internally *experienced* identity.

In the short term, however, feedback from outsiders might influence organization members' perception of identity in a way which can diverge from behavior. Occasionally, in an organization's attempt to achieve prominence, perceptions of its prestige or ranking come to the fore, taking precedence over what is concretely observable (Gioia and Thomas, 1996). Gioia and Thomas, and Elsbach and Kramer (1996), assessed the reactions of universities when *Business Week* published changed rankings of the top 20 US business schools. Elsbach and Kramer show how members of an organization sometimes select identity characteristics with the main purpose of comparing themselves favorably with peer organizations and how they change the set of comparisons in order to highlight more favorable characteristics. Members restored or affirmed positive dimensions of their organization's identity or highlighted their organization's membership in alternative comparison groups when negative image feedback was received (Elsbach and Kramer, 1996). People seldom or never seem to straightforwardly adopt the external view of their organization. Rather, they try to counter negative perceptions by emphasizing other aspects of their organizational identity which help them to rank more favorably in comparison to peer organizations. Comparison with other organizations can apparently substantially influence how members view their own organization, particularly if ranking with peer organizations. The pursuit of distinctiveness may lead members of an organization to creatively attribute certain characteristics to their own organization. They focus on what they do not share with others, and may distract their attention from what they do themselves. Such comparison processes heavily influence the identity professed by the group itself, that is, its *professed* identity (Soenen and Moingeon, 2002). Although there is some creativity involved in giving shape to a *professed* identity, this does not imply that members of an organization would not believe in it. If the identity is also professed at the shop-floor level, employees become committed to it (Salancik, 1977), and are likely to believe in it sincerely.

Evidence from the studies by Dutton and Dukerich (1991) and Fombrun and Rindova (2000) suggests that, in the long term, a certain degree of convergence between what members of an organization do and how they perceive their organization may be expected. On the other hand, the desire to compare favorably with peer organizations may lead members of an organization to emphasize particular aspects of their identity (Elsbach and Kramer, 1996). Creative attribution may be a not negligible factor in giving shape to the *experienced* identity. This leads to the second proposition in this research:

Proposition 2: How members of an organization experience their organization is closely related to the difference they perceive between their own organization and their peer organization(s).

Figure 5.1 illustrates both propositions. This study will investigate the selection of the aspects which members of an organization choose to describe their organization's identity. To what degree do members of an organization derive

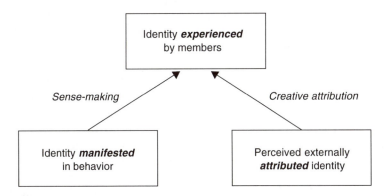

Figure 5.1 Basic sources of *experienced* identity.

inspiration from the sense they make of their own actions, and to what degree are they led by opportunities of comparing themselves favorably with peer organizations?

Deriving operational measures

In order to answer this question, three matters have to be determined: first, how people perceive identity; second, the sense people make of their own actions; and, third, how they rate their peer organizations in comparison to the own organization.

Members of an organization experience their organization's identity directly through everyday behavior and language (Hatch and Schultz, 2000). Reflections on the organization's identity take place at a conscious level. Organizational identity, from the representation perspective, is formulated and expressed through words (Rindova and Schultz, 1998). This relative accessibility to consciousness renders it quite explicit (Hatch and Schultz, 2000), and therefore more readily measurable. This enabled, for instance, Dutton and Dukerich (1991) to establish the identity of the New York Port Authority by asking members of that organization directly for their judgments.

Establishing the sense people make of their own actions is less straightforward. People perform many of their daily actions without too much thought, and the researcher may need to provide some means of provocation in order to establish what an action means to its performer (Garfinkel, 1967). Often, people may only know what their actions mean in retrospect. Through their actions, individuals become bound to beliefs that sustain their actions and their own involvement. A decision to act freezes one's motivational constellation for that action (Lewin, 1947). This enhances the inclination of members of an organization to adhere to and repeat these actions at future occasions. The sense people make of previous actions will drive their day-to-day behavior in the organization. The sense people make of their behavior constitutes the link between *experienced* and *manifested* identity.

The sense people make of their actions draws upon the ends sought, the conception of appropriate and effective means to these ends, and the cognitive structures which result from and are maintained by these actions (Weick, 1995). Thus, sense-making from action involves the means and ends associated with these actions. An *end* is an intended consequence which one or more members of an organization strive for. A *means* is an action or a consequence of a preceding action that the performer considers desirable or necessary to achieve the intended end. When people make sense of their own behavior, the consequences of an action are not given, but are provided by their beliefs (Salancik, 1977). A means–end relation is a perceived causal relation, where the actor has intended both the cause and its consequence. It is the relation the performer believes to exist between both. Ends themselves are often a means to more final ends (Simon, 1997). The end in one means–end relation is the means to achieve another end in a subsequent means–end relation. Motivation to provide continuity in action is more likely to result from intended consequences than from unintended ones. The crucial question in sense-making after action is: "Is this what I want to have done?" Actions and consequences not intended by members of an organization, at least not with hindsight, are not likely to gain their commitment. These would not be likely to incite them to repeat the same actions and to produce the same consequences again, whereas intended consequences would. This retrospective sense-making guides members of an organization to decide who they are and why they do things (Reger, 1998). In this way, retrospective sense-making allows members of an organization to observe and confirm the means and ends underlying their actions, which they may associate with "ways of doing things which are typical of our organization." This collective sense-making of members of an organization of their actions may bridge the gap between the "manifestation perspective" and the "representation perspective" on identity.

Figure 5.2 represents, by way of example, the sense that an employee from the housing corporation studied in this chapter made of "delivering really good work." It shows an extract from her means–end structure. The arrows represent means–end relations. To her, delivering really good work means that people will return to her for advice. This in turn gives her an overview of what other people in the organization do and therefore provides the opportunity to be consistent in the communication with stakeholders. This implies

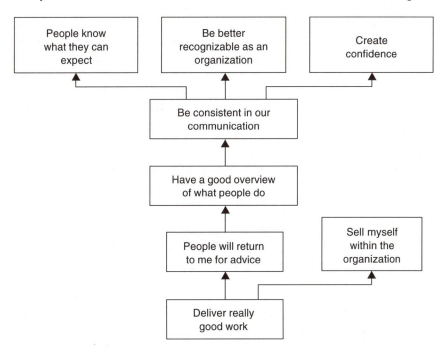

Figure 5.2 Sense made out of "delivering really good work." Extract from an employee's means–end structure.

that confidence is created, the organization achieves better recognition, and that stakeholders know what to expect from the organization. This way, pay-off from the behavior of individuals, in the end, is related to what could be important aspects of an organization's identity. The means and ends of interest in this research were those which appeared in the accounts of several interviewees. The more cognitions are shared among respondents, the more likely they are to represent sense-making at an organizational level, instead of representing one individual's particular way of thinking.

The research

The research was performed at a housing corporation in Alphen aan den Rijn, a medium-sized town in the west of the Netherlands. It took place on the eve of the merger between this organization and the only other housing corporation active in the same municipality. The focal organization was the larger organization with seventy-eight employees. Its counterpart was a small organization with eleven employees. The latter was the only peer organization which could serve as a reference for comparing the larger organization's identity. The research consisted of an exploratory phase, comprising qualitative interviews, and a subsequent survey among all employees.

First, interviews were held among fifteen employees of the organization, establishing the sense they made of what they did in their work. The two interviewers asked the respondents to give concrete examples of what they did. The interviewers then asked, "Why do you do it this way?" The answers to this question revealed the ends to which these actions were a means. Each time the respondent answered, the interviewers asked again, "Why did you want to do that?" or "Why is this important to you?" In this way, they reconstructed the chain of means and ends underlying the action, repeating the question time and again after each answer, "Why is that important to you?" In this way, the interviews build up whole "ladders" of means–end chains, from which this interviewing technique derives its name: "laddering technique" (Reynolds and Gutman, 1988). When respondents were unable to give further answers, the interviewers picked another concrete action, and started the questioning again. The fifteen respondents mentioned in total 508 different means and ends they had been working on. The means and ends of interest were those that were shared by several members of the organization, as these were the more common cognitions among the employees interviewed. Table 5.1 lists the means and ends mentioned by at least seven of the fifteen respondents.

These results were based on only fifteen interviews. One cannot be sure quite how representative these were for the whole organization. The means and ends that were selected for further research were those mentioned by the largest number of respondents. The cut-off level of seven ensured that each concept was mentioned by at least approximately half of all respondents. These were likely to play the most prominent role in the members of the

Table 5.1 Concepts mentioned by most respondents during laddering interviews

Rank	Aspect	Number of respondents mentioning the aspect
1	Enjoy your work	14
2	Work satisfaction	12
3	Achieve customer satisfaction	10
4	Perform properly	10
5	Make profits	9
6	Deal well with complaints	8
7	Retain your job	8
8	Everything goes smoothly	8
9	Earn my personal income	7
10	A good organizational reputation	7
11	Organizational continuity	7
12	Deliver service	7

organization's collective sense-making of what they did. Furthermore, the management of the organization was highly interested in investigating employee support for certain aspects not so frequently mentioned in the interviews. These were "being innovative," "alertly capitalizing on what is happening," "having a pleasant working atmosphere," "being sympathetic to people of modest means," "motivating people," and "respecting others." Column I in Table 5.3 (p. 101) lists the frequency with which these aspects were mentioned during the laddering interviews. In order to keep the questionnaires brief, the aspects "retaining your job" and "delivering service" were omitted in favor of these concepts. This brought the total number of identity aspects in the questionnaire to sixteen.

Regarding these sixteen aspects, the questionnaire assessed the degree to which respondents reported to have worked on these aspects, whether they believed the people around them had worked on these aspects, the degree to which the aspects applied to their own organization, and the degree to which they applied to the other organization, with whom the merger was planned. The questionnaire thus invited respondents to give three catchwords for the most characteristic aspects of the organization itself. The questionnaire included more questions, but they fall beyond the scope of the issues investigated in this chapter. The phrasing of the questions is given in the Appendix on page 114. Of the seventy-eight employees, seventy returned the questionnaire (an 88 percent response).

Table 5.2 lists the catchwords that at least two of the respondents gave. Two researchers coded the catchwords independently. The intercoder agreement (Kassarjian, 1977) was 0.88, pointing to a good intercoder reliability. Table 5.3 lists the average ratings on the survey questions. The average rating of 6.34 of the member's own organization's reputation (in column C in Table 5.3) confirms that the perceived *attributed* identity was not problematic at the time of the research. Moreover, a comparison between columns C and D in

Table 5.2 Most frequently mentioned catchwords

Rank of aspect	Aspect	Number of respondents mentioning
1	Innovative	23
2	Customer-oriented	16
3	Large	11
4	Customer-friendly	8
5	Delivers service	5
6	Professional	5
7	Alert	5
8	Continuity	4
9	Social	4
10	Good atmosphere	4
11	Commercial	4
12	Fast	3
13	Modern	2
14	Dynamic	2
15	Better	2
16	Co-operative	2
17	Solid	2
18	Good organization	2
19	Profitable	2
20	External image	2
21	Market orientation	2
22	Good human resources policy	2

Table 5.3 reveals that – in the eyes of its own members – the organization compared favorably to the peer organization on all sixteen aspects. The differences between the organizations (column E in Table 5.3) have been calculated by subtracting the rating of the other organization from the rating of the member's own organization on each of the sixteen aspects, and then calculating the average of these differences for each aspect. Most variables showed a distribution skewed to the right: a Kolmogorov–Smirnov test showed that at a 5 percent level, all of them had a distribution significantly different from normal. Spearman rank correlations were therefore used for further analysis. For each aspect, Table 5.3 shows the rank order correlations between the degree to which members of the organization reported that they worked on each of these aspects, the degree to which they perceived their peers to work on them, and the organizational identity experienced. The difference in ratings in Table 5.3 of both organizations did not bear much correlation with the *experienced* identity of their own organization. When analyzed aspect by aspect, only "having a good organizational reputation" showed a correlation which was significant at 5 percent. The results regarding members' self-reported activities and organizational identity are mixed. Table 5.3 shows how six of the aspects show correlations which were significant at a 1 percent level, and two weaker correlations, which were significant at a 5 percent level. The other eight aspects do not show a significant correlation. Of course, one can imagine

Table 5.3 Number of mentions, average ratings, and correlations regarding aspects of identity. Analysis for each aspect separately

Aspect of identity	I No. of people mentioning this in laddering interviews	II No. of people using this catchword	A "I work on this"	B "People around me work on this"	C Degree to which it applies to own organization	D Degree to which it applies to other organization	E Difference between own and other organization	Rank correlation (A*C)	Rank correlation (B*C)	Rank correlation (C*E)	No. of zero differences	No. of valid nonzero differences
Being innovative	5	23	5.43	4.94	6.28	5.48	0.95	0.05	0.06	0.16	27	13
Achieve customer satisfaction	10	1	6.07	5.70	6.28	5.98	0.58	0.12	0.24*	0.26	30	10
Organizational continuity	7	4	5.69	5.52	6.37	5.82	0.64	0.10	0.26*	0.12	32	12
Work satisfaction	12	0	6.41	5.87	6.02	5.76	0.41	0.39**	0.36*	0.07	30	4
Perform properly	10	0	6.49	5.96	6.19	5.82	0.56	0.22	0.30*	0.11	29	5
Alertly capitalize on what's happening	1	4	6.20	5.36	6.22	5.69	0.72	0.23	0.29*	0.10	30	9
Earn my personal income	7	1	5.47	5.79	5.88	5.42	0.45	0.51**	0.50**	0.26	27	6
Everything goes smoothly	8	0	5.86	5.47	5.63	5.29	0.37	0.22	0.12	0.07	29	6
Deal well with complaints	8	0	6.11	5.74	5.93	5.62	0.46	0.27*	0.30*	0.15	28	9
Have a pleasant working atmosphere	5	4	6.36	5.99	6.20	5.92	0.50	0.24*	0.35*	0.07	28	8
Being sympathetic to people of modest means	1	0	5.51	5.37	6.04	5.72	0.46	0.21	0.31*	0.01	33	6
Motivate people	3	0	5.49	5.26	5.91	5.64	0.50	0.12	0.32*	0.09	31	5
A good organizational reputation	7	2	5.99	5.67	6.34	5.93	0.56	0.23*	0.34*	0.35*	34	7
Enjoy your work	14	1	6.39	5.79	6.12	5.56	0.82	0.41**	0.35*	0.11	27	7
Respect other people	6	0	6.27	5.71	6.15	5.83	0.53	0.38**	0.49**	0.18	28	8
Make profits	9	2	5.21	5.14	5.93	5.57	0.52	0.39**	0.31*	0.22	32	10

Notes

* = significant at 5%.

** = significant at 1%.

perception of organizational identity depends more on what they see their peers doing instead of what they do themselves. Indeed, with regard to most aspects, the correlation between what respondents perceived their peers work on and how they *experienced* organizational identity was higher and more significant.

Only two aspects did not conform to this pattern: "everything goes smoothly" and "being innovative." It is feasible that with regard to "everything goes smoothly," the normal frustrations of everyday working life play a role. People strive for this aspect (half of the respondents mentioned it during the laddering interviews), but with mixed success. This was the lowest rating aspect of the organization's own identity. The respondents thought that they worked harder on this than their peers did (difference significant at $p = 0.001$, $Z = -3.4$ at a Wilcoxon signed rank test).

More striking is the other item where no link seems apparent: "being innovative." This is by far the most frequently given catchword for the organization (see Table 5.2). If we rely on the respondents' spontaneous characterization of their own organization, this catchword would be the most descriptive of its identity. People thought it well-applied to their organization (average 6.28) but they did not seem to work on it the hardest: it scored the second lowest with 5.43, just ahead of "making a profit." They perceived their peers to be working on it even less (4.94), which is the lowest rating of all. This is rather striking: for most aspects, the relation between what is done in an organization and its *experienced* identity seems to hold, but the most frequently used catchword for the organization seems to describe what members of the organization members do the worst. In fact, the catchwords seem to tap something different than the ratings of the organization on the survey items. Organization members' choice of catchwords seems to capture the *professed identity* rather than the *experienced identity*. In general, the themes of a *professed* identity are revealed by a word, label or short phrase which members of the organization perceive to adequately describe the organization's identity (Chreim, 2002). The question for the catchwords seems indeed to have tapped into this perspective on identity. The results from the catchwords clearly justify the distinction drawn in the five facets between *professed*, *manifested* and *experienced* identity (Soenen and Moingeon, 2002).

The next step was to make an overall analysis of all the aspects. Table 5.4 shows the rank order correlations between the averages of the questionnaire items shown in Table 5.3, the number of respondents giving that specific catchword, and the number of respondents mentioning the aspects during the laddering interviews.

One word of caution in the interpretation of the rank order correlations of Table 5.4 is necessary, though. All the measures in Table 5.4 are aggregate measures at the organizational level. Two of the variables are only available at this collective level: the total number of times a catchword is mentioned, and the total number of people mentioning a concept in laddering interviews. The other measures are averages from individuals' ratings in the survey. Correla-

Table 5.4 Rank order correlations between the averages of Table 5.3. Analysis of all aspects simultaneously

	People mentioning concept in laddering interviews	No. of people using catchword for own organization	"I work on this"	"People around me work on this"	Degree to which it applies to own organization	Degree to which it applies to other organization
Number of people using this catchword for own organization	−0.25					
"I work on this"	0.39	−0.28				
"People around me work on this"	0.47	−0.26	0.76**			
Degree to which it applies to own organization	−0.13	0.63**	0.19	−0.02		
Degree to which it applies to other organization	−0.02	0.06	0.44	0.33	0.65**	
Difference between own and other organization	−0.06	0.64**	0.03	−0.26	0.78**	0.22

Notes
N = 16.
** = significant at 1% level.

tions calculated from averages may not always accurately reflect what is going on at the level of the individual respondent (Robinson, 1950; Langbein and Lichtman, 1978). Table 5.5 contrasts the correlations in Table 5.4 with the results from the analysis of the correlations at the level of individual organization members. An overall measure of effect size can be computed by applying a Fisher Z transformation to the individual correlations. The average Fisher Z of the whole sample was calculated and the corresponding overall correlation was then derived from this average Fisher Z score (Rosenthal, 1991). Table 5.5 shows these derived overall correlations under the heading of "Effect size." One complication was that some respondents had correlations of exactly 1. In order to be able to make the transformations required, these were recoded as correlations of 0.99. The overall significance was computed by using Stouffer's (1949) method of computing the Z-score corresponding to the one-tailed individual significance levels. The individual respondents' Z-scores were added up. This sum was divided by the square root of N, the number of respondents (Rosenthal, 1991). The interpretation of this level of overall significance is slightly different from the interpretation of the significance of "plain" correlations. The compound null hypothesis is this: when the compound probability is as small as 5 percent, the overall null hypothesis can be rejected at the 5 percent level in favor of the alternative hypothesis, that for at least one of the studies the individual null hypothesis was false (Edgington and Haller, 1984: 265).

Five correlations in Table 5.4 are significant at a 1 percent level. It is not surprising that catchwords correspond to how people perceive their own organization (r = 0.63). People perceive themselves to be working on the same aspects as their peers: the correlation between "I work on this" and "People around me work on this" is 0.76, which is significant at 1 percent. In general, the pattern of differences between the member's own organization and the other organization is not large: the correlation between the degrees to which aspects apply at their own organization and to the other in Table 5.4 is 0.65 (p = 0.006) and the individual level size-effect in Table 5.5 is even 0.95. This is in line with the high number of respondents who did not really perceive much difference between both organizations. Table 5.3 shows how for every aspect, most people did not perceive differences between both organizations. Still, however, the frequency of catchwords is significantly correlated to the aspects in which people perceive a difference between their own organization and the other (r = 0.64, Table 5.4), confirming the research results of Elsbach and Kramer. The strongest correlation in Table 5.4 is between the "difference between the member's own and the other organization" and "degree to which the item applies to the member's own organization," derived from the survey: it amounts to 0.78, significant at a level of 1 percent. At the individual level, Table 5.5 still shows one of the stronger size effects for this relation, 0.59. In contrast to Table 5.3, the correlation between the degree to which an aspect applies to the member's own organization and the degree to which they think they work on the aspect is not significant in Table 5.4: it is only 0.19 (p = 0.49). This is exactly the same size effect as at the individual level (Table 5.5). Table 5.5

Table 5.5 Comparison of correlations at the aggregate and individual levels of analysis

Correlations between	and	Aggregate correlation from Table 5.4	Average Fisher Z	Size effect	Stouffer Z	Stouffer p (one-tailed)
"I work on this"	"My colleagues work on this"	0.76	0.40	0.38	10.56	0.00
"Applies to our organization"	"I work on this"	0.19	0.20	0.19	5.20	0.00
"Applies to our organization"	"My colleagues work on this"	-0.02	0.26	0.25	6.81	0.00
"Applies to the other organization"	"I work on this"	0.44	0.26	0.26	4.38	0.00
"Applies to the other organization"	"My colleagues work on this"	0.33	0.15	0.15	3.70	0.00
"Applies to the other organization"	"Applies to our organization"	0.65	1.80	0.95	27.48	0.00
Difference between our and the other organization	"I work on this"	0.03	-0.03	-0.03	-0.11	0.55
Difference between our and the other organization	"My colleagues work on this"	-0.26	0.16	0.16	1.70	0.04
Difference between our and the other organization	"Applies to our organization"	0.78	0.67	0.59	8.25	0.00
Difference between our and the other organization	"Applies to the other organization"	0.22	-0.82	-0.67	-9.29	1.00

shows, however, that this result is too strong to be neglected, confirming the results from Table 5.3 discussed earlier.

"Being innovative" was the only item from the survey that had a substantial number of mentions as a catchword describing the organization. In fact, it was the most mentioned catchword of all. Therefore, an additional analysis was performed on respondents' ratings in the questionnaire, in order to check whether people who mentioned the catchword "innovative" were different from those who did not. T-tests were performed for the degree to which people believed to work on "innovativeness," the degree to which they thought their peers worked on it, the degree to which they believed it to apply to their organization and to the other organization, and the difference computed from the two. Of these, only the last two t-tests were significant. This analysis will focus on the ratings underlying the computed difference score: the ratings of the own and the other organization on innovativeness. People who mentioned the keyword "innovative" rated the own organization on average 6.4 on a seven-point scale. Those who did not mention that catchword rated it 6.2 on the same scale. This difference was too small to be significant ($T = -0.82, p = 0.42$). On average, however, those who had used the catchword "innovative" rated the other organization 4.6 on a seven-point scale, those who had not used the catchword rated the other organization 5.8 (Table 5.6). This difference was significant ($T = 2.17, p = 0.04$).

The catchword "innovative" appears to reflect judgments of the other organization in comparison to the own organization, instead of perceptions of the own organization. The correlation of 0.65 between frequency of catchwords and degree to which an item was perceived to apply to the organization points to a close connection between *professed* identity as expressed in catchwords, and *experienced* identity, as expressed in member ratings of their own organization on survey items. Where *professed* identity diverges from experience identity, though, is in the choice of the catchwords. Catchwords seem to be related to how the own organization compares to the other organization, rather than to how organization members experience the identity of their own organization.

Following up from these empirical results, the way in which the organization further developed is noteworthy, as was reported a year and a half later by an informant from the organization. Before the research project, a small group in the organization had worked on innovative projects and the organization had presented itself to the outer world as innovative. The organization

Table 5.6 Average ratings of the innovativeness of the own and the other organization, related to the use of the catchword "innovative"

	Average rating of the own organization	Average rating of the other organization
People who used the catchword "innovative"	6.4	4.6
People who did not use the catchword "innovative"	6.2	5.8

seems to have been assessed at one particular point in its development. A year and a half after the research project, the organization had changed considerably. It had worked on a number of highly innovative projects, such as designing a residential area together with the prospective inhabitants of this area. Because of its innovative activities, it had been invited to participate in projects conducted by the European Community. At the time the data were collected, this innovation seemed to exist mainly in terms of a self-assigned predicate. Eighteen months later, this predicate has been transformed into concrete action, performed by more people than just a small group in the organization.

Discussion

This study set out with the question as to whether how members of an organization experience their organization corresponds with what they believe they are doing. In operational terms, this was elaborated upon as the correspondence between the sense people made of what they did in their job and how they experienced their own organization. For half of the sixteen aspects of identity in the survey, this relation seemed to hold. Proposition 1 could be accepted at a 5 percent level. The more members of an organization reported to have been working on the realization of an aspect, such as "dealing well with complaints," the more they believed that such an aspect applied to the organization. Aggregating over the aspects of identity, Tables 5.4 and 5.5 show a correlation of 0.19 between "I work on this" and the "degree to which it applies to the organization." This correlation is lower when respondents condense their perception of an organization's identity into a few catchwords. The correlation between the number of people using a specific catchword and the degree to which employees reported to be working on that aspect was even negative (–0.28, Table 5.4). The people who used the most common catchword, "innovative" were contrasted with those who did not. This analysis showed that people who used this catchword considered the organization about equally innovative as those who did not. However, those who used the catchword "innovative" for their organization rated the other organization significantly lower on this aspect. This result points to the second force influencing perceptions of organizational identity: the tendency of members of the organization to compare themselves favorably with peer organizations.

The presence of only one peer organization in the vicinity made interorganizational comparisons easy. Table 5.3 shows that, on an item-by-item basis, there were no significant rank order correlations between the organization's own rating on these aspects and the perceived differences between the two organizations, except for "the organization's reputation," which showed a correlation of 0.35, significant at 5 percent. On an aspect-by-aspect basis, the differences with the other organization seem to matter less than whether members of the organization perceive themselves and each other to be working on these aspects. However, when the rank order correlations between the average ratings of the sixteen aspects are calculated, a different pattern emerges

(Table 5.4). It seems that it does not matter much whether organization members work on an aspect or not. The correlations of "I work on this" and "people around me work on this" with "applies to the member's own organization" are not significant. The highest correlation of all in Table 5.4, however, is the one between the average perceived difference between both organizations and the degree to which an aspect applies to the member's own organization: 0.78 (p = 0.001), which at the level of individual respondents still amounts to 0.59 (Table 5.5). On an aggregate basis, the relation between the perceived difference between the two organizations and the *experienced* organizational identity seems strong, supporting Proposition 2.

Catchwords, as a measure of *professed* identity, correlate much stronger with *experienced* identity than with *manifested* identity: the former correlation in Table 5.4 is 0.65, the latter, 0.28. At first sight, these results suggest some tension between "theory-in-use" and "espoused theory" regarding the organization's own identity (cf. Soenen and Moingeon, 2002). "Espoused theory" is the theory to which organization members give allegiance and which they communicate upon request (Argyris and Schön, 1974: 7). Many people seem to take pride in how innovative the organization is, without necessarily putting it into practice themselves. The catchword "innovative" may perhaps best represent what Soenen and Moingeon (2002) call the *professed* identity of this organization. These results can be explained taking the delegation of tasks in an organization into account. Some people do work on it. In the qualitative interviews, five out of fifteen respondents showed concern about being innovative (Table 5.3, column I). As an informant confirmed, in the years before the research took place, a small number of people had been working very actively on innovative projects. These projects were highly prominent, both within the organization as well as within the municipality where the housing corporation was located. Only a small number of people in the organization had been involved in these projects. This explains the relatively low rating of "being innovative" that respondents gave to their peers (column B in Table 5.3). None the less, the high number of people mentioning "innovative" as a catchword to describe the organization seems disproportionate.

The research results provide evidence of a strong effect of perceived differences with other organizations on organizational identity and a weak, only partially significant effect of what people acknowledge working on. The perception of the members of the organization of their own organization's identity may indeed be influenced by the opportunities for drawing favorable comparisons with peer organizations, thus further confirming the results reported by Elsbach and Kramer (1996). The link between identity, as it is manifested in the actions of members of the organization, and identity, as members of the organization experience it, is weaker.

This is not to dismiss a link between *manifested* and *experienced* identity. The results point to the following conclusion: members of the organization do recognize a link between what they see their peers doing, what they are doing themselves, and the organization's identity, at least in certain aspects. However, what determines whether an aspect matters is the perceived difference between the member's own organization and the other organization. This conclusion applies to an even stronger extent to the relation between *professed* identity, expressed in catchwords, and the identity as it is manifested in actions. The organization appears to have made a considerable leap forward exactly in the area of innovativeness. If the research had been done one year later, the results would probably have been different. In other words, the relationship between *professed* identity and *manifested* identity may well be weak, but moreover, it is lagged. This lag effect deserves attention in future research.

However, the influence of sense-making of performed actions might be more enduring than the influence of any specific perceived difference. *Experienced* organizational identity may be subject to rapid change (Gioia, Schultz, and Corley, 2000), and *professed* identity even more so than *experienced* identity. In this case, we can discern two factors contributing to identity being short-lived, as it is captured in respondent ratings regarding the degree to which aspects apply to the organization (column C in Table 5.3). First, inter-organizational comparisons are often inspired by the in-topic of the moment. As topics change and rankings among organizations change, aspects of comparison change (cf. Elsbach and Kramer, 1996). They may change faster than people's jobs do. In the short term, what people do may seem the weaker factor explaining perceptions of identity. In the longer term, it might be stronger. In this case, the upcoming merger was highly influential in the perceptions of the members of the organization. After the merger, the organization would become the local monopoly. This could render the differences between the member's own and the other organization irrelevant. The factor for best explaining perceptions of identity would then disappear. This points to the volatility of *experienced* identity at any given moment in time (Gioia, Schultz, and Corley, 2000). However, most people would still do their work in a way which was not so fundamentally different from how they did it before. Over longer periods of time, sense-making from performed actions may play a more prominent role. After all, the weaker link between action and identity might turn out to be the more stable component.

Another factor making *professed* and *experienced* identity more fleeting than *manifested* identity is the rather exclusive allocation of innovative work to a small group of people. As long as those people are allowed to continue their innovative work, how innovative the organization is may be guaranteed. However, if these people are allocated different work in the organization, or worse, if they leave, how long will the perception of the organization as being innovative last?

The results suggest a process of development of identity over time. First, *professed* identity, that is, what people claim the organization to be, influences *experienced* identity. This is in line with Soenen and Moingeon's (2002) observation, that *professed* identity is rather desirable and future-oriented. *Professed* identity is primarily a promise. This organization provides an illustration for Kahane and Reitter's (2002) position that identity is expressed by keeping that promise: the "narrative" about being innovative has become "action." If members of the organization become committed to the *professed* identity, it becomes their *experienced* identity. This acceptance may be enhanced considerably if the *professed* identity applies more convincingly and positively to the member's own organization than to comparable organizations. Once a *professed* identity is accepted by members of an organization, it is more likely to be instantiated in their actions. In the case of this housing corporation, the restructuring of the organization, intended to give members of the organization more freedom to act upon the requests of customers, created the structural conditions by which individuals could further enact being "innovative." Of course, such a process does not necessarily follow this sequence of steps, as *experienced* identity may also take shape through the retrospective sense-making of performed actions. This research may have caught the organization at the moment that the *professed* identity had just been accepted by members of the organization, but when they had not yet transformed it into observable actions. This last conclusion, however, is tentative. The organization has only been assessed at one point in time and information about the organization in earlier and later times does not stem from comparable data collections at other points in time.

Limitations and suggestions for further research

This study represents one of the first empirical assessments of identity from two different perspectives, comparing the sense that members of an organization make of their self-reported behavior with their perception of the organization's identity. However, this study has its limitations. It addresses an organization in quite specific circumstances. The upcoming merger might have made the differences with the other organization much more salient, and therefore more influential, than otherwise might have been the case. Moreover, this study is a snapshot in time taken during a period of transition. There are no data on how stable aspects of identity were over a period of time. Furthermore, the differences between how respondents rated their own organization and how they rated their peer organization were calculated by the researcher. Given the interesting results which these data provided, in future research it may be advisable to have respondents directly rate such differences themselves, in order to be sure that the differences measured are what the respondents themselves regard as differences.

The results of the study also point to methodological implications for the measurement of identity. Catchwords can be interpreted as the primary, most readily available associations evoked for people by their organization. For organization members, the representations of identity most explicit and accessible to consciousness, may most closely correspond to the *professed* identity. The research results indicate that this *professed* identity is not identical to organizational identity, as organization members experience it. *Experienced* identity may thus well be more inchoate and less accessible to consciousness than *professed* identity. Careful in-depth interviewing or structured interviewing techniques such as Gustafson and Reger's (1999) and the Kelly Grid method may be more appropriate in order to establish the most relevant aspects of *experienced* identity.

What is new in this study is the empirical comparison between identity, as it is experienced by organization members, and identity, as it is manifested in the actions of members of an organization. The possible weak link between identity and what members of an organization do seems to have been overshadowed by the strong influence of the comparison with the other organization active in the area. What managers can learn from these results is that the perceptions of members of an organization of their own organization's identity may be influenced the fastest and most strongly in the short term by pointing to differences with other organizations. This may be particularly effective when such differences have implications as to whether the organization ranks favorably or not with those other organizations. If the members of the organization do indeed become committed to this *professed* identity and believe in it, this creates a fertile ground to successfully implement changes in members' behavior, as was illustrated by this housing corporation. This is in line with the dynamics Soenen and Moingeon (2002) posit in their five-facet framework. The *professed* identity may shape the *experienced* identity when it becomes actually projected. The relatively small size of the organization studied may imply that here this projection process is of minor importance. However, in larger organizations, the role of *projected* identity in mediating the relationship between *projected* identity and *manifested* identity is bound to be more salient.

A question still to be answered is what the results would look like if it had not been so obvious with whom the organization could be compared, for example, in the case of an organization which has a monopoly. Moreover, this study has been a cross-sectional one, held at a particular moment in time. Organizational identity, especially as expressed in catchwords, might be highly short-lived. Monitoring an organization over a longer period of time will bring more clarity. But above all, we may need a more theoretical underpinning of the relation between what organization members do and how they perceive their organization's identity. The discussion reported by Whetten and Godfrey (1998: 111–16), points to the link between *experienced* and *manifested* identity through the sense people make regarding what they do. This seems an interesting and promising road to pursue, uniting the work conducted in the disciplines which have conceived identity as "representation" with the work conducted from the perspective of identity as "manifestations" of what the organization is and what it stands for.

References

Albert, S., Ashforth, B. E., and Dutton, J. E. (2000) "Organizational identity and identification: charting new waters and building new bridges," *Academy of Management Review*, 25: 13–17.

Albert, S. and Whetten, D. A. (1985) "Organizational identity," in L. L. Cummings and B. M. Staw (eds) *Research in organizational behavior, volume 7*, Greenwich, CT: JAI Press, 263–95.

Argyris, C. and Schöm, D. (1974) *Theory in Practice*, San Francisco, CA: Jossey-Bass.

Baker, M. J. and Balmer, J. M. T. (1997) "Visual identity: trappings or substance?" *European Journal of Marketing*, 31: 368–84.

Barney, J. (1998) (contribution to) "A strategy conversation on the topic of organizational identity," in D. A. Whetten and P. C. Godfrey (eds) *Identity in organizations. Building theory through conversations*, Thousand Oaks, CA: Sage.

Chreim, S. (2002) "Reducing dissonance: closing the gap between *projected* and *attributed* identity," in B. Moingeon and G. Soenen (eds) *The five facets of organizational identities: an integrative perspective*, London: Routledge.

Dutton, J. E. and Dukerich, J. M. (1991) "Keeping an eye on the mirror: image and identity in organizational adaptation," *Academy of Management Journal*, 34: 517–54.

Edgington, E. S. and Haller, O. (1984) "Combining probabilities from discrete probability distributions," *Educational and Psychological Measurement*, 44: 265–74.

Elsbach, K. D. and Kramer R. M. (1996) "Members' responses to organizational identity treats: encountering and countering the *Business Week* rankings," *Administrative Science Quarterly*, 41: 432–76.

Fombrun, C. J. and Rindova, V. P. (2000) "The road to transparency: reputation management at Royal Dutch Shell," in M. Schultz, M. J. Hatch, and M. H. Larsen (eds) *The expressive organization: identity, reputation and the corporate brand*, Oxford: Oxford University Press.

Garfinkel, H. (1967) *Studies in ethnomethodology*, Englewood Cliffs, NJ: Prentice Hall.

Gioia, D. A. (1998) "From individual to organizational identity," in D. A. Whetten and P. C. Godfrey (eds) *Identity in organizations. Building theory through conversations*, Thousand Oaks, CA: Sage.

Gioia, D. A., Schultz, M., and Corley, K. G. (2000) "Organizational identity, image, and adaptive instability," *Academy of Management Review*, 25(1): 63–81.

Gioia, D. A. and Thomas J. B. (1996) "Identity, image and issue interpretation: sensemaking during strategic change in academia," *Administrative Science Quarterly*, 41: 370–403.

Gustafson, L. T. and Reger, R. K. (1999) "Beyond collective organizational identity: empirical evidence for multiple subidentities," paper presented at the Academy of Management Meetings, Chicago, IL, August.

Hatch, M. J. and Schultz, M. (1997) "Relations between organizational culture, identity and image," *European Journal of Marketing*, 31: 356–65.

Hatch, M. J. and Schultz, M. (2000) "Scaling the Tower of Babel: relational differences between identity, image and culture in organizations," in M. Schultz, M. J. Hatch, and M. H. Larsen (eds) *The expressive organization: identity, reputation and the corporate brand*, Oxford: Oxford University Press.

Huff, A. (1998) (contribution to) "A strategy conversation on the topic of organizational identity," in D. A. Whetten and P. C. Godfrey (eds) *Identity in organizations. Building theory through conversations*, Thousand Oaks, CA: Sage.

Kahane, B. and Reitter, R. (2002) "Narrative identity: navigating between reality and fiction" in B. Moingeon and G. Soenen (eds) *Corporate and organizational identity – integrating communication, marketing, strategy and organizational perspectives*, London: Routledge.

Kassarjian, H. H. (1977) "Content analysis in consumer research," *Journal of Consumer Research*, 4: 8–18.

Langbein, L. I. and Lichtman, A. J. (1978) *Ecological inference,* Sage university paper series on "Quantitative applications in the social sciences," No 07–010. Beverly Hills, CA: Sage.

Lewin, K. (1947) "Group decision and social change," in T. M. Newcomb and E. L. Hartley (eds) *Readings in social psychology*, New York: Holt.

Pratt, M. G. and Foreman, P. O. (2000) "Classifying managerial responses to multiple organizational identities," *Academy of Management Review*, 25: 18–42.

Reger, R. (1998) (contribution to) "A strategy conversation on the topic of organizational identity," in D. A. Whetten and P. C. Godfrey (eds) *Identity in organizations. Building theory through conversations*, Thousand Oaks, CA: Sage.

Reynolds, T. J. and Gutman, J. (1988) "Laddering theory, method, analysis and interpretation," *Journal of Advertising Research*, 28(1): 11–31.

Rindova, V. (1998) (contribution to) "A strategy conversation on the topic of organizational identity," in D. A. Whetten and P. C. Godfrey (eds) *Identity in organizations. Building theory through conversations*, Thousand Oaks, CA: Sage.

Rindova, V. P. and Schultz, M. (1998) "Identity within and identity without: lessons from corporate and organizational identity," in D. A. Whetten and P. C. Godfrey (eds) *Identity in organizations. Building theory through conversations*, Thousand Oaks, CA: Sage.

Robinson, W. S. (1950) "Ecological correlations and the behavior of individuals," *American Sociological Review*, 15: 351–7.

Rosenthal, R. (1991) *Meta-analytic procedures for social research*, Applied Social Research Methods Series, Volume 6, Beverly Hills, CA: Sage.

Salancik, G. R. (1977) "Commitment and the control of organizational behavior and belief," in B. M. Staw and G. R. Salancik (eds) *New directions in organizational behavior*, Chicago, IL: St Clair.

Simon, H. A. (1997) *Administrative behavior. A study of decision-making processes in administrative organizations*, fourth edition, New York: The Free Press.

Soenen, G. and Moingeon, B. (2002) "The five facets of collective identities: integrating corporate and organizational identity," in B. Moingeon and G. Soenen (eds) *Corporate and organizational identities – integrating strategy, marketing, communication and organizational perspectives*, London: Routledge.

Stimpert, L. (1998) (contribution to) "A strategy conversation on the topic of organizational identity," in D. A. Whetten and P. C. Godfrey (eds) *Identity in organizations. Building theory through conversations*, Thousand Oaks, CA: Sage.

Stouffer, S. A. (1949) "How these volumes came to be produced," in S. A. Stouffer, E. A. Suchman, I. C. DeVinney, S. A. Star, and R. M. Williams, Jr. (eds) *The American soldier: adjustment during army life, volume I*, Princeton, NJ: Princeton University Press.

van Rekom, J. and van Riel, C. B. M. (2000) "Operational measures of organizational identity: a review of existing methods," *Corporate Reputation Review,* 3: 334–50.

Weick, K. E. (1995) *Sense-making in organizations*, Thousand Oaks, CA: Sage.

Whetten, D. A. and Godfrey, P. C. (1998) *Identity in organizations. Building theory through conversations*, Thousand Oaks, CA: Sage.

Appendix I: The survey questions

On the job, I very actively take care that . . .

> 1 = completely disagree, 2 = disagree, 3 = disagree somewhat, 4 = don't agree, don't disagree, 5 = agree somewhat, 6 = agree, 7 = completely agree

	completely disagree					**completely agree**	

- everything goes smoothly   1   2   3   4   5   6   7

The people with whom I work very actively take care that . . .

> 1 = completely disagree; 2 = disagree; 3 = disagree somewhat; 4 = don't agree, don't disagree; 5 = agree somewhat; 6 = agree; 7 = completely agree

	completely disagree					**completely agree**	

- everything goes smoothly   1   2   3   4   5   6   7

Could you please indicate in the table below to what degree each of the aspects mentioned applies to your own organization and the other organization? You can assign a number from 1 to 7 and fill it in in the box. If you don't have an opinion, please fill in an X.

> 1 = does not apply at all; 2 = does not apply; 3 = applies hardly;
> 4 = neutral; 5 = applies somewhat; 6 = applies; 7 = applies completely

Applies to:	Our organization	The other organization
Everything goes smoothly		

Please state in three catchwords, in order of importance, what you think are the most characteristic aspects of your organization:

	Our organization
1	
2	
3	

Note: where this appendix mentions "your/our organization" and "the other organization," in the original phrasings the names of both organizations were mentioned. The original questions have been translated into English.

6 Narractive identity

Navigating between "reality" and "fiction"

Bernard Kahane and Roland Reitter

Introduction

The narrative perspective in strategy has been introduced and developed by several authors (Boje, 1991; Barry and Elmes, 1997; Czarniawska-Joerges, 1996) who adopt a "post-modernist" approach toward organizations. These authors argue that organizations are losing their boundaries and are dissolving themselves in their environment. Furthermore, within the organization, several "polyphonic" voices are fighting each other, trying to become the "official," "dominant" strategy. These authors emphasize the importance of listening to dissonant and often minority voices in order to construct and implement a sound strategy, but this goal seems elusive. The main limit of these post-modernist approaches is that they are too relativist and thus fail to explain how an organization can formulate and implement what would be a "good" strategy, or at least a better one. Moreover, in such a perspective, identity also loses its consistence since no one knows any more what it is and where it lies. What, then, is identity when an organization has no boundary and expresses itself through several conflicting voices?

Despite these limitations, however, narration seems to have much to offer to strategy. Managers themselves (Shaw, 1998) recognize that they constantly tell and have to tell stories, both inside and outside of their organizations. Even for more traditional and leading organizational theorists such as James March, the interaction between narratives and strategy appears to be a central issue (March, 1999). March argues that organization members, in their search to escape chaos and ambiguity so as to perform collective and coordinated action, must create and exchange narratives. In doing so, they allow themselves to interpret and communicate their own history and are thus able to live through it and by it. Since these organizational narratives are built by and for action, we qualify them as "narr-actives," and the strategic process linked to them as "narration." In this perspective, "a group" is constituted by members exchanging related narr-actives.

In this chapter, we analyze the relation between the various facets of identity and narration and explore its consequences for strategy formulation and implementation. To do so, we use the five-facet framework developed by Soenen and

Moingeon (2002). The categories of collective identity developed by these authors enable us to define narraction as a *professed* identity that is actually being *projected* and gradually reinforced or disconfirmed in the evolving *manifested* identity. We show that narraction has its roots in the works of "central identity" authors, such as Erikson and Ricoeur. A reinterpretation of Apple's communication and our own research on the emergence and development of gene therapy in France are used to tell these stories of action, called narractions.

Collective identity and narration

Apple's response to threat: integrating identity, narration, and action

What is identity? In Apple's approach, identity appears as the interaction of three different types and levels of narrations put together in a coherent manner. Apple seems to build deliberately on these three stories, reinterpreted and presented to serve its action and its goals: the story of its founder (Steve Jobs), the story of mythical personalities, such as Gandhi, that are used in its communication, and the story it uses to make users feel that they are part of Apple.

Steve Jobs

Steve Jobs was one of the founders of MacIntosh and is seen as the soul of Apple. Working nearly alone, he put himself at risk, worked in a garage to secretly develop an object destined to change the world (making computing fun and diffusing it to the world). Once he succeeded and managed to develop a successful firm, he was driven away by bureaucrats and managers who, trying to reap the benefits of a great idea, applied conventional financial and managerial rules and who, in the end, tore the firm down. When Apple was in disarray, actors both inside (employees, the Board) and outside the company (consumers, financial markets) forced the firm to look for radical solutions to rescue itself. When all conventional solutions seemed to have failed and when there was no more hope, its founder was called back in, and with his magical touch, helped clean the house and led the company to a new and bright future.

The story of Apple is similar to that of its founder. Working almost on its own, Apple put itself at risk, worked to develop an object designed to break the old order (the monopolistic and outrageous dominance of a big brother firm: IBM). Once it succeeded in destroying IBM's monopoly, new actors entered (Microsoft and Intel) with "dirty" tricks (marketing and coalition) and managed to create a new monopoly, cornering Apple. When everything seemed to be lost and when there was no more hope, Apple looked to its roots and found in itself (the originality of its design and its products) the solution to its problem. The potential was there and needed only to be recognized and exploited.

Gandhi

Interestingly, Apple, in its communication evokes certain historical characters because they tell the same story. One of them is Gandhi, who is shown
working alone in his rags, affirming and standing up for a message he wants to
deliver and to be recognized by the rest of the world: violence only brings
more violence and will always destroy, be it now or later. By putting myself at
risk, I will show you the way that will allow others to recognize where truth
and justice lie. By sharing this way of doing things, we will become an
increasingly large group, our position will be accepted by everyone, even those
who now fight against us.[1]

The users

The beauty of these stories is that on the one hand, they are all the same, and on
the other hand, they ask Apple's users to adopt them for themselves, as they
would fairy tales. Those who reject them must accept that they position themselves as the "bad guys" (the "bureaucrats," IBM, the oppressors of Gandhi's
time). All of these stories convey the same meaning, that is, we, who work
inside Apple, and you, users, are the same as Jobs, the company, and Gandhi,
and we think "different," as an "avant-garde" (which makes us a minority,
proud of ourselves and accepting of our destiny). In addition, as highlighted in
Propp's works on fairy tales, these stories share a common structure: in the age
of homogeneity, some, like us, accept defiance of the existing rules, and we
must fight for our convictions, and ultimately, we will be recognized and
rewarded for showing the path to the "masses." According to Propp's (1970)
view, what we have here is a crisis situation (an existential crisis where a
minority could disappear) where something is missing (truth is ignored in
this age of darkness) and a hero is needed to perform a function that will
resolve the problem (the ultimate power of truth will be recognized). Those
who listen/read the story, accept and share it, can identify themselves to the
proposed main characters, feel that they are indeed the "hero" as much as Steve
Jobs, Gandhi, or the firm through which the "good" and the "truth" (our
technology is the best) will succeed.

For Apple, identity and strategy are the two faces of the same coin and
narration is the tool to connect one with the other. Actual and potential users
are asked to engage themselves with Apple, just as Gandhi had asked the
Indians to join him in his own time. Interestingly, Gandhi's affirmation of his
engagement and its translation into a strategy for action for the Indian people
was studied by Erik Erikson, the American psychoanalyst.

Narration, identity, and action in Erikson's work

Erikson played a key role in the construction of our knowledge about identity;
he offered, from a psychoanalytical perspective, a framework for reflecting upon

human identity. His interest in identity led him to study the formation of the human psyche during the entire life cycle, and especially during adolescence. He concluded that identity is a construction. It is not given, nor is it cognitively acquired. It is the output of a fragile work on oneself and on the world. It is never simply a self-representation. It is a social construction, evolving through time, marked by conflict and doubt, simultaneously conscious and unconscious.

Erikson showed that there were episodes in the construction of one's identity: moratoria, crises. He also described the usual pathologies: confused, diffused, and split identities. Notably, he depicted the connections between identification and identity. The construction of identity is achieved through identification to valued social roles. In turn, the social glue is constituted of individual identifications, micro commitments and libidinal investments, the origin of which can only be individual. Thus, the relation between individual and collective is a core issue.

In his work, Erikson often relied on his experience as a psychoanalyst. However, he was also an anthropologist, and this enabled him to speak about collective identity. For example, he studied and compared two American Indian tribes: the Sioux and the Yurok. His two masterpieces combine the individual and the collective approaches: *Gandhi's truth* (Erikson, 1969) and *Young man Luther* (Erikson, 1962).

Gandhi

Erikson describes the textile mills strike of 1918 in Ahmedabad. Gandhi, approaching 50 years of age, was no longer a young man in quest for identity. In Gandhi's narration, this quest had taken place earlier, in South Africa, where he had discovered Apartheid. In 1918, he was preaching nonviolence and had some political influence – but no political weapon. The strike allowed him to work through two ideas: fasting and promise. Gandhi sat on the riverbank under a big tree, which he had baptized Ektek: *keep your promise*. He asked the workers to commit themselves not to give up. And he committed himself to fast to death if the employers did not give up. This commitment was not impulsive. It followed a clear analysis of the situation and of the actors. There was some form of staging: ultimatum, announcement, reformulation, negotiation, and proclamation that Gandhi wished no harm to anyone.

This episode demonstrates the inner strength of a man who committed himself to fight, using nonviolence and its newly codified weapon (fasting) on all the battlefields he selected. It is only one episode, but not the most dramatic one. The Salt March in 1930 and the London Conference in 1931 contributed more to the creation of collective meaning. However, Erikson chose this 1918 textile mills strike episode because on that occasion, Gandhi took on a new public stature. Furthermore, it is a good illustration of one of Erikson's favorite conceptual creations: the generativity phase of the human life cycle. Generativity is the transmission of meaning to the future generation, implying the primacy of the collective over the individual. While generativity is an important episode in the construction of identity, it cannot be understood in and of itself. It must be related to the rest of the text. *"La vie est un roman."*

Luther

The French title – *Luther avant Luther* (Luther before Luther) – accurately describes the book's content. It depicts the evolution of the son whose father, a Saxon miner, wanted him to become a lawyer and who became a monk instead, rebelled against the established Papal authority and led the traumatic split of the Reformation. Martin Luther was a troubled young man in troubled times.

Young man Luther is a narrative. It takes place at a specific period in time (1505–12 : Luther before Luther), at a specific place (Erfurt, Wittemberg), portrays a specific scenery (a monastery, a forest) with characters (Martin, his parents, his superiors, his mentor), and has a plot. The idea is to give coherence to a stream of dramatic events: God's call in the middle of a forest, reminiscent of Paul's conversion on his way to Damascus; a spectacular convulsive fit in a choir in the middle of a mass when Luther screamed: "Ich bin's nit"; paralysis at the very moment he was about to perform his first mass; a great mystic vision in a tower. One can imagine a film starting in 1517, with Luther nailing his ninety-five theses on the door of Wittemberg's Church. A flashback to 1501 would then show the 17-year old adolescent entering university. Critics would claim that this is a film about identity. It shows a young man, faced with an authoritarian father, doubting of himself. God calls him out of his dilemmas, but the young man is no more at ease in his new life. He must undergo some real soul searching in order to give some content and form to his conflicts and to limit them (the primacy of faith over works, the humanity of Christ, the necessity of a direct relation to God, the individuality of conscience . . .). These issues have a strong resonance in the city. Many Catholics are experiencing an identity crisis at that time. The Catholic establishment is guilty of some leniency (as in the indulgences affair) while printing provides a great vehicle for the strengthening of national languages and also deepens the gap between upper clergy and the masses.

Contrary to the film, Erikson the psychoanalyst must offer concepts. Identity diffusion or moratorium must credibly apply to the case. If they do not, we start feeling that the text is a narrative, not about the object (Luther), but about the author (Erikson): the book would be an episode of Erikson's narrative identity. As a matter of fact, this very concept of narrative identity would have greatly helped Erikson, by the distance it creates with objective reality. Erikson speaks about Luther's identity as if it were some natural object that we could comprehend without the help of existing texts and concepts posterior to Luther's time (although Luther, without these concepts, certainly had to ponder about the paradox of Theseus' ship, which remains the same, although through time, all of its parts had been replaced). Unfortunately,

Luther never laid on Erikson's couch, neither could one study him as a rat in a laboratory. He cannot react to stimuli or to interpretations, his "identity" is an intellectual reconstruction. Erikson must convince his readers and calls on our own adolescent crises to help. In order to have us share the mental equipment of a Saxon peasant of the fifteenth century, he chose to be very familiar in his language. He spoke about young Martin, a normal young adolescent with whom we can identify. In the process, we lose sight of the social construction of the Reformation. Luther's texts are seen as outputs of his psychic conflicts and not as semi-autonomous objects which lend themselves to political and social appropriations after they are issued.

To a certain extent, for Erikson, history is like a fairy tale. In the cases of Gandhi and Luther, personal identity and collective identity merge because the time was ripe. This proposition has some merit, but we can only be a little skeptical in the face of such a miracle. Let us turn to Ricoeur, who can help us to better clarify how individual and collective identity merge.

Identity and promise in Ricoeur's work

The concept of narrative identity comes in his early works and is central to *Soi-même comme un autre* (Ricoeur, 1990). Its great contribution is to understanding the connections between the two canonical dimensions of identity (both personal and collective): sameness and ipseity.

One understands the importance and the limitations of sameness. My identity is what the others recognize me to be. Does Theseus' ship have an identity? If I say no, on the basis that all its parts have been changed, only what is immutable has an identity. If I say yes, what is the basis of its identity, since none of its components is the same? Ipseity also can be ambiguous. To say that specificity is the basis for identity may well lead to a reification of qualities or characteristics that cannot (and should not) be fixed forever. In business administration, we have a clear demonstration of that trap: flexibility is a fact of life. A company should be different from others so as to enjoy a competitive advantage. Yet this specificity is constantly questioned and, in addition, it cannot be instrumentalized (bought or sold at will): it is a social construction.

Ricoeur wants to go beyond this idea. For him, ipseity is not manifested by identity traits, but is expressed by promising and keeping a promise. It is the decision of a subject, of somebody who speaks out and acts, who says: "here I am, I commit myself for the future: I will sustain, preserve, keep up, be loyal to my commitment." Narrative identity is the means to keep a certain coherence between sameness/continuity and ipseity/promise. Constructing and reconstructing the text of one's life builds coherence into continuity and, at the same time, specifies who speaks and acts and will be accountable in the future. The word can be trusted only if the speaker is credible.

Ricoeur could have commented Luther's fit in the choir ("Ich bin's nit") along those lines. It is the core of Luther's personal conflict. Luther had been through the opposition to his father; he was no longer "Martin," but still a rebel. Could one survive opposing God? How could one express one's rebellion and find justification from God? Luther had reached rock bottom. He was *not* (not mad, not possessed, not rebel). Yet this very nothingness allowed commitment. This commitment was at first very personal (he submitted to God, without intermediaries), but as soon as Luther could express himself through preaching, he extended it to his community. There was a risk: Luther had to flee and hide. However, he continued to keep his promise, which was later amplified by politics. The Reformation was a matter of power. Luther became an actor in a game. In 1517, he was not conscious of the consequences of his symbolic action. But Leon X was shortsighted, and the Elector of Saxony chose to protect Luther and to use him as a political weapon.

For Ricoeur, narrative identity is more than playing political chess. "Soi-même comme un autre." When the troubled adolescent became Luther and nailed the ninety-five theses, he was acceding to something universal. He became justified by other people's expectations. He was the one who was invested with power. He proposed a new attitude toward God: direct, personal, humble, genuine, in the name of others, with strong collective symbols (as the Bible in German).

Erikson and Ricoeur thus help us understand what we mentioned for Apple: the importance of narratives for identity building; the interrelations between individual and collective identities; the strength of promises to commit oneself and to influence the course of events. Let us now test this on our fieldwork: gene therapy.

Narrative identities and the development of gene therapy in France

In this section, we report the findings from research we undertook on the development of gene therapy in France. First, we present the innovation, gene therapy, its context and its main actors. Then, we look at the dynamics of collective identities in this context. We show that identity is a complex question with many potential groups vying to answer. Then we show that as a narration, identity stands at the crossroad between reality and fiction. Finally, we highlight the dynamic nature of identity, as narrations are continually evolving.

Addressing the innovation's context: gene therapy emergence and development in France

Gene therapy is a radically new therapeutic method proposed to cure diseases such as cancer, AIDS, and degenerative syndromes such as Parkinson's or Alzheimer's diseases. Using a modified viral vector or a synthetic one, an external gene is introduced inside a patient's cells to cure the cause of the disease linked to the absence, deficiency, or over expression of an internal gene. Due to the therapeutic targets involved, the number of potential patients to be cured and the solvency of the countries where these patients live, stakes on gene therapy are high for pharmaceutical companies, research organizations, and states. Further, because it offers a possibility to cure "orphan" mono-genetic disease, patients' associations play an important role in promoting this approach and have become prominent actors in the field. Such is the case for AFM (French Association against Muscular Dystrophy) and AFLM (French Association against Cystic Fibrosis), both of which position themselves in France between state research organizations, such as CNRS (Centre National de la Recherche Scientifique (National Center for Scientific Research)) (which can be compared in some way to the NSF (American National Science Foundation), and profit driven pharmaceutical companies. These organizations help bring donators, clinicians, researchers, and patients closer, and have become themselves strategic actors in the innovation process.

In France, most of the top academic laboratories are affiliated to one or the other of the national research organizations such as CNRS, Inserm, Inra, Cea, etc. Researchers inside these laboratories "belong" to these organizations which pay them on a permanent basis and which also provide a substantial part of the laboratory's annual budget. Nevertheless, since laboratories need more resources to conduct their research, and since they possess rare and valuable knowledge and expertise, they accept contracts with external actors, such as pharmaceutical companies and patients' associations, to work on matters of common interest. For these external actors, working with academic laboratories is a flexible way to conduct strategy. On the one hand, research projects inside one laboratory evolve with scientific evolution, and on the other hand, decisions to support one or another set of laboratories can be changed along the way for similar reasons. This way, organizations avoid committing resources internally when uncertainty surrounding the various options and components of an innovation is too high.

The five years from 1990 to 1995 were crucial for the development of gene therapy. This period saw the establishment of the first genetic map of the human genome, the organization of the human genome sequence identification project, and successful and unsuccessful clinical trials of this approach. Throughout the entire period, we studied at an operational level the main French organizations involved in the research effort, namely CNRS, the biggest French research organization; Rhône-Poulenc, the biggest French pharmaceutical company; AFM and AFLM, the two patients' associations previously mentioned, which were strongly involved in gene therapy (Kahane, 2000). To implement their strategy for gene therapy research, each of these organizations established numerous links with academic laboratories which had the rare and crucial skills and knowledge (e.g., in vectors, sequencing, transfection, etc.) needed for gene therapy. All the organizations we studied implemented a common strategy centered on networking, which featured the mobilization of academic laboratories, sometimes several simultaneously. Since they played such a strategic role, academic laboratories became the center of our investigation. Our objective was to understand how the "mobilization" strategies are translated, interact, and are reinterpreted at the ground level. In other words, we studied "strategies in action," with a specific focus on the relationship between narrations and actions. To that end, more than one hundred face-to-face interviews, lasting 3 hours each, were conducted, and a questionnaire was addressed to all the teams involved in the project in each organization.

Uncertainty is the first intrinsic difficulty of innovation (van de Ven, Angle, and Poole, 1989). The aim of innovation is to create and develop something new that will transform the world in which action takes place. Due to scientific evolution and organizational action, new elements are continuously incorporated in the action system, changing the environment as well as the determinants of action. In such a context, anticipation of the future appears as an elusive game that needs to be reconstructed again and again as action progresses. Can we construct the vector we have in mind? Will it work? Will we be able to incorporate the gene in it? How will the target cells react to penetration? All these questions cannot be answered at the beginning of the journey and only organizational actions and experimentation will enable progress. So, action is needed (without action, no progress), but its results are uncertain. It is because AFM decided to build the "Genethon infrastructure"[2] that the bet on obtaining a genetic map of the human genome was taken, and in the end, was won.

Identity as a complex matter

Our research points that, in such a context of radical innovation pursued by interacting actors, identity is an open and difficult question. Who can legitimately speak on identity matters? The potential voices are numerous: one of the funding organizations; a committee in charge of projects assessment and/or management; participating laboratories and/or networks of them; small operational teams inside them; individual researchers. The same difficulty applies to issues on strategy formulation. All these actors have their own distinctive goals. For instance, CNRS wants to further scientific knowledge at large to fulfill is role towards society and the government; Rhône-Poulenc ultimately wants to make money by operating gene therapy on major diseases; AFM and AFLM, each for its specific groups of patients, want to foster hope and offer a possibility to survive deadly diseases; laboratories and researchers want to advance their research projects to gain knowledge and prestige. Although all these actors turned to academic laboratories as part of their strategy, they differed in the actual tactics used for implementation. However, at the same time, they shared a common interest in the successful development of this innovation. Together, they were to succeed or together they were to fail. This common interest led them to interact together in numerous networks and projects that questioned their identity. What is identity for an organization such as AFM and AFLM (or even the part of Rhône-Poulenc which is concerned with gene therapy) when most of its resources are provided by ad hoc expert committees from external entities such as academic laboratories? What is identity for a research organization such as CNRS when its academic laboratories receive most of their funding from external sources and can decide almost freely their goals and strategies? What is identity for an academic laboratory when, on the one hand, researchers come and go, assemble and disband, depending on research subjects, and when, on the other hand, the resources are mostly external, coming from grants and contracts? "What is identity?," then, can be a tough question when organizations' boundaries tend to dissolve in networks and when the source and the results of action lie as much inside the organization as outside it. Thus, we found that identity was a complex matter in an innovation process, such as the one we studied (similar observation would have probably been made in other sectors like information technology where network configurations change continuously).

Further, compared to Apple, the context of gene therapy development does not facilitate the narration of identity through mythical stories. First, we have seen that defining the border of an organization is not simple. Organizations dilute themselves in numerous academic laboratories and a laboratory can be considered as a strategic integrator belonging to various organizations. Second, like the boat of Theseus, organizations change their parts contin-uously, supporting different laboratories at different periods in time. Third, although the goal (gene therapy for a given disease) is fixed, how it will be reached is unknown and it changes during the journey. Thus, in our story, the boat of Theseus has a consistency that is somewhere in the middle between a virtual object and a physical one. Not only does it change its parts as it proceeds along its journey, but it also reinterprets the journey itself.

Evolving narration: identity at the crossroad of "fiction" and "reality"

In such a context, how do organizations implement strategy? How do they decide which laboratory and which research subject they will support? How do they decide which is the best way to achieve what they have in mind? Similarly, how do academic laboratories and individual researchers choose their research topics, the support they will seek, and the collaborations in which they will engage themselves?

We found that, faced with a messy reality, such as the one previously described, organizations build their stories not only on "reality" and its "interpretation," but also on "fiction." They use "fiction" to engage them-selves and deliver a promise both on a future to be reached and on ways to reach it. Narration is the tool used to relate the present "reality," its "interpretation" and the proposed "fiction" into a single story to obtain something consistent and convincing. These stories enact the conditions for future experimentation and they will be validated or challenged by it, that is, narration by and for action. In this sense, these narrations are narractions. In this interpretative, continuous knitting process between "reality" and "fiction," organizations define themselves as well as their actions. Thus, narraction is identity and identity is narraction.

As in Erikson's and Ricoeur's works, or as in the case of Apple, in our work on gene therapy we discovered an intimate interaction between narration and identity. In the example of AFM, one of the patients' associations, it is because AFM, through its leader Bernard Barrataud, claimed that gene therapy was feasible, showed some results, and decided it would use all of the resources necessary to place itself at the forefront of this research that gene therapy became a core feature of AFM's identity and that AFM became its incarnation in France. The narrations that we identified were individual as well as collective. They interpenetrated and answered each other. The efficiency of AFM's narration came from its similarity or complementarity with those of others. Patients and the public alike wanted to believe in it, became interested in science, and participated in AFM's actions, both financially and through the time and energy spent on the manifestations organized by the association. Academic laboratories were glad to see the public interested in their work. They also shared AFM's goals, which allowed them to work on interesting topics they wanted to address, to obtain funding, and to expand their recognition beyond their peers to reach public opinion and the media. Thus, AFM's narration was the narration of all the components that participated in it. The more actors that shared a part or the totality of the narration, the more consistent and credible it appeared. Finally, we also discovered that narrations allow organizations to engage themselves, and help others engage in action. It is because AFM offered and claimed a promise of a way to cure patients on death row that it raised media interest and public funding. It is because it said it would commit itself, and indeed did, that others committed their intellect, time, and funding to the same interest.

Thus, actors at each level (organizations as well as committees, academic laboratories, teams and individual researchers) involve themselves through stories they build on a known "reality" (the result of previous actions) in order to reach a new "reality" (the result of the actions they engage themselves into). The shape of the future reality will depend on the validity of the proposed initial story in its essence (will scientific results foster or invalidate the story) and in the capacity of organizations (will the organization be able to transform the story into action). As one of the scientists involved in the Genethon recalled, "From what was known, we considered that there was a good chance we could achieve the genetic map if we put together a specific set of people and tried to develop new instruments."

Reconfiguring narractions

Yet there is no direct and sure way to link what already exists in the present to the expected future that actors want to attain. As we have seen, actors must create "fictions" to connect one to the other. "If we do this, we will achieve that from which we will be able to do this." "Fiction" allows for creative and constructive ambiguity between what exists and what will exist.

However, these narractions are not fixed forever. Fictions are regularly put to the test by action (e.g., scientific experimentation, market need or expectations) which either confirm them or ask for their reconfiguration when things do not go as expected. Thus, actors must navigate between "reality" and "fiction" in a never-ending iterative process. "Fiction" allows them to escape temporarily the constraints of what is known of "reality" (existing science and actors) to explore new territories in order to come back later to a "transformed reality" (new elements of science and new actors). Narration is what they mobilize in order to organize consistency between "reality" and "fiction." As AFM stated,

> First, we will develop automates, and if they work, we will use them to construct our genetic map, and if we achieve that, then we will identify target genes, then we will incorporate them in vectors, etc., and in the end, we will have a way to cure people.

As these narratives must respect, at each step, the results of past actions in order to engage credibly in new actions, they are narrations (narratives by and for actions). Who tells and shapes the story as well as the set of characters involved is at the core of identity.

Through the clear definition of its targets and of its "call for tenders," through the concentration of its resources on a limited set of actions periodically assessed and reconfigured, through its impressive communication, AFM succeeded in making gene therapy a central feature of its *professed*, *experienced*, and *manifested* identity. Gene therapy became a core feature of the identity AFM projected and of the identity that actors in the environment attributed to AFM. Aside from its centrality, gene therapy also became one of AFM's distinctive features: AFM came to be associated with gene therapy far more than CNRS, even if laboratories, teams, and human resources of this latter institution were at the core of AFM action. To all actors involved in this process, gene therapy in France is the result of AFM action. The intelligence of AFM was to let the narration progress and reconfigure periodically when new or already existing actors or scientific elements came into play. Once a result was achieved (or, on the contrary, seemed out of reach), the entire story and the set of actions to be conducted were reinterpreted in this new light. Significantly, the way AFM operated at its organizational level is similar to that of laboratories which regularly reconfigure their projects and composition depending on what has been achieved by them and by others. Thus, at the organizational level as well as at the laboratory level, narration was conducted as a novelist would do to advance in his story: defining a plot inside a context and exploring what it can give, introducing new characters or eliminating those no longer needed, modifying the plot as the story progresses, and at all times respecting consistency so that the readers, the characters, and the author do not get lost. What science and organizational action add to the narrative plot is that validity tests should be passed. Either the narrative convinces readers, passes the validity test and goes on, or it fails and has to be modified.

Can the experiment and the organizational action conducted be successful and will it succeed in the end? This is the test. This is what differentiates narraction from narration as we have shown in our previous works (Kahane, 2000).

Further, it is because there is this regular reconfiguration of the fiction told under the test of reality that the promise and the engagement of AFM on the one hand, and of academic laboratories, patients, and the public on the other hand, can be renewed, strengthened, and pursued. Reality testing of fiction and the reconfiguration of narractions (from the results obtained) are the conditions of these never-ending, reciprocal promises and engagements obtained through narraction. As the story progresses and the reality tests are passed, the organization strengthens itself. When the past and present narrations have been through numerous and/or difficult reconfigurations, the organization's ability to knit together reality, its interpretation, and fiction in a creative and fruitful way is increased, and makes it more capable of leaving and conducting its future narration. This capacity is traditionally termed "resilience" by psychologists (Cyrulnik, 2001). Developing resilience is a great achievement for organizations.

Conclusion: narraction, promise, and the theory of collective identity

We believe that these notions of narraction and promise are helpful if we wish to deepen our understanding of collective identities. The conceptual framework proposed by Soenen and Moingeon (2002), because it introduces a differentiation between several perspectives, reminds us that identity is a complex matter. It is not sold on the market, nor can it be decreed. It can be dreamed and proclaimed, but it becomes a social reality only when it is experienced, manifested, and perceived by outside observers (which entails that it is supported by "real" events). In other words, identity becomes real – but always precariously – only if it flourishes in the imaginary world of the players and the observers, and this requires that they share a collective experience thanks to a symbolic elaboration on reality and a possible future.

Identity relies on the effective creation of a collective narraction. Any researcher and/or consultant knows how difficult it is for top executives to create mythologies, because powerholders are always tempted to adopt a functionalist stance; they are obsessed by what seems functional to them, and are rarely aware of the ambivalence of identity issues. They are easily tempted to create mythologies from scratch and find arrangements with truth. We know that symbolic elaboration does not work that way. It requires:

1   a clear connection with reality
2   a deep connection to felt identity issues
3   the use of strong symbols.

Narraction connects reality and fantasy through symbolic elaboration. It does it in an iterative manner. Whenever action is highly uncertain, the leader becomes a central figure because he can take charge of uncertainty-engendered anxiety by making a promise, *a personal commitment*. A promise constitutes a hallmark in the narrative chain. It creates an "ante" and a "post." A promise is made unilaterally. It establishes the prominence of the speaker, staging himself in his capacity to interpret the dynamics of the world and the organization's identity, in his resolution to construct solutions to strategic problems, and to take uncertainty upon himself. A promise is also the sign of a leader's intrapsychic work, the result of fusing formal and personal sources of legitimacy.

The strength of a promise lies in trust. In a world of uncertainty, trust is not associated, in the mind of followers, with fulfillment, but with the knowledge that if circumstances and events become disadvantageous, he who speaks will stage his exit. Such is the case of de Gaulle who did it twice. Such also is the case of Christian Blanc, who saved Air France and left when the government refused its denationalization. The leader is like a film director. He organizes the course of a story for the actors, except he is not the master of the text. He must ensure the credibility of the script, and narraction helps him to reconcile script and events. Life is a novel but a novel in which we live.

Notes

1   This is a personal interpretation of Gandhi's motto.
2   The Genethon infrastructure is a central facility that was created and supported by AFM and located near Paris. Its aim was to create the human genome map using an industrial approach. Its cumulative budget from 1991 to 1995 was 500 million FF ($100 million at that time). Nearly 150 people worked in a 3600 m² building equipped with a significant amount of apparatus (102 PCRs, 20 multiblotters, 17 sequencers), some of which were developed specifically for this facility.

References

Barry, D. and Elmes, M. (1997) "Strategy retold: toward a narrative view of strategic discourse," *Academy of Management Review*, 22(2): 429–54.

Boje, D. M. (1991) "The story telling organization: a study of story performance," *Administrative Science Quarterly*, 36(1): 106–26.

Cyrulnik, B. (2001) *Les vilains petits canards*, Paris: Odile Jacob.

Czarniawska-Joerges, B. (1996) *Narrating the organization: dramas of institutional identity*, Chicago, IL: University of Chicago Press.

Erikson, E. (1962) *Young man Luther*, New York: Norton.

Erikson, E. (1969) *Gandhi's truth*, New York: Norton.

Kahane, B. (2000) "La 'narraction' comme mode d'élaboration de la stratégie en situation d'incertitude: le cas de la thérapie génique et des 'innovations technologiques de rupture'," unpublished doctoral thesis, HEC School of Management, Paris.

March, J. G. (1999) "Les mythes du management," *Gérer et Comprendre*, 57: 4–12.

Propp, W. (1970) *Morphologie du conte*, Paris: Seuil.

Ricoeur, P. (1990) *Soi-même comme un autre*, Paris: Seuil.

Shaw, G. (1998) "Strategic stories: how 3M is rewriting business planning," *Harvard Business Review*, 76(3): 41–4.

Soenen, G. and Moingeon, B. (2002) "The five facets of collective identities: integrating corporate and organizational identity," in B. Moingeon and G. Soenen (eds) *Corporate and organizational identities – integrating strategy, marketing, communication and organizational perspectives*, London: Routledge.

van de Ven, A. H., Angle, H.L., and Poole, M. S. (1989) *Research on the management of innovation, the Minnesota studies*, New York: Ballinger.

Part III
Managing identities

7 Creating a new identity for France Télécom

Beyond a visual exercise?

Monique Brun

Introduction

The objective of this chapter is to investigate the role of visual identity in corporate communication. More precisely, we intend to show that while firms often consider visual identity to be a graphic exercise, the implementation of a visual identity program is in fact linked to more strategic issues. After defining the concept of corporate communication in relation to corporate image and corporate identity, we will focus on the process of creating a new brand identity. Writing from a marketing perspective, we use the term corporate identity. We will specify how we position this term with regard to Soenen and Moingeon's (2002) five facets of collective identity. Visual identity will be treated as one of the components of corporate identity.

To illustrate our proposition, we studied the case of France Télécom, a major French telecommunications operator that recently adopted a new logo and visual identity system. The company has undergone a spectacular evolution over the past few years as it shifted from being a state-owned company operating in the sector of fixed telecommunications to an international group with markets in mobile communications and the Internet. For our research, we collected secondary data and conducted in-depth interviews with both France Télécom and Landor, a design agency with which France Télécom worked. We tracked the entire process and show the interactions between the different participants involved. Based on these data, we discuss the main issues at stake for France Télécom in its development of a new position in the market. More specifically, we address the relationships between the different facets of identity (Soenen and Moingeon, 2002), and show how the creation of the new visual identity and corporate brand can be seen as a turning point that supports the company's future evolution.

The issue of corporate identity in corporate communication

This section is intended to enable the concept of corporate identity to be positioned within the context of corporate communication. According to Soenen and Moingeon (2002), marketing and communication research on corporate identity tend to focus on two categories of collective identity: on the one hand, the identity *projected* by the firm toward its many audiences, and on the other hand, the identity *attributed* to the firm by its various publics. Both types need to be taken into account in corporate communication, just as do other facets of identity, that is, the identity that the organization *professes*, the identity experienced by organizational members, and the identity actually *manifested* over time in organizational routines, structure, and culture. From a marketing and communication perspective, a central issue is developing a coherent strategy for managing the *projected* identity, which we will refer to as "image strategy."

Defining what this image strategy should be implies (i) distinguishing between different types of communication, (ii) clarifying the concept of image, and (iii) considering corporate identity as a key element in communication strategy. We will argue that corporate identity is composed of several elements. Since it has notably a symbolic dimension, in the last section, we will explore (iv) the symbolic dimension and the role of design in managing visual identity.

The concept of corporate communication

Literature about companies and brand communication emphasizes complexity. Following Palo Alto's school of research, in particular, awareness that the environment is no longer an exogenous factor, but forms part of the individual, implies that everything is based on communication. From being a "field of knowledge," communication has become the envelope that encompasses any activity (Sfez, 1988). However, marketing communication, and especially advertising communication, has long been presented as a linear process, with little room for interaction with other types of communications. Considering that communication extends beyond the sole scope of the marketing division's activities and involves the entire company has multiplied the definitions for this term.

Some authors make a distinction between global communication at the marketing level, which involves choosing between the different means available (advertising, direct marketing, corporate sponsorship and patronage, public relations, etc.), and global communication at the corporate level (President's speech, relations with the press, lobbying) (Lendrevie and Lindon, 1996). Others distinguish nine modes of communication (Gayet, 1998): territory communication, product communication, management communication, environmental communication, published communication, direct communication, promotional communication, advertising communication, socio-relational communication. Such a classification, however, does not allow for a clear distinction to be made between communication objectives, communication types, and media. Authors in general, though, do agree on the meaning given to marketing communication, which is product-related and directed at customers. Many books and articles, which we will not explore here, cover this subject. A consensus seems to have developed in support of integrated marketing communication, that is, the different means of an organization's commercial communication are integrated to create more consistent messages and to benefit from greater efficiencies.

However, communication with other types of audiences gives rise to different definitions. Some authors make a distinction between organization and company communication on two different levels: the company, on the one hand, and the institution, on the other (Schwebig, 1988). The discourse about the company deals with the human, technical, or financial resources that it deploys to fulfill its economic and social role of producer. The institutional discourse concerns the organization as a social whole. Beyond its role of producer, the company expresses its mission, vocation, and contribution to society's general welfare.

The danger of fragmented communication emanating from a large variety of internal sources has led to the necessity of harmonizing all forms of communication. In this sense, corporate communication has been defined as

> an instrument of management by means of which all consciously used forms of internal and external communication are harmonised as effectively and efficiently as possible, so as to create a favourable basis for relationships with groups upon which the company is dependent
>
> (van Riel, 1995: 26)

A total communication strategy raises the issue of the creation of a specific territory that will be involved in all communication actions (Westphalen, 1998). The creation of this territory is strongly related to the question of corporate image.

Corporate image

The term "image" has been used in a wide variety of contexts. In *Images of organization* (1986), Gareth Morgan pointed out the metaphorical basis of organization theory and showed how all the different perspectives could be used to "read" the nature and significance of different aspects of organizational life. Marketing has popularized the concept of image. Different methods make it possible to determine the image of a brand as perceived by customers, to compare it to the desired image, and to try to modify it by means of marketing communication. No doubt the concept of image is a multidimensional one if we consider all possible corporate publics that form an impression of the company when they, directly or indirectly, interact with it: customers and suppliers, opinion leaders, distributors, employees, shareholders, etc. Moreover, the multiplicity of image types – product class image, brand image, country image, corporate image, and sector image – has also contributed to a certain confusion of the term.

According to G. R. Dowling, the confusion between the different types of images can be clarified if we adopt the following definition of image:

An image is the set of meanings by which an object is known and through which people describe, remember and relate to it. That is, it is the net result of the interaction of a person's beliefs, ideas, feelings and impressions about an object.

(1986: 110)

According to this definition, the word "object" can be replaced by brand, product, or company to specify the type of image concerned. It is also obvious that the company will not have one, but several, images, as the image is determined both by the object and by the person who observes and selectively perceives the different aspects of the company's communication.

For a variety of reasons, companies are paying increasing attention to corporate image. Corporate image can be a strategic asset, a source of competitive advantage, and an investment for the future, particularly when there is little or no difference between competitor brands. Corporate image can affect the buyer's judgement about the company's products and contribute to increasing sales; notably, it can help in new product development and launches. It can also be used to strengthen financial relationships, to harmonize employee relations, and to attract higher quality employees (Diminopolu, 1999). More and more, the word "reputation" is being substituted for that of "image" but the arguments remain the same. In the next section, we argue that corporate identity is central to the creation of a favorable image for the company.

Corporate identity, a key element in communication strategy

Balmer has proposed a comprehensive definition of corporate identity: "Corporate identity is what the organization is, i.e. its innate character. Everything an organization says, does and makes impacts on an organization's identity, e.g. products and services, formal and informal communications, company policies, the behaviour of staff, etc." (1995: 25). Birkigt and Stadler suggest a narrower definition of corporate identity – "the way in which a company presents itself to its target groups" – and qualify image as "the picture of an organization as perceived by target groups" (cited in van Riel, 1995: 28). These authors introduce the idea of a corporate identity mix where "corporate strategy" is linked with "communication in the broad sense." The corporate identity concept is broken down as follows:

- Personality, described as "the manifestation of the company's self-perception." In order to present itself clearly, the company must have a clear picture of its real situation. This presentation is made through:
- Behavior: the company will be judged by its actions; therefore, behavior is the most important medium;
- Communication: communication in the "narrow sense" refers to verbal or visual messages. It is linked to behavior, as the message enables positive aspects of the company's actions to be emphasized;

- Symbolism, which gives an implicit indication of what the organization represents.

From a visual identity perspective, symbolism plays a central role. We focus on this element in the following section.

Symbolism, design, and image strategy

Research on the concept of identity has shown the importance of symbolic elements in the expression of a company's identity. Besides the official discourse, myths, rites, legends, or taboos form part of an organization's identity (Larçon and Reitter, 1979). Symbolism is of special concern to the design field. Graphic design and environmental design, including product design and packaging, all contribute to the visual identification of a company and its products (Brun, 1990).

As of 1980, the *Union Française des Designers Industriels* (UFDI) identified different fields in design activities (industrial design of products, visual communication, packing and packaging, amenities, and environment). According to *Association Design Communication* (ADC), created in 1988 by design agency leaders in their domains, design covers three main sectors:

1   Graphic design, including visual identity, packaging and publishing;
2   Environmental design, including points of sale, workplaces, exhibition spaces and signage;
3   Product design applied to mass-marketed convenience goods, capital equipment, industrial product, and different forms of packaging.

The association insists that design should not only involve the aesthetic appearance of a product or the *ex nihilo* creation of a company's logo. In their view, prior to the creation stage, any approach involves a strategic reflection with which the design agency must be closely involved.

For a company, then, design investment can include multiple sources of added value and differentiation from competitors. For product design and packaging, design contributes to a company's competitiveness through both the product's use value and esteem value. Performance, practical use, and ergonomics are crucial for the use value, while the esteem value allows for the object to be characterized in relation to the target aimed at, and for the product recipients to be marked with identification signs, enabling recognition.

An examination of the reality of design professions shows that the different fields of design application are grouped according to technical performance. Graphic design includes visual identity, packaging, and publishing, while product design includes the design of products and three-dimensional packaging. Environmental design refers to the commercial architecture, creation of booths, amenities at the workplace, and signage. From the viewpoint of a company requiring a designer's skills, it seems crucial to us to adopt a classification with two different design levels:

1   Product and packaging, relating to marketing reflection and brand;
2   Visual identity and environmental design, expressing the organization's identity.

Awareness of both these levels does not mean that they should be dealt with separately. On the contrary, the coherence of the whole must be a major objective for the company. Symbolic identity, which deals with what design professionals call "visual identity," thus plays a key role in image strategy. The decisions relating to the development of an image strategy that relies upon symbolic communication are of crucial importance in any approach aiming at eventually ensuring a company's competitiveness. However, work on visual identity too often remains limited to a mere graphic exercise.

We proposed, in a previous study, an analytical framework for the creation and management of a company's visual identity in relation to image strategy (Brun and Rasquinet, 1996). The diagram below illustrates the main aspects of this approach (Figure 7.1).

The diagram evokes three strategies – monolithic strategy, branded

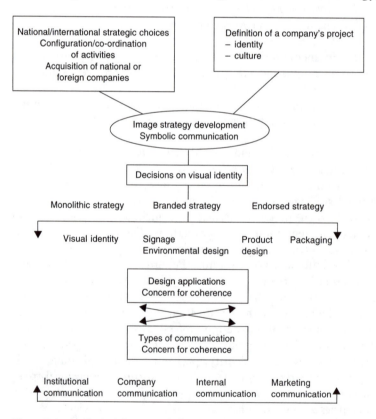

Figure 7.1 Analytical framework for the creation and management of a company's identity.

strategy, and endorsed strategy – which correspond to the three categories defined by W. Olins (1989) relating to the expression of identity:

1   Monolithic identity: the organization uses one name and one visual style over a vast range of activities;
2   Endorsed identity: the organization wants to tie together a group of activities and companies by using, besides the identification of individual parts, the group's name and logo. They all appear as part of a larger whole;
3   Branded identity: the organization operates through a series of brands that are quite separate from that of the company.

Managing design in a company implies managing the interface between design and communication. The different visual applications of identity, different types of communication and their interactions should be taken into account. Therefore, explicitly choosing one or the other of the three visual identity strategies above is essential in the implementation of a global communication strategy. Certainly, the implementation of a visual identity program requires both the definition of strategic objectives and the explicit formulation of company values.

Reflection on image strategy development must also consider the company's international development choices. In recent years, companies have increasingly aimed to develop in size, and the market base has now become global for many of them. We first present the new issues for a company's visual identity in a perspective of change through the case of France Télécom. We then interpret the case, demonstrating the links between visual identity and the other different facets of identity: controllable *projected* identity (e.g., formal communication), partially controllable *projected* identity (e.g., staff behavior), *professed* identity, and *experienced* identity.

The France Télécom case

France Télécom's revolution

Very few sectors have experienced such radical evolution as the telecommunications sector. In the 1960s, post, telephone, and telegraph (PTT) operators had to connect each call manually. The installation of telephone lines was a lengthy process. The evolution of this sector and what France Télécom has become took place in several stages.

Early 1970s to mid-1980s: the technological challenge of implementing infrastructures

The Delta LP project to increase the network of main lines, initiated by the French government and conducted by the General Directorate for Telecommunications at the time, was implemented from 1972 to 1983. It was a vast program for network expansion and modernization that drastically changed telecommunications infrastructures in France. The Directorate General of Telecommunications was influenced by a strong culture in which technical excellence was considered a fundamental value. In the beginning, this period was characterized by heterogeneous procedures and a decentralized management style aimed at enhancing innovation and ensuring fast and effective implementation. However, the risk of dysfunction quickly resulted in the development of centralized management.

Evolution of the competitive context and France Télécom's status from 1984 to 1995

British Telecom's privatization in 1984 was the starting point for a number of significant changes in the telecom industry. As of 1986, the French Minister of Telecommunications suggested that the national operator change its legal status but, given the personnel's vehement rejection of any initiative that questioned their civil servant status, and in view of the many strikes, the project was abandoned. In 1987, an internal survey on the evolution of staff regulations was conducted. In December of that year, the Directorate General of Telecommunications chose the name "France Télécom," thereby showing a willingness to change its identity. The July 2, 1990 law allowed for the creation of a distinct, state-owned company. On July 9, 1990, the majority of social partners signed a social agreement on staff redeployment. Once this necessary change in status was completed, France Télécom became on January 1, 1991, an autonomous, public-law institution.

Staff redeployment was carried out between 1991–2. This complex procedure involved repositioning all the employees – over 150,000 people – according to a new job logic. Created in 1992, France Télécom's visual identity was to be maintained for eight years. In 1993, the European Community announced the deregulation of the telecom sector as of January 1, 1998. The French government's announcement of partial privatization caused a general strike with a record 75 percent employee participation rate in October 1993.

Implementing the identity change at France Télécom occurred in several phases from 1990 to 1995, the most significant of which were the following:[1]

- A strategic formulation process, leading to the publication of "CAP 98" (CAP: Clients–Adaptability–Performance), a restructuring plan aimed at preparing France Télécom for total deregulation on January 1, 1998;
- The PAC (Plan for Actions of Change), a guide for implementing change and new management methods;
- An evolution towards global quality;
- The creation of a decentralized social observatory, a structure specialized in the surveying of employees' opinions; and
- The 1994 debate, a real communications exercise in the form of questions and answers within the company at large.

The arrival at the end of 1995 of a new chairman at France Télécom also emphasized a new challenge, that of growth in a market stimulated by deregulation and new technologies.

1995–2000: new challenges, new services, and internationalization

Several elements have emphasized France Télécom's evolution in recent years. The law enabling the partial privatization of France Télécom was voted through in 1996. In 1997, France Télécom became partially listed on the Paris and Wall Street stock exchanges, with 4 million private shareholders. In 1998, the market not only in mobile communications, but also in fixed telecommunications, was opened up completely to competition. In 1999 and 2000, the evolution of France Télécom's activities, with fixed telecommunications amounting to only 50 percent of the consolidated sales in comparison to 75 percent in 1995, was confirmed. International revenues, which amounted to 2 percent in 1995, rose to 25 percent in 2000, and are expected to be close to 50 percent in 2003.

In 1999, France Télécom's consolidated sales amounted to 27.2 billion euros. The company currently has a presence in seventy-five countries and employs 174,000 people worldwide. Oriented toward large businesses, private customers, and other operators, its range of services includes local and long-distance calls, data transfer, mobile communications, multimedia, the Internet, cable television, and broadcasting. France Télécom's international development is one of the company's strategic priorities. The purchase of Orange, Britain's third largest mobilecommunications operator in August 2000, confirmed this new orientation. Orange, part of the capital of which is already quoted on the stock exchange, will group all of France Télécom's and Orange's activities and investments in mobile communications. With the purchase of Orange, France Télécom has become the second largest mobile operator in Europe, and the third worldwide.

Internet activities for the public and professionals have been grouped together under the banner, Wanadoo, since June 23, 2000. Wanadoo, an Internet access provider launched in 1996, has enjoyed an impressive development. From 1998 to 2000, the number of Internet users in France increased from 2 to over 7 million, and Wanadoo's market share rose from 17 to 39 percent. In 2000, France Télécom made several major corporate acquisitions (alapage.com, kompass, marcopoly.com, and librissimo) and was able to launch the instant mobile (WAP). As a result, the company's evolution in recent years has been spectacular. The change in visual identity, image, and brand strategies has formed part of this evolution.

From France Télécom to france telecom: the change in visual identity and brand strategy

France Télécom's former visual identity, a digital dialing keypad inside a circle, was launched in 1993 and replaced the handset over a digital dialing keypad inherited from the Directorate General of Telecommunications. The 1993 logo, created for a state-owned monopoly, reflected the issues at the time. The digital keypad symbolized the technical evolution and the circle, the beginning of internationalization. The objective was to confirm the existence of the France Télécom entity and to federate all staff in the context of the thorough transformation mentioned earlier. Both the blue color and the keypad emphasized the company's technical competence. However, with the arrival of new stakeholders in the market, internal and external surveys revealed the discrepancy between the visual identity (i.e., what it evokes) and the company's goals. France Télécom's logo was ranked below those of its main competitors. As a result, the company was incited to introduce new forms and colors as well as increasingly humanized logos connoting youth and dynamism. The important areas of change were the following:

- Logo: descriptive, dynamic, connoting openness and movement, but mainly described the telephone; it was outdated, technical, and emotionless;
- Color: light and suggested trust and reliability, but was cold and monolithic;
- Typography denoted trust, leadership and power, but also rigidity, distance, and impersonality.

Using the five-facet framework (Soenen and Moingeon, 2002), we note that in this case there was a gap between the *projected* identity, and more specifically, the visual identity of which it is a part, and the identity *professed* by the company's management (notably its strategic intent). As a result, a new visual identity was launched in March 2000. It features a symbol (the ampersand (&)) in warm colors (orange and red), with the "france telecom" name attached and written all in lower-case letters, whereas it was previously written in all capitals. The blue color was kept for "france tele," to which "com" was added in orange. This new visual identity was clearly supported both internally and externally. It ranked first in surveys when compared to those of its main competitors. Six months after the logo's launch, the adjectives respondents used to describe it revealed the great success of this operation (see Table 7.1).

The statistics in Table 7.1 could be interpreted as the satisfactory result of

Table 7.1 Logo survey results 6 months after launch (%)

	External	*Internal*
Creative	70	77
Friendly	69	85
Warm	61	78
Internet	55	89
Modern	57	92
Dynamic	53	83

a successful graphic exercise. Understanding the reasons for such a success, however, requires going beyond the visual expression of identity. It requires a complementary analysis of the image strategy and the implementation process used. We will see that the process leading to the creation of a new *projected* identity (composed in part of the visual identity) has its origins in an acute awareness of the *experienced* identity and *attributed* identity.

Beyond visual identity: the territory of relationship, the new brand driver

The creation of France Télécom's new *projected* identity is a result of an in-depth reflection on brand strategy and image strategy. The company has undergone major changes both internally and externally. The transition from a situation of monopoly to the status of a company listed on the stock exchange, the international commitment, and the presence in new markets are all challenges in a highly competitive telecom market.

Since France Télécom's strategy was founded on three growth engines – mobile communications, the Internet, and international development – the company began to study, in 1998, a new brand strategy expressed in the new visual identity system. The most significant change, however, occurred internally. The company evolved from a context in which the determining element was technology to a vision in which the customer is of central importance. The structure implemented in 1996, integrating highly developed marketing techniques and an upgraded commercial function, reflected this evolution. Aside from the main transversal functions – corporate communications, public affairs, finance and human resources, corporate secretary – the company was restructured into four divisions: mass market products and services, large businesses, networks, and development. Two figures sum up the employees' support for France Télécom's new goals and status. In 1993, 75 percent of the personnel went on strike to protest against the company's privatization. In 1998, 90 percent of the employees had become shareholders, indicating that they had accepted privatization and competition.

The company's cultural background was used to underpin the company's values and, in particular, its taste for challenges: important in this were the historical technological challenge the company had undertaken of installing telephone lines for the entire French population; the challenge to innovation of having launched numerous new products; and the challenge of the change in its status. The company's current ambition is to present itself as an historical telecommunications operator opening out to the world, settling on all continents, and becoming a reference point in the provision of services – this is France Télécom's corporate *professed* identity. Enacting this *professed* identity is certainly a considerable challenge.

In 1996, a new brand strategy was implemented in preparation for the opening up of markets to competition in 1998 and for the company's introduction on the stock exchange. The entire communication campaign was aimed at

Figure 7.2 Enhanced relationships: France Télécom's new brand driver.

establishing a relationship with the public and was intended to be optimistic in a rather pessimistic climate. *"Nous allons vous faire aimer l'an 2000"* (We'll make you love 2000) featured a new start, since France Télécom had always been perceived as a technically-oriented enterprise. This transitional communication necessarily changed again in 2000. The latest institutional communication campaign – *"Bienvenue dans la vie.com"* (Welcome to life.com) is closely related to the definition of a brand driver based around the concepts of relationship, convergence, and service.[2] The idea of being linked to the Internet suggests that France Télécom has moved from the "one-to-one" relationship of traditional telecommunications to the richer and more diverse relationships of the new telecommunications world, that is, "one-to-the-world," "many-to-one," and "many-to-many." Likewise, the symbol chosen for the visual identity (the ampersand (&)) means you and me, that is, France Télécom and its customers. France Télécom can now offer this new type of relationship, with its new range of products and services, including the Internet and mobile communications. Its new brand driver is illustrated in Figure 7.2. This brand driver and the resultant visual expression permeate through all of France Télécom's brand manifestations (advertising, promotion, sponsorship). We will evaluate in the next section the main stages of the process implemented.

Implementing the new projected *identity: from the brand driver to the brand universe*

General process

This change process was pushed on further when a significant gap was noticed between the company's visual identity (the *projected* identity) – what was experienced internally by France Télécom's employees (the *experienced* identity) – and the company's image as perceived by customers (the *attributed* identity).

The staff, especially those in marketing and sales, who had been readied to face competition in 1998 and to respond to the customer service challenge, felt that the old visual symbol was a handicap that reminded them of the past. The role of the outside design agency was not limited simply to the design of the logo's graphics. Rather, the resultant collaboration was a case of genuine interaction between France Télécom and the agency, so as to integrate the different facets of identity throughout a period of change. The full transformation process, which led to the launch of a new visual identity, lasted nearly two years. The initial brief was laid down in the summer of 1998. Surveys were carried out through the year, at the end of which time a final brief was written to take into account both the market's and the company's evolutions. In October 1999, the visual identity was finalized. It was launched internally on February 29, 2000 and disclosed to the public on March 1, 2000 (see Figure 7.3).

The design applications for all media were developed over a two-year period from March 1, 2000 to the end of 2001, as detailed below:

- Websites: all of them have carried the new identity since March 1, 2000;
- Products and brochures: they have been using the new identity since March 1, 2000;
- Phone cards: a new series has been created;
- Phone booths: the new identity was displayed at tourist sites from May to October 2000; carrying on through until the end of 2001, stickers were progressively applied to the remaining phone booths;
- Fleet of vehicles: stickers were applied to all vehicles by the end of 2000;
- Business cards and headers: on March 1, 2000, Net FT provided employees with headers and business cards for download. New headers have since gradually replaced the former upon stock renewal;
- Points-of-sale: all of them were provided with a presentation kit. Signage was changed between March 1 and April 1, 2000, in priority points-of-sale and were subsequently modified in the remainder by the end of 2001.

The interaction between the company and the design agency has indeed played a major role in the definition of the new *projected* identity. Hundreds of applications were involved in a largescale identity program. The approach adopted by Landor, the design agency responsible, is schematized in Figure 7.4.

The first ten to twenty applications were used to develop and validate the brand design and the brand universe. The brand universe creates a house style, that is, a visual code identifiable beyond the logo itself. It involves all the visual identity components, including secondary graphic elements, color palette, photographic style, etc. After the graphics chart was established, the

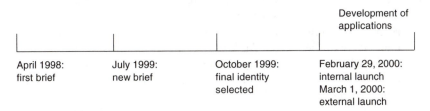

Figure 7.3 Key dates in the program.

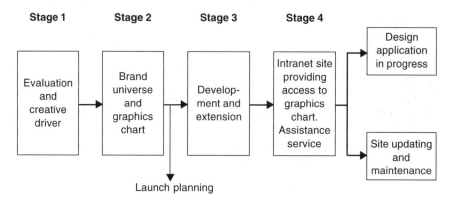

Figure 7.4 The implementation process for the new visual identity adopted by the design agency, Landor.

launch was planned at the end of stage 2. Stage 3 consisted of implementing and performing stage 2 applications. About a hundred additional applications were developed and validated. Stage 4 involved documentation and assistance. Documentation describes the technical aspect, while assistance refers to the human aspect, that is, helping people to understand the new identity and to get involved in the change. Interaction was constant throughout the development stages, but was particularly essential during stage 1, which resulted in the definition of France Télécom's visual identity and brand universe. The following section focuses on this first phase.

Creating a new brand universe for France Télécom

The creation of a new brand universe for France Télécom required at first a detailed analysis of France Télécom's strategic context. The next step consisted of identifying the key points of the brand driver so as to best take advantage of the current situation and to build up a competitive advantage in the longer term. The approach adopted by Landor is presented in Figure 7.5.

In this respect, the brand project is a genuine company project. The steps schematized in Figure 7.5 are detailed below.

- Strategic axes – worldwide actor/exhaustive services, and Innovator/"the" reference point in terms of services.
- Brand positioning – vision: a world that communicates more and better is more likely to "be" better. Ambition: being the brand that, more than any other, helps and encourages people to communicate more and better.
- Driving statement – it is to be expressed by the ampersand and the relationship concept that we have discussed earlier. It is keyed to different axes: smart society, homo connectus, ergonomics, technology, life+, and lifeblood, etc.

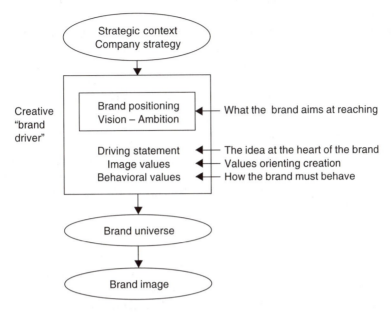

Figure 7.5 Creating a new brand universe and brand image for France Télécom – key steps of the process adopted by the design agency, Landor.

- Image values – image values are keyed to functional issues (the broadest offer – heritage – technology – competence – experience – adequacy – proximity) and emotional issues (responsibility – reliability – accessibility – equity – seriousness).
- Behavioral values – the closest and most responsible brand, making the fairest offer. Behavioral values are directly translated into actions (behavioral evidence): refunding when errors are made, proactive attitude.

In practice, to deploy this process to create a new brand universe, the design agency carried out a visual audit on France Télécom and its main competitors and assessed the brand's architecture in its environmental setting. Existing surveys were reviewed and completed using internal and external interviews. Throughout the process, working groups constituted of both France Télécom and Landor members were formed. The project was conducted by France Télécom's Corporate Communications division.

First, the project was defined in meetings (brief reevaluation, identification of key partners, definition of roles and responsibilities, project planning, etc.). Many interviews were then carried out at different France Télécom sites, involving managers, field managers, marketing and sales people. These interviews helped Landor to better understand the company, its expectations, and its relationships with customers. Sensory and colorful universes were tested on internal actors, both to refine the data collected and to determine if the people recognized themselves in these universes or if, on the contrary, these universes were inadequate. In addition, specialists in the field and representatives from the different subsidiaries of the design agency in France and abroad brainstormed on the future telecom market and on its consequences for brand positioning and architecture. Subsequent follow-up involved the Executive Committee and a group of marketing and sales executives.

Launching the new visual identity

In our view, there were three key features in the new identity implementation process: (i) confidentiality, (ii) the importance given to the internal launch, and (iii) the synergy of communication elements for the external launch.

CONFIDENTIALITY

Although everybody knew that France Télécom's visual identity was to change, the logo was kept secret until the internal launch. A simulation was performed to assess the cost of applications. A sham logo was therefore developed. It took exactly the same space as the actual logo and the same number of letters was attached to it.

IMPORTANCE GIVEN TO THE INTERNAL LAUNCH

The privilege of discovering the new logo first was given to France Télécom employees. To this end, 800 people, all France Télécom employees, were trained by an external company to be relays in 800 meeting rooms of the France Télécom network spread across the entire national territory. On the day before the external launch, all the staff were invited to an internal press conference. A 35-minute video presented the change. The President and each member of the Executive Committee explained, in their respective fields, what the new identity represented for each of them. The 800 people responsible for the different rooms completed the presentation and answered all staff questions. On the same day, the head office employees were given business cards and header paper. The graphics chart was available on the company's intranet. Each France Télécom employee was given a specific brand launch book, entitled "Welcome." This brochure presented the new group logo and the communication universe. A number of objects bearing the new identity were distributed to the staff for their offices. The new identity was also explained in the internal newsletter and a specific campaign was launched internally on the theme "The world changes, this is another sign." To comply with the President's message, "in the year 2000, all thrifty," the new identity was implemented over a two-year period. Stocks of commercial brochures had been managed with great care in the preceding months in order to prevent waste. In-company enthusiasm seemed to indicate that the launch was a success.

The new identity was adhered to and strengthened the pride of belonging to the company. A faster updating of all media, according to the new graphics chart, was even desired, although some feared a lack of understanding about the related costs.

SYNERGY OF COMMUNICATION ELEMENTS FOR THE EXTERNAL LAUNCH

The external launch of the new identity gave rise to a press conference held by the President and Vice President for Corporate Communications. Beyond the promotional aspects (head office and network animation, distribution of objects, etc.), it should be noted that the launch date chosen, March 1, 2000, coincided with the publication of the 1999 annual report and launch of the new brand signature "Welcome to life.com." On the following day, the quoted stock exchange price rose by 25 percent. Combining the announcement of good annual results with the launch of a new institutional campaign strengthened the message that the new identity was intended to convey and, at the same time, reinforced the coherence around the brand driver: relationships, convergence, and service.

Case interpretation – from *projected* identity to corporate identity management

The previous section has focused on the creation of a new visual identity for France Télécom. We now focus on the connections between the visual identity, that is, the *projected* identity, and the other facets of identity defined by Soenen and Moingeon (2002). To do so, we first review the identity diagnosis carried out prior to the identity change. We show that in the case of France Télécom, the new *projected* identity was derived through a process in which due attention was paid to the *experienced* and *manifested* identity. The case also shows evidence of the interaction between the *professed* identity, the *manifested* identity, and the new *projected* identity. We conclude the chapter by looking at the role of visual identity in corporate identity management.

France Télécom's new visual identity: more than just a design exercise!

Diagnosis of identity

As mentioned earlier, organizational identity is at the heart of any corporate image and communication strategy. In theory, several elements should be taken into account when diagnosing an organization's identity (Moingeon and Ramanantsoa, 1997). First, a distinction needs to be made between culture and identity. Allaire and Firsirotu (1984) proposed that organizational culture be viewed as the interrelation of three components. There is a socio-structural system made of formal structures, strategies and management processes and of all components of the organization's reality and functioning. Then there is a "cultural" system that is composed of the organization's expressive and affective dimensions (myths, ideology, values, and cultural artifacts such as rites, metaphors, legends, design, architecture, etc.). Finally, the interaction of the individual actors constitutes the third component of organizational culture. While culture, composed of symbolic productions, represents the visible part of identity, the organizational imagery represents its hidden face. Organizational imagery is defined as the "set of basic assumptions, impulses and values which govern (not necessarily consciously) the behaviors of organization members" (Moingeon and Ramanantsoa, 1997: 386). This part of identity is the most difficult to evaluate since it refers in particular to "internal" images in the minds of individuals. Second, in diagnosing an organization's identity, one must acknowledge the link between identity and history. Identity is the product of the organization's history, but identity also molds history by acting either as a force of inertia or as a force of progress. Third, it is necessary to recognize both dimensions of identity: sameness, that is, shared values, and conflict (Moingeon and Ramanantsoa, 1997). According to these authors, who refer to Bourdieu's "objective complicity" concept, there are struggles in organizations, but also an agreement between the agents about what is worth struggling for.

In the case of France Télécom, the creation of the visual identity was preceded by a genuine diagnosis of identity. Indeed, the pilot committee – the Corporate Communications Division and the external design agency – integrated the new brand policy into the global approach described earlier. This global approach incorporated the company's history, its evolution over time, its change in status, and the drastic change in its competitive environment. It also considered the possible internal conflicts and their high stakes – public versus private, technical versus commercial – and focused on those elements with which the staff at large could identify themselves (sameness, that is, shared values linked to what is felt as high stakes). In addition, this approach developed over time, which made it different from a great number of approaches on the creation of visual identity, where the evaluation stage is extremely short, if not nonexistent. Furthermore, Landor truly accompanied France Télécom's change, as the interaction between France Télécom's internal team and the design agency's team lasted approximately two years. Referring to the taxonomy of corporate identity programs, as defined by J. Balmer and G. Soenen (1999), one can call this is a fullscale, multidisciplinary, strategic corporate identity program.

Links between the different facets of identity

Obviously, the visible change achieved by the process implemented at France Télécom is related to the *projected* identity, or what is controllable. In concrete terms, it dealt with the creation of a new logo, a new visual environment, and a new institutional communication campaign. The attention paid to the company's staff, and in particular to marketing and sales people, shows that the *experienced* identity was also a strong focus in the change process. The aim was to bring *experienced* and *projected* identity into alignment. The same applies to the *manifested* identity, since the history of the company was taken into account during the identity development process.

The *professed* identity, which is related to the notion of the company's mission or project, and which was mainly intended for the internal public, is very closely related to the *projected* identity. As emphasized earlier, the change in identity was backed by strong external communication: the publication of group results and the launch of the new institutional campaign. The internal launch, which preceded the external launch, was a privileged opportunity to internally communicate the company's project. On this occasion, the main managers expressed their vision of the company and its development. The links demonstrated by Gioia and Thomas (1996) – links through which the projection of the future desired image is a means to accelerate the change in *manifested* identity – are here again present.

The *projected* identity is also related to the *experienced* identity insofar as the visual identity program was initiated at a time when the internal request for a change in the external image was strong, particularly among the marketing and sales people. There was a gap between the image attributed externally (the *attributed* identity), which was reinforced by the former visual identity (the *projected* identity), and what was experienced internally (the *experienced* identity). The company was perceived as being technical, whereas employees were becoming increasingly customer-focused. One knows how organizational members' views of their company's external reputation are important in the identification process (Dutton, Dukerich, and Harquail, 1994). This led us to think about identity management from a perspective of change.

Visual identity, a turning point in a changing environment

An evaluation of the processes implemented at France Télécom aimed at defining a new brand driver and a new visual identity emphasizes an aspect that is too often neglected: the preparation of possible futures. One of the fundamental changes that took place within the company was its accelerated internationalization, or rather, a change in the nature of its international development. Until recently, for its international penetration, France Télécom had acquired local companies. Each operated in its own market, and France Télécom's visual identity and name only applied to operations in France. The group is currently entering a new stage in its development and is preparing to become a truly global company, as defined by Porter (1986), that is, developing competitive advantages by means of its international presence. Service-providers, which have recently become increasingly international, are being confronted with new issues that extend beyond the mere preoccupations of country selection, penetration modes, and local marketing strategies. More precisely, these companies are confronted with the necessity to review their internal organization in order to respond to environmental evolutions. Bartlett and Ghoshal (1997) demonstrated that changes in management roles and personal capabilities are part of a more general and fundamental change in organizational philosophy:

- Companies are rethinking the old top-down approach and are paying more attention to the small, front-line, operating units;
- The emerging organizational model is characterized by cross-unit, integrative processes designed to break down the vertically-oriented relationships of the classic authority-based hierarchy;
- The role of top management has evolved from being the formulators of corporate strategy to the shapers of a broader corporate purpose with which personnel can identify and feel a sense of personal commitment.

In an increasingly turbulent environment, the reactivity model is required (Lerch and Llerena, 1995). It follows on from previous models of standardization (Taylorian and Fordian models) and variety. The gradual transition from homogeneous demand to a more diversified demand, characterized notably by a stronger requirement for services, has influenced economic evolution. Neither of these models, however, question the logic of an independence between the company's organization and the state of the environment. The reactivity model radically breaks away from the previous models insofar as it argues that the company must be able to meet the requirements of exacerbated competition and of constantly evolving demand to rapidly restructure its organization. Both vivacity, defined as the "promptness to act," and flexibility are then essential (Spitezki, 1998). For G. Hamel, the challenge for organizations today is to become the architect of the revolution in their industry and to be able to change the rules of the game. It involves implementing a "structured anarchy" in order to consider apparently contradictory poles:

> Typically, when we talk about innovation, we emphasize diversity; but coherence in strategy is equally important. At one extreme, fragmentation results in anarchy – there is no structure that unites individuals in common causes. At the other extreme, coherence becomes authoritarianism or groupthink – uniformity kills a company's ability to experiment and adapt.
>
> (Hamel, 1998: 24)

In such a context, what is at stake is not to be bigger, nor even to be better, but to be different.

At the end of 2000, France Télécom reorganized the Executive Committee to take account of the differentiation between Internet activities with Wanadoo, mobile communications with Orange, and fixed telecommunications. The mass-market division is therefore divided into three branches, with a newly created division responsible for the sales network. Although technologies are increasingly interrelated (in particular, mobiles and the Internet), all stock exchange markets require a marked visibility in the different activities introduced, or to be introduced, on the stock exchange (France Télécom, Wanadoo, Orange). As a result, one of the key areas for thought is the brand architecture. The creation of the new visual identity is both the achievement of a process and the turning point that will enhance the group's flexibility in its development strategy. Notably, France Télécom's name is much less present in the new visual identity than in the former one. While surveys have shown that France Télécom's name was beneficial to the group and differentiated it clearly from many start-ups in the same field, this name is of most use in France. By contrast, the logo on its own, which has become the priority identification sign, is more capable of endorsing varied identities.

The example of France Télécom clearly demonstrates that, today, corporate identity management leans heavily on elements of stability and coherence, while preserving some fluidity. This fluidity, according to Gioia and Thomas (1996), is essential. Indeed, it enables the firm to confront a diversity of activities and environments and to prepare for the future. The investigation into France Télécom's case has therefore led us to suggest the following model for corporate image management (Figure 7.6).

In this context, visual identity can be seen as being fully integrated with brand identity and brand strategy in a global approach. The processes implemented go beyond occasional interactions, extending to genuine support for a strategy of evolution.

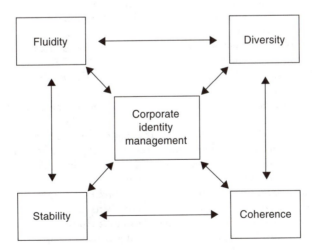

Figure 7.6 The new stakes in corporate identity management.

Notes

1   See France Télécom – Transformation Organisationnelle, 1972–1985, 108–1996 et 1980–1995, 109–1996, Theseus Institute, Sophia Antipolis, 1996.
2   Brand driver is a registered trademark of the Landor design group. It can be defined as the exclusive and specific brand concept driving and harmonizing all brand manifestations.

References

Allaire, Y. and Firsirotu, M. E. (1984) "Theories of organizational culture," *Organization Studies*, 5(3): 193–226.

Balmer, J. M. T. (1995) "Corporate branding and connoisseurship," *Journal of General Management*, 21(1): 24–46.

Balmer, J. M. T. and Soenen, G. B. (1999) "The acid test of corporate identity management," *Journal of Marketing Management*, 15: 69–92.

Bartlett, C. A. and Ghoshal, S. (1997) "The myth of the generic manager: new personal competencies for new management roles," *California Management Review*, 40(1): 93–116.

Brun, M. (1990) "Le design au service de la stratégie," *Revue Française du Marketing*, 129: 13–38.

Brun, M. and Rasquinet, P. (1996) *L'identité visuelle de l'entreprise*, Paris: Editions d'Organisation.

Diminopolu, C. F. E. (1999) "Shaping corporate images: attributes used to form impressions of pharmaceutical companies," *Corporate Reputation Review*, 2(3): 202–13.

Dowling, G. R. (1986) "Managing your corporate images," *Industrial Marketing Management*, 15: 109–15.

Dutton, J. E., Dukerich, J. M., and Harquail, C. V. (1994) "Organizational images and member identification," *Administrative Science Quarterly*, 39: 239–63.

Gayet J. (1998) *La totale communication*, Paris: Top Editions.

Gioia, D. A. and Thomas, J. B. (1996) "Identity, image and issue interpretation: sense-making during strategic change in academia," *Administrative Science Quarterly*, 41: 370–403.

Hamel, G. (1998) "The challenge today: changing the rules of the game," *Business Strategy Review*, 9(2): 19–26.

Larçon, J. P. and Reitter, R. (1979) *Structures de pouvoir et identité de l'entreprise*, Paris: Nathan.

Lendrevie, J. and Lindon, D. (1996) *Mercator. Théorie et pratique du marketing*, Paris: Dalloz.

Lerch, C. and Llerena, P. (1995) "Integration et méthode d'évaluation: l'expérimentation d'une nouvelle approche," in Nathalie Lazaric and Jean-Marie Mounier (eds) *Coordination économique et apprentissage des firmes*, Paris: Economica.

Moingeon, B. and Ramanantsoa, B. (1997) "Understanding corporate identity: the French school of thought," *European Journal of Marketing*, 31(5/6): 383–95.

Morgan, G. (1986) *Images of organization*, Newbury Park, CA: Sage.

Olins, W. (1989) *Corporate identity*, London: Thames & Hudson.

Porter, M. E. (1986) "Changing patterns of international competition," *California Management Review*, 28(2): 9–40.

Schwebig, P. (1988) *Les communications de l'entreprise*, Paris: McGraw-Hill.

Sfez, L. (1988) *Critique de la communication*, Paris: Seuil.

Soenen, G. and Moingeon, B. (2002) "The five facets of collective identities: integrating corporate and organizational identity," in B. Moingeon and G. Soenen (eds) *Corporate and organizational identities – integrating strategy, marketing, communication, and organizational perspectives*, London: Routledge.

Spitezki, H. (1998) "Innovation et vivacité, les stratégies d'offre dans le secteur financier et des services," *Vie et Sciences Economiques*, 151–2: 87–109.

van Riel, C. B. M. (1995) *Principles of corporate communication*, London: Prentice Hall.

Westphalen, M. H. (1998) *Communicator, le guide de la communication d'entreprise*, Paris: Dunod.

8 Conversion of organizational identity research findings into actions

Cees B. M. van Riel and Jan-Jelle van Hasselt

Introduction

Research into organizational identity can be divided into several lines of thought (Balmer, 1996). The variety in definitions and measurement instruments does not simplify discussion about the concept (what is it?), the preferred measurement tools (how to best measure it?) and implementation conditions (how to implement a desired identity most effectively?).

Most academics from a variety of disciplines and paradigms tend to focus primarily on the concept (Albert and Whetten, 1985; Gioia and Thomas, 1996; Hatch and Schultz, 2000) and, although less prominently, on the measurement of organizational identity (van Rekom and van Riel, 2000) and its diagnosis (Moingeon and Ramanantsoa, 1997; Moingeon, 1999). Representatives of the business world (design, corporate advertising, employee communication, etc.) are, however, more interested in the implementation of activities that will vividly express the desired identity characteristics, both internally and externally (Olins, 1989; Chajet, 1997). Publications about this aspect of organizational identity are limited (Larsen, 2000) and tend to focus primarily on "success stories" and less on the systematic approach in which these organizational identity programs are rooted.

In this chapter, we will attempt to fill this gap by focusing on the methods that organizations can use to transform research findings into actions. Summarized, our research question is: "How can an organization transform the perceived organizational identity into change programs that will enable it to gain acceptance for the chosen *projected* identity?"

We will first focus on several methods that can be used to reveal the perceived organizational identity (beliefs of organizational members about characteristics that describe the continuity, centrality and distinctiveness of their firm).[1] Thereafter, we will explain the different methods that can be used to gain acceptance for the *projected* identity (those characteristics that are used by the firm to express the organization's identity).

We will present four strategies to implement programs aimed at gaining acceptance for a new organizational identity. We will pay specific attention to the role of the three identity instruments (behavior, communications, and symbols) within the context of each strategy. This will be illustrated with practical examples. Finally, we will draw conclusions about the practical consequences of our discourse, and will suggest the types of studies that need to be implemented in the near future to elaborate on our findings.

How to uncover the perceived organizational identity

Academic literature provides several examples of methods that can be used to discover the perceived organizational identity. Bernstein (1986) assesses organizational identity as part of a research session where the desired organizational identity and the current organizational identity are elaborated and contrasted within the same dimensions. His method is particularly useful for obtaining a rapid consensus on the dimensions that are relevant to organizational identity and on those that need to be improved. At the start of the session, each of the managers makes a list of the corporate features that they believe to be important now and for the organization's future development. A group discussion then follows, at which time the total number of values is to be reduced to eight. When a consensus is reached on the eight values, each manager rates the organization on these values on a nine-point scale, both for the degree to which each value applies to the organization right now and for the degree to which it should ideally apply to the organization in the future. In this way, organizational identity is assessed in the form of perceptions by top management. Such a method fosters discussion in the management team and clarifies the direction toward which management believes its organization should be steered.

Dutton and Dukerich (1991) assessed how interpretations of identity shape organization members' actions when more and more homeless people populated the premises of the New York Port Authority. From twenty-five open-ended interviews with New York Port Authority employees, eighty-four items were established for the study. They were classified into seven major categories, based on a very general classification of theme substance. One of these categories was "the Identity of the Port Authority," the items of which were eventually summarized into five dimensions (Table 8.1).

Atamer and Calori (1993) developed method of a measurement to assess organizational characteristics; this method ultimately contributes to the diagnosis of an organization's long-term competitive position. These authors distinguish four components of identity, each to be measured separately by the organization's managers. These are the organization's goal orientation ("finalité"), its norms and values ("culture"), its management system ("système

Table 8.1 Dimensions used by Dutton and Duckerich (1991)

1	Professional organization with unique technical expertise
2	Ethical, scandal-free, and altruistic
3	First class, high-quality organization and provider of superior service
4	Highly committed to the welfare of the community
5	Fixer, "can do" organization

de management"), and its dominant logic ("recette stratégique"). Goal orientation is measured as priority ratings on the organization's growth, yield, societal
value, independence, and prestige. To assess values, managers are asked to
identify the values in the corporate mission statement that they believe are
brought into practice. If the organization lacks a mission statement, each
member of the management team names the five values he or she perceives to
be most characteristic of the organization, along with two practical examples
for each. The management system is assessed with four questions: "Which
practices make the planning system clear?"; "Which practices reflect the organization's attitude toward risk?"; "Which practices reflect the decentralization of
decisions?"; and "Which reflect their centralization?" The fourth component
measured by this method is the organizational strategy, as perceived by
management. If managers differ in their opinion, the opinion of the majority
determines the research output. Atamer and Calori's method is intended
mainly to be a quick organizational diagnosis. With this method, consultants
can explain strategic difficulties by identifying the imbalances in the system.

Foreman and Whetten (1994) addressed the issue of how to manage multiple and partially conflicting stakeholder interests by applying a multiple-
identity perspective to organizations. Using a large co-operative in a rural area
as the case study, they first held focus group interviews among members.
Here, they identified the metaphors that could best capture the tension with
the dual identity of a co-operative. The resulting metaphors, "family" and
"business," served as input in a survey. From these focus group interviews,
Foreman and Whetten also developed the scales to measure these two
identities. In the survey, members' identity perceptions and expectations of
co-operatives in general were measured, as well as their attitudes about the
legitimacy of co-operatives as an organizational form. The results show how
conflicting identities for one organization can also exist at the level of individuals. This requires that management frame strategies and actions in such a
way that they can be interpreted from multiple perspectives simultaneously.

Gustafson and Reger (1999) addressed explicitly the issue of multiple
identities in one organization. They investigated the different views held
among organization members at different locations and different hierarchical
levels at Intel, using the Kelly Repertory Grid technique (Kelly, 1955). Cards
were prepared representing different perspectives on Intel: "Intel today,"
"Intel three years ago," "top management's belief about Intel," and so on. The
ten cards were randomly grouped into triads. For each triad, respondents
determined which two elements were most similar, and therefore, different
from the third in terms of organizational characteristics. They were then asked
to write down one or two ways in which the two similar elements were alike
and the ways in which they differed from the third. Then, for each
organizational feature noted, respondents rated the ten elements on 7-point
Likert scale. This method enabled Gustafson and Reger to identify the characteristics that were specific to the business units, geographical locations, and
hierarchical levels, as well as those that were shared organization-wide.

Gioia and Thomas (1996) investigated organizational identity in order to develop a framework for managing change. Taking a grounded-theory approach (Glaser and Strauss, 1967) to the beliefs of managers at universities, they found that identity is an important lens through which issues are interpreted. In a survey sent to university administrators, they allowed managers to rate their organizations on items derived from previous theory and research on universities. Building on Albert and Whetten's (1985) work, Gioia and Thomas asked managers from different universities to rate the degree to which their university was "utilitarian" as apposed to "normative." Additionally, they included a six-item scale to measure the strength of identity, which is referred to as managers' beliefs about various facets of their organization's cultural values. Gioia and Thomas then demonstrated how organizational strategy was linked to perceptions of identity.

How can acceptance for the projected organizational identity be gained?

The various methods presented and discussed in the previous section all produce lists with words that describe the organizational core. In 99 out of 100 situations, these lists do not create the ideal starting point for communication initiatives destined to portray the firms' identity in an appealing manner to stakeholders. Consequently, organizations combine internal research with external data and – rather often – also with the "dreams" of top management about the desired future situation. Stakeholders will, in our view, be more receptive towards corporate messages if they perceive the contents of organizational messages to be appealing (i.e., favorable to them personally and, most importantly, not a source of irritation) and coherent. Communication, then, will be more effective if organizations can rely on a so-called "sustainable corporate story" as a source of inspiration for all internal and external communication programs. Stories are difficult to imitate and they simplify the management of consistency in all corporate messages.

Created in an open dialogue with the stakeholders on whom the organization depends, an ideal (normative) sustainable corporate story is a realistic and relevant description of an organization. A corporate story will be more effective if four criteria are met. First of all, the story must be *realistic*. This is the case if stakeholders perceive the contents of the story to fit the organizational characteristics that they perceive to be "distinctive," "enduring," and, above all, equally extended throughout the entire organization. Second, the story must be *relevant*. Stakeholders must perceive the story's key message as being of added value for them. Third, the style that the organization uses to communicate the corporate story, that is, the "two-way symmetrical communication style" (Grunig, 1992), should be typified as *a responsive attitude*. A corporate story is a dynamic entity invented and reinvented by the permanent interaction between external and internal stakeholders. A continuous dialogue with stakeholders testing the relevance and the reality of the sustainable corporate story and being prepared to apply changes resulting from this dialogue will improve the appealing nature of the story.

Recent developments in technology (websites) make it much easier for organizations to show a responsive attitude. However, it is not the technology that is relevant here, but the mentality behind it. Referring people to a website does not make much sense if the company does not want to react to the messages sent to them at the site.

The fourth characteristic that will improve the effectiveness of corporate stories is the degree to which the story appears to be *sustainable*. A corporate story will only be sustainable if it succeeds in finding and maintaining the right balance between the competing demands of all relevant stakeholders and the desires of the organization itself.

Corporate stories should not be seen as goals in and of themselves, but as aids to the stimulation of reflective conversation and the creation of shared understanding, which in turn enable an organization to find an inspiring frame of reference for orchestrating the future communication of the company as a whole. An ideal way to create a sustainable corporate story is to gather information, based on a combination of internal (garnered from meetings with top management and surveys from a sample of employees at all organizational levels) and external data (multiple stakeholders approach). A sustainable corporate story should be founded on an aggregation of a set of words evoked by qualitative and quantitative research among internal and external audiences. These words should be combined in such a way as to create a story that is perceived as relevant (having added value for society in the broadest sense of the word), realistic (typical for the organization), and having a responsive attitude (stimulating supporters and opponents to engage in open dialogue with the firm about its ambitions and operating choices). There are various ways to create a sustainable corporate story, depending on the type of change strategy a company wishes to implement. Top management (or the dominant coalition in general) can take the initiative as part of a political play involving powerholders within the organization, or as a learning process extending throughout the entire organization, involving large groups of stakeholders with an equal opportunity to contribute to the story.

Winning acceptance for the sustainable corporate story

Once agreement has been reached about the creation process for the sustainable corporate story, management must focus on the programs that need to be created and implemented in order to gain acceptance for the story's key message. Firms can apply three mutually-complementary instruments to stimulate acceptance of the *projected* identity (summarized in a sustainable corporate story): the behavior of organizational members, communication (advertisements, press releases, brochures, etc.), and symbols (logo, house style, architecture, etc.).

In the following section, we will present four strategies that a company can implement to gain acceptance for the *projected* organizational identity. For each of these strategies, we will focus specifically on the different ways in which "behavior," "communication," and "symbols" are applied. The main determinants of the four strategies are:

- rigidly planned change versus the open planning of change;
- focus on planned instruction as a vehicle for group change versus focus on individual explorative learning.

The four strategies, color-coded, were originally developed by De Caluwe and Vermaak (2000) primarily to implement organizational change programs.[2] Naturally, these strategies represent ideal types.

Four change strategies

Blue-print – projects and results. Rigidly planned change; focus on instructed group change

The color blue is assigned to theories of change that are based on a rational design and implementation process. Project management forms one of the most striking examples. The change agents focus on planning and organizing the change, irrespective of individual opinions and preferences. It is their aim to realize the result of the change, which has been agreed on in advance.

Yellow-print – power and coalitions. Open planning of the change; focus on instructed group change

The color yellow represents schools of thought based on socio-political views of organizational change. The underlying train of thought behind yellow-print thinking is the search for common interests in the effective pursuit and implementation of complex goals in an environment characterized by many conflicting goals and influences. The color yellow symbolizes power – "the sun," "fire" – and the nature of coalition formation, "hatching processes" and "fireside chats."

Green-print – learning. Rigidly planned change; focus on individual learning

Green-print thinking concentrates on changing people or stirring them into action by motivating them to learn, bringing them into learning situations and increasing their learning potential. To a large extent, the result depends on this learning potential. Green-print thinking is aimed at encouraging people to move, "giving them the green light." It is also associated with "growth," just as the green in nature.

White-print – chaos and energy. Open planning of the change; focus on individual learning

The last strategy is white-print thinking, the philosophy behind which is that everything changes spontaneously and permanently. The change agent removes obstacles through painstaking observation and interpretation of the situation. White-print thinking draws on people's inner strength and direction rather than on external safety or reassurance. It focuses on giving things meaning. The color white is the combination of all primary colors and therefore affords the most space for self-steering: everything is still open.

The role of three organizational identity instruments within the context of change programs

The four strategies for organizational change each represent different convictions about the effectiveness of change interventions. They also embody different beliefs about the perceived effectiveness of each identity instrument within the context of a campaign aimed at winning acceptance for a new organizational identity. When implementing any one of the four strategies, companies will apply the three instruments – symbols, communications, and behavior of organizational members – in a specific way. Each strategy will emphasize different instruments, depending on their perceived attractiveness in a specific situation. Before presenting an overall picture of the role of each instrument within the four change strategies, we will first elaborate briefly on the typical characteristics of each instrument.

Behavior

How to stimulate a change in organization member's behavior depends on the preferred change strategy, as illustrated in Table 8.2.

Communication

In 1998, van Ruler (inspired by Grunig, 1992) developed "a communication typology," a model in which four basic strategies for communication were incorporated. The model is based on a choice: "(controlled) one-way versus two-way communication" and "communication that is aimed at purely 'informing' people versus messages that want to persuade people in a direction that is seen as preferable by the transmitter of the information." This choice leads to the formulation of the following four strategies: informing, persuading, forming coalitions, and dialogue. These four communication strategies can be linked to the four change strategies described earlier. The blue-print change strategy will predominantly make use of a communication strategy of well-planned persuasion, while the yellow-print change strategy will predominantly make

Table 8.2 Assumptions about behavioral changes in the four strategies for identity implementation

	People will change their behavior, if you . . .
Blue-print – project and result	– give a clear idea about the aim and the result of the change – focus on planning and phasing the change – reduce complexity where possible
Yellow-print – power and coalitions	– are able to convince people of their common interest in the change – can form coalitions and win/win situations – can close ranks
Green-print – learning	– can make people aware of new views – are able to motivate people to learn – can increase people's learning potential
White-print – chaos and energy	– can point out the dynamics and complexity of the change – allow people to use their own energy as drivers of change – lift blockades and optimize conflict situations

use of a communication strategy of forming coalitions. The green-print change strategy will predominantly make use of a communication strategy of creating learning experiences by both informing and holding dialogues with stakeholders. Finally, white-print change strategy will predominantly make use of a communication strategy of following an exploration process, of creating a dialogue.

Certain communication activities will form a common basis for all change processes: for example, group meetings, an Intranet site, a manager's letter, and information for the home front. Other choices, however, will directly relate to the chosen change strategy. In Table 8.3 we provide an overview of the types of typical communication activities best adapted for each of the four change strategies.

Symbolism

The third identity instrument, symbolism, is considered to be a very effective tool for showing tangible change effects to the entire organization and its external stakeholders. The most common form of symbolism can be found in organizations' house styles. The introduction of a consistent house style contributes to the identification with an organization, giving a coherent representation to internal and external stakeholders. Other forms of symbolism can be encountered in logos, office and shop fittings, company clothing, and

Table 8.3 Overview of the communication activities for each change strategy

Blue	*Informative group meetings*: planned gatherings where the objectives and the contents of the change are explained.
	Newsletter motivating the change: temporary printed or digital medium that provides target groups with information and motivation about the change process.
	Fact sheets: compact overviews that explain the change progress, with an emphasis on the positive aspects.
	Dashboard: a visual printed display of the key indicators that illustrate the progress of the change activities.
Yellow	*Opinion media*: printed or digital media where representatives of stakeholder groups have the possibility of expressing their views on the objectives and the contents of the change.
	Forum discussions: meetings where representatives of stakeholder groups discuss the objectives and contents of the change. The chairman is carefully selected by the change manager.
	Lobbying activities: the deliberate influencing of specific stakeholder groups to accept the change and to support the change process by specified actions.
	Search conferences (Emery and Purser, 1996): participative planning method that enables stakeholders to identify, plan, and implement their most-desired future.
Green	*Gaming*: a learning method in which people participate in a structured activity or simulation. In this way, they can experiment in a safe environment with the new behavior that is linked with the organizational change (learning by doing).
	Real-time strategic change (Danemiller and Jacobs, 1992): a large-group (300–2500 participants) intervention where, in a highly-structured way, within a period of 2–3 days, by making use of internal and external experts and the available common database, a vision and an action plan are developed for the future.
	Inter vision meetings: a periodic meeting, constituted of a small group of colleagues, at which group members introduce cases. Others are encouraged to ask questions and share their thoughts about the chosen solution and possible alternatives.
	Sessions for sharing learning experiences: meetings where colleagues exchange their personal learning experiences, and in this way, increase their knowledge about the change and the ways in which the change can be realized.
White	*Brainstorm*: unstructured meeting where participants can freely air their personal ideas about the change, and further build on others' ideas.
	Open space technology (Owen, 1993): discussion and exploration of issues, where the participants themselves create agenda topics and form groups around these topics.
	Customer panels: a representation of the client system is being used to reflect on the actual and the desired situation. During the change process, these panels periodically meet with representatives of the organization.
	Adventures and heroes: a selection of specific symbols and "champions" of the change process in order to stimulate organizational members during the change process.

company architecture. Companies like Coca-Cola, Rolls Royce, or Sony are known for the distinctive use of symbolism in their product design.

The difference between communication and symbolism is rather artificial: both could be labeled as "communication." However, the topic of symbolism belongs traditionally to the design and logo specialists. A change of identity will logically be reflected in a certain change of symbolism. This creates an instant, visible change for internal and external stakeholders and can fuel their sense of change.

From their study of symbols (specifically logos), van Riel and van den Ban (2001) draw several conclusions. First, a well-designed logo, through its graphical properties "only," is able to evoke a limited, but essential, amount of desired organizational characteristics among external stakeholders. Second, the fit between external perceptions of a new logo and organizational intentions will increase if the logo is shown in combination with the company name. This seems especially true if the company behind the logo has a high degree of familiarity and appreciation (reputation) among external stakeholders. Third, the fit between external perceptions of a new logo and organizational intentions will increase if the launch of the new logo is embedded within a nationwide advertising campaign that explains the values the company wants to express with this logo.

Within the scope of the four change strategies, a change of symbolism can be a vital part of the change program. However, how new symbols will be perceived depends greatly, in our view, on (i) the timing of the launch of the new symbols and (ii) the involvement of a small or large group of people who were part of the decision-making for the new symbol. We distinguish the following options:

- The new symbols are designed and implemented at the beginning or at the end of the change process;
- The new symbols are designed by an expert designer, who works exclusively for, or together with, top management and uses help from specific groups of stakeholders.

We assume that these options can be linked to the four change strategies. In the blue-print change strategy, the new symbols are designed by an expert designer working for management and will be implemented at the beginning of the change process. Likewise, in the yellow-print change strategy, the new symbols are designed by an expert designer working for management and will be implemented at the end of the change process. In the green-print change strategy, the new symbols are designed by an expert, with input from stakeholders, at the beginning of the change process. Finally, in the white-print change strategy, the new symbols are designed by an expert, with input from stakeholders, at the end of the change process.

Four change strategies for gaining acceptance for a new identity

In the previous section, we discussed (a) four change strategies and (b) the conditions that determine the potential added value of three so-called organizational identity mix instruments: behavior, communications, and symbols. A combination of the four change strategies and the most preferable application of the three organizational identity mix instruments in each strategy are summarized in Figure 8.1.

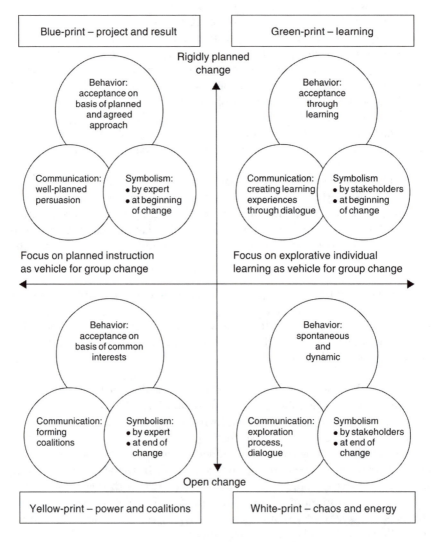

Figure 8.1 Four change strategies for gaining acceptance for a new organizational identity.

The choice of one of the four strategies should, in our opinion, be guided by two principles: (i) Do we have time to gain acceptance (i.e., there is no crisis situation inside or outside the organization)?; and (ii) Does management have a clear idea about the desired situation the organization wants to attain in the near future? If time is limited (crisis) and strategic directions are clear, it is quite understandable that organizations will choose a blue-print strategy. However, if time is not limited and/or clarity in strategic intents still need to be created, then one of the three other strategies will be preferred. Which of the three will be chosen, then, depends greatly on the management style of the dominant coalition in the specific organization.

Practical examples

To what extent is organizational identity truly discussed during organizational change? If it is discussed, how is an identity change translated into specific actions relating to behavior, communication and symbolism? Which change strategy is applied? In this section, we provide three examples of organizational change in practice (van Hasselt, 2001).

Central government: specialist consultancy group (CG-scg)

Description of the organizational change settings

This first case deals with one of the ministries of the Dutch government. Within this ministry, several separate consultancy groups working in the same professional field were active in different sectors. The ministry decided to merge the consultancies into one single group of approximately 400 consultants and supporting staff. The merger led to the implementation of a matrix structure and changes in the contents of the consultancy process from linear to integral consulting. The focal points of the organizational change were corporate strategy and human resource management. The new corporate strategy, labeled "vision," aimed to bring together expertise and improve the exchange of knowledge and expertise. This implied new working processes and a new organizational structure. The starting point for the change process was a discussion about CG-scg's core values and its vision for the future (i.e., envisioned future). The change was then realized through the implementation of a new strategic vision in the consulting process and services, a new organizational structure, and a redefinition of the organizational culture. Key players in the vision process were the general management, the management of the four newly created departments and the appointed process manager. During the ensuing change process, every staff member was involved in the definition of the core values and purposes.

Implications of change

BEHAVIORAL CHANGES

The new vision encouraged the following behavioral changes:

- professional: improving consulting skills;
- knowledge-sharing: from a group of specialists with separate knowledge bases to a new organization with a knowledge-network that would make CG-scg a key player in its field;
- pro-active: from a risk-averse attitude toward much more proactive behavior;
- stimulating: from oppositional to mutually stimulating learning- oriented behavior.

COMMUNICATION

Within the new organization, the communication was typified as more open and focused on the exchange of knowledge and ideas. The focus was discussion and learning.

SYMBOLISM

Prior to the change, the separate consultancy groups used their own interpretations of the ministry's symbols and visual identity. During the change, a single new house style and visual identity, in accord with the ministry's rules, was applied to the new organization. The consultants were involved in the design and selection process for the symbol.

Communication activities during the change process

These were as follows:

- special magazine;
- e-mail discussions: over a set period, the general manager sent an e-mail with the daily position to all staff members. The recipients were invited to react, and their reactions were summarized both in the following e-mail and in the special magazine;
- transferer game: a two-day management game was organized to introduce all staff members to the new culture and vision;
- conference: a conference was organized for the entire organization. The central theme was the new vision and its implications for daily work;
- video-production: the video, produced by a group of internal consultants and assisted by a professional editor, focused on the change process within the organization.

Conclusion

As "learning" was a recurring theme, the change strategy pursued was the green-print strategy. A game simulation and sessions to collectively develop vision fits this approach well.

Rabobank

Description of the organizational change settings

The Rabobank, with approximately 53,000 employees, is organized as a co-operative of 424 local banks. In order to strengthen its market position (triggered by several mergers of competitors and the introduction of a handling fee for money transfers), an organizational change process was initiated in the early 1990s. The change included mergers with several local banks, the closing of smaller branches, and a repositioning of the bank in the market. The areas on which change was focused included corporate strategy, organizational structure (organizational restructuring and internationalization), marketing, and technology (increased office automation). The starting point for the change process was a discussion, repeated several times during the process, with all 4,500 members of the governing bodies of the member banks. The central board of directors, which involved the local banks at a very early stage, was the initiator of the change. All staff members were also involved in the change process.

Implications of change

BEHAVIORAL CHANGES

The change was defined as a change in core values. The new emphasis on core values was translated into desired new behavior. A central theme was being customer-friendly, and every staff member was trained to be customer-friendly in the in-house training program. Furthermore, as the organizational restructuring implied a completely new management style, managers too were trained and coached.

COMMUNICATION

External communication focused far more on co-operation, the personal attention given to customers by professionals. Apart from campaigns, sponsoring and public relations were recognized as the strongest tools in communicating core values to stakeholders.

SYMBOLISM

The change of visual identity played a key role in the final part of the change process. The new logo (a human figure walking on a compass rose/ dial plate, use of warm colors (orange and blue)) reflects the core values, "personal," "co-operative," and "professional."

Communication activities during the change process

These were as follows:

- meetings;
- road shows: nine spectacular gatherings attended by approximately 38,000 employees, at which time the CEO presented and explained the new visual identity;
- video presentations;
- parallel media;
- a mass media campaign, "You'll never walk alone," aimed at external audiences, supported the introduction of the new visual identity.

Conclusion

In this case, the manner in which common interests were sought in a complex environment fits well the yellow-print change approach. The emphasis on meetings and forums as communication instruments to achieve a common view about the change fits well with this strategy, as does the approach and timing of the new logo's introduction on the market.

Nuon

Description of the organizational change settings

The entire Dutch energy sector is in the process of changing from a state-owned, monopoly-oriented sector towards a privatized, commercialized one. Mergers, internationalization, and increased size are recurring themes. Four Dutch energy companies in the east, north, and south of the Netherlands decided to co-operate through a total merger. There were no lay-offs. The change process involved several functions: corporate strategy, human resource management, financial management, and marketing. It was realized by the introduction of a new organizational structure, new systems, a new strategy, an adapted management style, and a new human resource management policy.The initiator of the change process was the newly-formed central board of directors (with equal representation for the four merger partners), which worked closely with the Department of Corporate Communication. The chairman of the board played a key role. After the initial phase, change was to be implemented at all levels of the new organization. Even in the smallest organizational unit (team level), the change was to be made visible and understandable by translating it into practical consequences and their implications for the daily routine.

Implications of change

BEHAVIORAL CHANGES

A change in behavior, where line-management leadership played a key role, was considered crucial for effective change. To equip managers to perform this task, management training was necessary. As a result, Nuon College was founded. A curriculum was designed for all management, containing all the elements that were considered vital for effective change: vision, the coaching of people, communication, and newly shared values (decisive, dynamic, durable, nearby). On average, all line-managers spent two days a month training at Nuon College.

COMMUNICATION

A new, commercially-oriented organization demands a new professional communications approach. Within the new organization, a set of parallel media was introduced for internal communication. These media were used during the change process. A key role was given to an internal magazine with a journalistic approach and to audio-visual media. Furthermore, a communications professional participated in all of the important organizational bodies. This expressed the important role of communication in the change process. Apart from the parallel media, line communication was emphasized as a crucial communication tool.

After an analysis of periodic measurements, employee commitment was judged to be at a relatively low level. Nuon therefore decided to invest in a series of group activities. In June 1996, a big event was held for all 8,000 Nuon employees in Papendal. All kinds of activities were organized and linked to Nuon's sponsoring activities.

External communication was also employed to reflect Nuon's commercial orientation. An extensive use of the mass media and a sponsor program were intended to make Nuon and its new core values highly visible.

SYMBOLISM

A new house style with bright colors (yellow and purple) was designed early in the process to demonstrate the new, commercially-oriented organization. Its substantial auto fleet made Nuon's new house style extremely visible. The new name, Nuon, is a "fantasy" name, chosen because of favorable associations with the new core values.

Communication activities during the change process

These were as follows:

• magazine

- audio-visual media
- intranet
- Nuon College
- staff meetings.

Conclusion

The emphasis on management's role and on the well-planned process is closely related to blue-print thinking. New behavior was stimulated predominantly through instruction at Nuon College. The communications means used and the process and timing of the introduction of the new house style fit well the blue-print strategy.

Conclusions

A sustainable corporate story should be conceived with the help of internal and external stakeholders and should reflect the key values that form the basis of the desired identity. The four basic change strategies that can be applied to realize the desired change differ, depending on whether the change can be planned and whether the focus should be on group instruction or on individual learning. Each change strategy implies a different use of the three identity instruments, referred to as the corporate identity mix (CI-mix): behavior, communication, and symbolism. The application of these elements should be consistent with the change strategy. For a change to be visible to a broad internal and external audience, a change of symbolism can be considered as an effective tool. The cases presented support our assumptions about the different applications of the CI-mix during change processes, based on the chosen change strategy.

A number of questions remain for future research. Notably, to what extent is the choice of a specific change strategy dependent on the organization's cultural setting? What cultural preferences can be identified? Which stake-holders are most often involved in discussions about symbolism, and how does their involvement affect the acceptance of the new symbols as a reflection of the desired identity?

Notes

1   We use the notion of *perceived* identity whereas Soenen and Moingeon (2002), in this volume, refer to the *experienced* identity, that is, what members feel, more or less consciously, toward their organization.
2   De Caluwe and Vermaak (2000) distinguish a fifth strategy: red-print thinking. This strategy typically achieves change by stimulating people in the right way by deploying human resource management tools. From a communication perspective, this strategy can be closely linked to the blue-print strategy, with the well-planned human resource management tools as a central theme. In view of this similarity, we have decided to focus on only four strategies in this chapter.

References

Albert, S. and Whetten, D. A. (1985) "Organizational identity," in L. L. Cummings and B. I. M. Staw (eds) *Research in organizational behavior, volume 7*, Greenwich, CT: JAI Press, 263–95.

Atamer, T. and Calori, R. (1993) *Diagnostic et decisions strategiques*, Paris: Dunod.

Balmer, J. M. T. (1996) "The nature of corporate identity: an explanatory study undertaken within BBC Scotland," unpublished Ph.D. thesis, No. T8755, University of Strathclyde, Department of Marketing.

Bernstein, D. (1986) *Company image and reality*, London: Cassells.

Chajet, C. (1997) "Corporate reputation and the bottom line," *Corporate Reputation Review*, 1(1/2): 19–23.

Danemiller, K. and Jacobs, R. W. (1992) "Changing the way organizations change: a revolution in common sense," *Journal of Applied Behavioral Science*, 28: 480–98.

De Caluwe, L. and Vermaak, H. (2000) *Leren Veranderen; een handboek voor de veranderkundige*, Alphen aan den Rijn: Samsom Management Selectie.

Dutton, J. E. and Dukerich J. M. (1991) "Keeping an eye on the mirror: image and identity in organizational adaptation," *Academy of Management Journal*, 34: 517–54.

Emery, M. and Purser, R. E. (1996) *The search conference: theory and practice*, San Francisco, CA: Jossey-Bass.

Foreman, P. and Whetten, D. (1994) "An identity theory perspective on multiple expectations in organizations," paper presented at the Academy of Management Conference, August.

Gioia, D. A. and Thomas, J. B. (1996) "Identity, image and issue interpretation: sense-making during strategic change in academia," *Administrative Science Quarterly*, 41: 370–403.

Glaser, B. and Strauss A. S. (1967) *The discovery of Grounded Theory. Strategies for qualitative research*, Chicago, IL: Aldine Publishing Company.

Grunig, J. (1992) *Excellence in public relations and communication management*, Hillsdale, NY: Lawrence Earlbaum Associates.

Gustafson, L. and Reger, R. (1999) "Beyond collective identity: empirical evidence for multiple identities, Academy of Management Conference, Chicago, IL, August.

Hatch, M. J. and Schultz, M. (2000) "Scaling the Tower of Babel: relational differences between identity, image and culture in organizations," in M. Schultz, M. J. Hatch, and M. H. Larsen (eds) *The expressive organization. Linking identity, reputation and the corporate brand*, Oxford: Oxford University Press.

Huff, A. (1998) (contribution to) "A strategy conversation on the topic of organizational identity," in D. A. Whetten and P. C. Godfrey (eds) *Identity in organizations. Building theory through conversations*, Thousand Oaks, CA: Sage.

Kelly, G. A. (1955) *The psychology of personal constructs*, New York: W.W. Norton and Co.

Larsen, M. H. (2000) "Managing the corporate story," in M. Schultz, M. J. Hatch and M. H. Larsen (eds) *The expressive organization. Linking identity, reputation and the corporate brand*, Oxford: Oxford University Press.

Moingeon, B. (1999) "From corporate culture to corporate identity," *Corporate Reputation Review*, 2: 352–60.

Moingeon, B. and Ramanantsoa, B. (1997) "Understanding corporate identity: the French school of thought," *European Journal of Marketing*, 31: 383–95.

Olins, W. (1989) *Corporate identity: making business strategy visible through design*, London: Thames & Hudson.

Owen, H. (1993) *Open space technology*, Potomac, VA: Abott Press.

Soenen, G. and Moingeon, B. (2002) "The five facets of collective identities: integrating corporate and organizational identity," in B. Moingeon and G. Soenen (eds) *Corporate and organizational identities – integrating strategy, marketing, communication and organizational perspectives*, London: Routledge.

van Hasselt, J. J. (2001) "Organisatie-identiteit: verandermethoden," in C. van Riel (ed.) *Corporate communication – het managen van reputatie*, Alphen aan den Rijn: Kluwer.

van Rekom, J. and van Riel, C. B. M. (2000) "Operational measures of organizational identity: a review of existing methods," *Corporate Reputation Review*, 3: 334–50.

van Riel, C. B. M. and van den Ban, A. (2001) "The added value of corporate logos: an empirical study," *European Journal of Marketing*, 35(3/4): 428–41.

van Ruler, B. (1998) *Strategisch management van communicatie. Introductie van het communicatiekruispunt*, Deventer: Samsom.

9 Corporate brand and organizational identity

Jean-Noël Kapferer

Introduction

Corporations have just recently realized that they are brands. In our modern global village, where the irruption and widespread development of the Internet and worldwide events relayed through global media link us even closer together, corporations' names and associated signs (marques) are reaching across the continents to touch very broad and diverse audiences, beyond restricted circles of customers and sectorial audiences. Moreover, corporations' names are associated with a number of values in people's minds, which may affect their behavior, be they a future employee, investor, supplier, or purchaser. These names encapsulate a reputation.

Suddenly, with companies' recognition that they are, *de facto*, brands, came the necessity to manage this reputation and the corporate brand that sustains it. In many major companies, the first sign of this revolution is the Corporate Communication Director position being renamed "Director of the Corporate Brand." Interestingly, as a rule, this position is not linked to the marketing department. Usually, the Director of the Corporate Brand reports directly to the CEO and the Executive Committee. The second sign of this revolution is the widespread emergence of intensive investigations to establish what is called the "brand platform" (Kapferer, 1991), that is, what the corporate brand should mean in the long-term to its various stakeholders and audiences if the corporation wants to develop its business, gain social and community-wide acceptance, and increase the quality of its human resources.

In this brand charter elaboration process (Macrae, 1996), however, it soon became obvious that corporate brands had something special that made them not as easily manageable as the classic product brands. In fact, the classical tools based on image were rather inappropriate. Image stands for the mental representation of a stimulus by a group of people. It is the subjective idea these people have of this stimulus (a person, a country, a brand, a corporation, etc.). Let us be reminded of the often overlooked fact that image is a reflection of past actions stored in people's memory. Image is a mirror, more or less reliable. In and of itself, it is only a measure of the gap existing between communication intentions and results. Brand management is about defining these intentions beforehand. Moreover, as a rule, there are as many images as there are audiences, not to speak of the differences in image at the international level. How can one manage an organization's identity on the basis of images if they are so different from one person to another, from one country to another? Identity is about the truth of the brand. It is self-driven, not mirror-driven. For corporate brands, in particular, the organizations that they represent provide elements of truth, of inner authenticity, of inner relevance; the brand's meaning is not invented, or derived from market analysis: it is revealed. The truth of corporate brands lies within themselves. This is why the process of defining a corporate brand's identity so stresses the necessity of understanding the organization itself, its identity. In turn, understanding an organization's identity calls for distinguishing the different facets of collective identities (Soenen and Moingeon, 2002).

Interestingly, although a classic topic in human personality research, cultural anthropology, and to a certain extent, in organizational behavior studies, the concept of identity is recent in marketing, advertising, and brand management. Certainly, for a long time, there used to be design agencies that redesigned corporations' logos and the brand symbols often associated with their names. These agencies called the output of this design work "brand identity" (Olins, 1989). However, what is at stake behind the present use of the concept of brand identity is no longer the graphics, name, or attractiveness of the marque itself (the visual symbol). Rather, it is the clear definition of what this brand wants to represent. Interestingly, the introduction of the necessity to consider identity as central to brand management originates in Europe, elaborated in books such as *Strategic Brand Management* (Kapferer, 1991), in which the concept of brand identity was first theorized. Certainly, in Europe, there had been a tradition of research on organizations' identity as the basis for corporate strategy (see Larçon and Reitter, 1979, 1984). The extension of these works, thus far concerned primarily with the internal aspect of corporations, to issues of the interface between organizations and their environment (e.g., corporate brands, reputation) should not come as a surprise. In modern competition, authenticity is a success factor: corporations need to promote their own truths, to start their own crusades. It is interesting to note that US brand management manuals never mentioned the concept of identity until very recently. The most quoted one, D. Aaker's 299-page textbook, *Managing brand equity* (1991), never mentions the word "identity" nor the concept of brand identity. Two years later, identity is still absent from even the most advanced book, *Brand equity and advertising* (Aaker and Biel, 1993). In his book, *Building brand identity* (1995), L. P. Upshaw acknowledges clearly the European source of thinking in the conceptualization and formalization of methods for brand identity.

The purpose of this chapter is to investigate the links between organizational identity and brand identity, especially from the perspective of corporate brands. Indeed, not all brands are corporate brands: Tide is a product brand, that of a leading global low suds detergent. Axa and Renault are corporate brands. Obviously, Tide is one of the many brands (among more than a hundred) of the Procter and Gamble corporation. Its identity is based on the willingness to optimize its market share and profits within a specific market segment. This identity is entirely externally determined. The influence of Procter and Gamble's corporate culture and identity on Tide's identity is minimal. For Axa, a leading insurance company, however, the question is very different. Since the brand is intimately linked to the company, which is the body behind the brand, one cannot suppose that such intimacy does not give way to identity transfers between the corporation and the corporate brand. Before addressing these central issues, it is necessary to first review the two aforementioned conceptual revolutions: the shift from brand image to brand identity and that from mere organizations to companies as brands. Thereafter, we shall develop the methodology for defining the corporate brand identity. This methodology will demonstrate how organizational identity is an essential input. Numerous examples will be developed, in particular a comparison between two major corporations, Renault and Peugeot.

From brand image to brand identity

A conceptual shift

Classic brand management is based on image. Madison Avenue advertising moguls have long been denounced for being image-makers. Most books on corporate communications used to be called *The company image*, or something similar. The focus on image, be it for product brands or for corporate brands, was a reflection of the discovery that buyers are guided by their own perceptions. In marketing, there is no such thing as reality; perception is reality. As a consequence, it became of the utmost importance to know this image and to manage it in a profitable way. Image, like automobiles, must be driven. The emergence of scores of market research companies corresponded to this need to permanently assess the brand's image, which was an indefectible sign of the brand' s progress and status in audiences' minds. Curiously enough, image has never had a good reputation as a word. It hardly hides a flavor of superficiality. Image-based brand management seems to be about managing impressions, on the surface. As a matter of fact, in our modern mature markets, as brands increasingly experience difficulty in differentiating themselves from competitors (the essence of a brand's role) in what they do, corporations find that projecting what the brand believes in – its own personal truths – is felt to be more engaging by audiences and a source of long-term relationships.

Such an evolution raises an interesting question: although everyone can immediately understand what it means to describe what a person is (for example, what are his or her deeply held values and beliefs and visions), how can brands have inner beliefs? The answer is simply by considering brands as persons. The metaphor of brands as persons is a classic one in qualitative marketing research. For instance, the projective technique, known as "the

Chinese Portrait," asks interviewees to think freely and to associate the brand with a flower, an animal, a planet, or a person (e.g., a movie star, a political figure). This technique can be reversed for action purposes. Instead of trying to convince a wide audience that there are significant performance differences between two brands, the role of communication has been to build identities for brands, however inanimate. Hence, brand characters, especially if they are living characters, have become increasingly important. Advertising has become a veritable zoo of animals, each symbolizing a brand: most of Kellogg's cereal brands use an animal as their emblem, for instance. Likewise, the character of alcoholic spirits is depicted by an emblem, most often an animal: for example, The White Horse (a horse), Glenfiddich (a deer), Black and White (two dogs), Wild Turkey (a turkey), Baccardi (a bat). The Italian insurance company Generali uses a lion as its symbol, Exxon uses a tiger, Shell, a shell. Another way to give flesh, and therefore a soul, to a brand is to link it to a person over a long period of time. The purpose is to produce a transfer of identity from the person (most often a star) to the inanimate product, thus creating a lively brand. J. Seguela (1982), one of the most famous creative directors of European advertising in the 1970s and 1980s, and a prolific writer on brands and advertising, built an advertising empire based on a simple but most repeated assertion: brands are like persons. As such, they have a physique (e.g., a body, strengths, know-how, and specific abilities), a personality, or character, and a style, or a specific and recognizable way of acting or behaving. This metaphor created a considerable revolution and represented a paradigm shift in managerial thinking, for it clearly separated the brand from the product and made it the "source" of the product – a living source.

The brand identity prism

Extending Seguela's approach, the "brand identity prism" (Kapferer, 1991, 1998) recognizes six facets of a brand – six leverages of added value. Two of them capitalize on Seguela's legacy, and stress (i) the "physical facet" and (ii) the "personality facet" of the brand. However, the brand identity prism also emphasizes (iii) the "relationship facet" and (iv) the "cultural facet" of the brand. Finally, the last two facets are the (v) "customer reflection" and (vi) the "customers' self concept." It is not our purpose here to fully describe this tool of diagnosis and decision, but rather, to analyze in-depth some of those facets most relevant to the question of the link between organizational and brand identity.

The third facet, the relationship facet, is particularly important for service brands and corporate brands. Engaging in specific transactional modes, corporations are in permanent interaction with their environment. Some act like teachers, others like partners or friends. Some of them dominate, or like to lead. Naturally, the same holds true with service brands, whose added value is precisely an interaction, a relationship. Product brands, however, can also have a distinctive relational facet, as is exemplified by Nike's "just do it" slogan, which explicitly states the nature of the brand's relational facet. Nike stimulates, acts like a sting.

The cultural facet digs deeply into the cultural underpinnings of the brand's mission and vision. It is based on the assumption that all strong brands are based on values (end goals worth thriving for, according to M. Rokeach). For instance, behind the Amex brand there is a hymn to modern and triumphant capitalism. Its symbols are a centurion and the dollar. The centurion represents a warrior for modern economic competition and warfare, whereas money, and in particular the dollar, is held as the yardstick of value, that is to say, of a person's value. Visa is based on an entirely different vision of the world, as its name indicates. A visa is a door opener, an agent of fluidity of exchanges, travels. Visa is in an open world, without frontiers.

Certainly, not all companies or brand executives are aware of these underpinnings, emitted meanings and deep truths. Often, they continue to believe that the brand is only a name that represents a product's specific performance. They believe Amex stands for a number of specific services in restaurants, hotels, auto rental companies, and so forth. Amex is much more than that – it is an ideology. It is a zealous priest of the dollar religion. Today, the mantra of modern marketing is "bond the clients," "create loyalty," both internally and externally. However, one should be aware that the roots of this brand attachment are rarely found in the physique (i.e., the performance facet of the brand). As in enduring marital couples, the intimacy is based on shared values and visions, common commitments. Are suburban kids crazy about Nike because of the quality and originality of its ever changing shoes? Or do they simply worship Nike because of what it does to them (i.e., the relationship facet of the brand identity prism) and because they can identify with the Nike values (i.e., the cultural facet of the brand)?

These facets define brand identity, that is, the long-term meaning of the brand, its intrinsic difference, its coherence through time, its reason for being, its own personal truth, the key values it wants to fight for. A product may have a specific performance. The brand puts it in perspective with the organization's value system; the product's performance thus seems to be an output of this value system. The brand identity prism is programmatic: it communicates the purported identity. What is the brand trying to do with the market (relationship)? What is it trying to contribute (physique)? By what kind of end values is it motivated (culture)? Brand identity signals the limits of a management obsessed by image or by "reputation" (Fombrun, 1996), the modern buzz word replacing "image management" in corporate circles. As former L'Oreal CEO, F. Dalle once said: "I do not measure the image of my brands, for such studies just tell me nothing. Consumers only play back what we had said ourselves to them." As previously stated, image is on the reception side of the communication interaction, whereas identity is on the emission side. In the modern international world, a single brand may have different images in different cultures or countries. If this is the case, how then can brands be managed? Either by specific and local programs or by choosing one specific image. In contrast, by focusing on identity, one takes a different stance on these issues. Instead of painstakingly attempting to match images of the brand to different markets around the world, one considers that the brand is unique, with but one identity and but one truth.

Certainly, when one creates a product brand, one enjoys a wide degree of freedom. In the target market, the clients are king and the brand will seek to maximize their satisfaction through a specific blend of material and immaterial values. However, through time and the steady mental sedimentation of experiences, images and feelings, a brand-extended meaning slowly accrues in clients' collective memory, and therefore, in the market. Over time, then, like cement, many degrees of freedom are lost, as the brand becomes locked-in, attached to specific meanings in the clients' long-term memory. Soon, the brand can no longer turn its back on this instilled meaning; it can no longer shy away from its emerging *attributed* identity. What is true for any brand is *a fortiori* even truer for a brand based on an organization with its own culture, personality, and style. This is typically the case with corporate brands.

The modern emphasis on the old concept of "reputation," which takes the goal of corporate communications to be that of maximizing the corporation's reputation, is a close parent to the former emphasis on image. The corporation's obsession is to maintain a good reputation, with no one badmouthing it. However, the obsession with reputation and reputation-based management is clearly a dead-end street for management. It leads to conformism and provokes the fear of taking bold stances on key issues. They erode identities. Reputation management as an extraverted obsession is too outward oriented – in practice, it means that one is willing to please all stakeholders, even by expressing conflicting positions. Instead, in our view, identity fixes the locus of the corporation's energy and action on itself; its goals and its missions are under the auspices of its very personal values, irrespective of whether they are shared by everyone outside the organization. Strong brands can be compared to religions. Let us remember that all religions started by promoting a value system that was at odds with the one existing at the time. All religions were initially perceived as being deviant, and had bad reputations. However, they created proselytes and developed into what they are now. If they had been obsessed with reputation management, they never would have thrived.

Thus far, we have revealed how management thinking, prompted by European schools of thought, has integrated the concept of identity in brand management as a substitute for that of image building. We have also showed that so-called "reputation management" is a modern avatar of image-driven brand management, and leads to a management style that is detrimental to the building of a corporate brand identity. In the next section, we focus more specifically on corporate brands.

From company to corporate brand

In this section, we show how companies discovered that they are also brands, or "corporate" brands. (This term has gained a greater international recognition than its exact equivalent, "company brand.") Why is it so, and what are the implications of this discovery?

For most companies, especially those engaged in business-to-business activities, branding issues seem remote, or merely tactical. Executives generally believe branding deals with product or service brands, that is, names that have gained recognition thanks to a specific registered trademark, extended communication efforts, and distribution. These executives have a simple, dichotomous view, with the corporation on one side, and the commercial field of products and brands on the other. Consequently, speaking of "corporate brand," or even more so of "branding the corporation," may seem odd, or in any case, very unclear to many executives. Let us clarify these issues.

Companies often think of themselves as mere companies, corporations, or bodies (the English word "corporation" stems from the Latin word *corpus*, meaning body). They forget that we live in an age of communication and widespread diffusion of economic information to the public at large, and not only to a small group of expert analysts or buyers. In this context, companies become known, at least by their names, to which will be steadily attached chunks of information found, heard, and memorized here and there. In fact, most people have no direct first-hand experience or relationship with the corporation and its living parts or bodies: they have never seen the plants, the headquarters, the CEO, the Executive Committee, or the employees. They only see its productions and its communications in all their forms. They hear about a profit warning, of a product recall, or of a strike. They catch hearsay about working wages, labor conditions, or atmosphere. They read about the company's ethical conducts, etc. As a result, the brand is the corporation's visible profile.

For many executives, then, the corporate brand will often be reduced to its "marque" (the actual set of signs by which it is represented), a visible facet of the corporation that aims to identify with it. By identification, we mean that this sign must meet certain criteria:

- it should be easily recognized, both internally and externally;
- it should be attributed uniquely to that company;
- it should become associated with key attributes and values that position the company as a nonsubstitutable partner in all the markets in which it competes – the market for products and services, the market for employment, the market for financial investments, etc.;
- it should foster employees' identification with the company, and similarly, prospective clients' desire to interact with the company, that is, the brand should be inspirational.

The corporation uses a marque to convey some aspects of its identity, and a name to convey others. Now, as we shall see, the brand cannot be reduced to its graphic and nominal vehicles. To paraphrase a famous saying, the word dog does not bite. The corporate brand is in fact the corporation's profile that has been, purposively or not, diffused and has achieved significant recognition.

This profile may be inherited, if it is not managed. As a strategic lever for growth, it should be managed. Its goal is to *symbolize the contract* passed between the corporation and its audiences and markets. Basically, the corporate brand should identify the added values, either material or immaterial, that it intends to deliver. How does it do it? With what tools?

From company legal names to corporate brand names

What are the vehicles used by the brand to express a corporation's values and identity? What relationship is there between the brand, the company name, and the "marque" itself (the set of signs: symbols, logos, etc.)? There is a clear distinction between the brand and the company (legal) name. The company name obeys the necessities defined by the law and the legal identity of the organization and its shareholders. It refers to a tangible reality. The brand name obeys the rules of the information economy, that is, that it should encapsulate and communicate rapidly key differentiating dimensions to the relevant targets. It need not be the mirror of the organization, but its identification sign in auditory, and, as we shall see, in visual terms. However, as the brand tries to encapsulate the corporation's strengths and added values, there is a structural tendency to contract the corporation's name in order to make it suitable for branding purposes. For example, Elf Aquitaine Corporation's brand was simply Elf. Many companies, such as Sema Group, have selected a (legal) name to describe their specific organization and structure. Sema Group's name was a reflection of its organizational structure, as it was known as a group. This type of legal name may be kept for legal reasons or merely for billing purposes. However, the clients had already "branded" that corporation, by speaking of it simply as "Sema." Indeed, it is the vocation of brands to symbolize the contract passed between the corporation and its many publics, and not to mirror its internal structure. As a result, brand names tend to be a contracted version of the company's legal name, as they are easier to memorize and have a stronger impact.

Brands and trademarks

A brand needs a number of supports to convey and store its message. It will make use of a visual template, called the trademark, that encompasses, in a fixed and invariable way, a name, a logo-type, colors, graphics, and eventually, a symbol (often referred to by designers as the "marque," before lawyers intervened to make it "a trademark," a proprietary asset). Naturally, the trademark is an important brand property (both legally and in stakeholders' minds). The trademark will itself convey some aspects of the meaning the corporation wants to create in its customers' and stakeholders' minds. The key questions for the corporation then become: What values and impressions does the visual symbol convey about the company? Are these values in line with the future brand platform? Is the symbol a good vehicle for expressing the identity and values of the organization? Does the symbol have a built-in emotional value, a high symbolic voltage? Is it unique and attractive? For instance, BT, formerly British Telecom, has selected a flute player as the visual symbol of its brand because it conveys humanitarian values, softness, harmony, and pleasure. However, it says nothing about BT's other dimensions, such as its unique expertise, its customer orientation, etc. This is normal, for a simple sign cannot by itself convey the corporation's entire profile. For this reason, communication is needed to associate these other dimensions with the trademark. This can be done through advertising, PR, press relationships, sponsoring of activities such as the Olympics or the local football team, and naturally, also through the interaction with all of the corporation's agents at all hierarchical levels. Having clarified the conceptual distinction between the company and the brand, and between the brand and its vehicles, in the next section, we introduce a conceptual tool central to the management of brands – the brand platform.

Building the corporate brand

Building a corporate brand is a complex task. First, one needs to define clearly the brand's meaning for tomorrow: What is the contract that the brand wishes to forge with its targeted audiences? This contract can be summarized in a single-page document known as the "brand platform." A typical brand platform asks six questions, listed in Figure 9.1.

Such questions can be answered for any brand, even FMCG (Fast Moving Consumer Goods) brands, from Signal to Kleenex. However, when working on a corporate brand, unlike product brands, which are a virtual reality, we are speaking of a true body, a living system and organization. Branding is about shaping the company's profile for the purposes of communicating and influencing audiences. Branding is intimately linked to the vision of extended competition and the need to persuade, at distance, people who may, tomorrow or in future years, be voting for or against the company, as buyers, bankers, or employees.

THE BRAND PLATFORM

What are the brand's foundations and its heritage?

What is unique about the brand?

What is the brand's personality?

What are the brand's values?

What is the brand's mission?

What is the brand's positioning versus that of its competition?

Figure 9.1 The brand platform.

The brand platform is a medium-term engagement with consistency, most useful in decentralized global companies. It defines what the brand will say about the corporation's profile and its implicit contract, that is, the customer value it must deliver at all levels of the company and at all points of contact with the environment (clients, suppliers, journalists, bankers and analysts, employees, students likely to be attracted professionally). This is why corporate brand platforms cannot be invented from the outside or by external consultants alone. More than any other type of brand, the corporate brand's truths must originate from within the company. Management must dig into the organization to find its truths and purposes. In other words, building the brand platform requires that the brand identity be unveiled. We now turn our attention to this self-exploration process.

Inferring the brand identity

Experience indicates that direct questioning is not the most effective means of eliciting the responses that the brand platform requires. For instance, typical answers to questions about the values that the brand symbolizes include: customer respect, customer satisfaction, reactivity, quality, humanity, group cohesiveness, etc. These qualities are all the idealized virtues of the model organization. However, while it is extremely useful for any organization to try to please its clients beyond simple satisfaction or to pursue a high standard of quality, these virtues are not very useful as statements for the purpose of identity. They define the conditions for remaining in the market, for still being able to compete in markets where the basic standards are continually rising. These virtues or qualities lack any differentiation potential. This is why they are useful benchmarks in terms of output and processes for an organization. However, these measures tell nothing about the brand's specific "contract." This is why brand identity, the inner self of the brand, its motivating system, and genetic program are to be inferred and not simply asked. If a brand has an identity, it should have been revealed over time and through consistent signs given in its behavior and productions, be they material (products for instance) or immaterial (communications). The task of making a brand identity, and *a fortiori* a corporate brand identity, explicit requires three major steps, which we will now discuss.

Step one: "brand archeology"

We call the first step in uncovering brand identity "brand archeology." Identity refers to something that exists from the start, something that is almost in the genes. Therefore, when investigating the organization's early days around the time of the corporate brand's birth, traces of the identity should already be present. Hints of the identity can be found in the personalities of the organization's founding fathers, their inspiration, personal, educational, and professional backgrounds, their values, and even their religion. It is interesting to know, for instance, that traditionally, the Peugeot family is Protestant. This essential differentiating facet of the family, still in power today, could not but have a long-lasting influence, certainly on the way the Peugeot organization was managed throughout an entire century, but also on the specific nature of its productions (Kapferer and Gaston-Breton, 2001, 2002). Exploring the name initially chosen for the organization is also part of this archeological task, for the name remains an active symbol of what the creators had in mind, either implicitly or explicitly. For instance, not just any organization in the high-tech market would have chosen to call itself Apple. In this market, all other names seem to have been simply inherited or are apparently descriptive, often being the creators' family names or the main location of the business (e.g., Texas Instruments). It is important to remember that markets decode names, not as a notary would, but as messages, or purposive decisions that are meant to convey a specific and important message. Each name has a potential latent symbolic meaning that, through lack of any other information, exerts some influence on the molding of the organization's profile. "British Tele-com," meaning Telecommunications for Britain, was simply a description of a monopoly, just like the names of all former telecom monopolies (Belgacom, France Telecom, Telecom Italia, Telecom Argentina, etc.). However, in an era of deregulation and open frontiers, the symbolic meaning of nations is very different in the home country compared to beyond its borders. This is why either this name is maintained, which in practice means that its latent connotation is kept alive, or it is changed. Finally, another part of the archeological work should consist of analyzing all the communications support from the founding era: annual reports, President's speeches, advertisements, etc. The goal is to unveil the founding fathers' sources of inspiration and their hidden values.

Step two: unveiling the brand's organizational foundations

The second part of the task of understanding a brand's identity involves analyzing how the organization's structure produces the dimension of brand identity through a set of differentiating behaviors relevant to the market. After all, unlike simple product brands that have no "hinterland," corporate brands are based on an active organization, a living system with a formal structure, a culture and specific values that strongly affect its internal and external functioning. Now, let us not be misunderstood: there is a difference between identifying a company's culture and identity and identifying a brand's culture and identity. The former relates to the internal processes and behaviors (i.e., the *manifested* organizational identity) while the latter is outward oriented (i.e., the *projected* organizational identity). Certainly, since the brand's products are ultimately made by the corporation, there must be some link between the two. However, they are not synonymous. For instance, hired to help define the Salomon brand identity and its differentiating values, we discovered that somewhat parallel work was being conducted on the company's culture and identity. These two endeavors, though, yielded two different results, for they were not oriented toward the same goals. Markets are not aware of what happens inside organizations; they experience only its externalized deeds and productions, its projections. To clarify this point, it is useful to refer to Soenen and Moingeon's (2002) five-facet framework, which draws a distinction between the *manifested* identity and the *projected* identity. The corporate brand identity is closely related to the *projected* identity. However, in order to establish a sound identity for the corporate brand, one must also consider the *manifested* identity. Indeed, *manifested* identity (i.e., the enduring and central features of an organization's structures and processes) exerts a profound influence on the company's ability to establish and sustain its contract with its many audiences.

Step three: analysis of symbolic productions

The third part of the task consists of an analysis of the corporation's most symbolic productions, those that have left a long-lasting mark on people's minds, in other words the "landmarks" that are characteristic of the identity *attributed* to the organization. That these productions are still remembered tells the brand analyst that they are living ashes, with fire and emotion still attached to them. For instance, Citroën's most symbolic productions are not its recent best-selling cars, but the unique DS, SM, 2CV, and the "Croisière Jaune," a famous cruise from Paris to Peking at the turn of the last century. These symbolic productions are the genes of the Citroën brand. Whether or not the Citroën corporation is still able to meet the challenge of keeping up with this former brand identity is another story, for the conditions of competition in the automotive industry have drastically changed.

Clearly, not all productions need to be analyzed and their implicit meanings exhumed and made explicit. Only those considered to be very representative, that is, only what cognitive psychologists (Rosch and Lloyd, 1978) would call the "best exemplars of the concept" or "prototypes of the concept" (the concept here being the brand) need be evaluated. Who decides what is a best exemplar? – the markets. Have these productions left an enduring memory? A positive answer would indicate that they have strongly marked the brand's collective perception and played a structuring role in the brand's meaning. It is also interesting to analyze productions that, internally, are considered to be the most symbolic, the ones of which employees are most proud. For instance, Sema, formerly Sema Group, still remembers with emotion what the Royal Navy Chief Commander once said to P. Bonnelli, former Sema CEO: had the Royal Fleet been equipped with Sema's information technology and customized software, it would not have lost its famous warship, which was hit by an Exocet missile during the Malvinas war with Argentina. Sema's specialized software would have immediately acted to prevent the fatal shock between the vessel and the missile. Information is critical to a mission.

Links between brand and organizational identity

The corporate brand sketches the organization's external profile. This is not an idle task, as it aims to create value in the eyes of the receivers, be they buyers, investors, potential staff members, young MBAs, bankers, trade unionists, political figures, or the layman. The use of the word "brand identity" stresses modern brand management's recognition that truth is a basic long-term success factor. A brand identity must be true. One should remain oneself. Actually, very few brands know who they are. While scores of marketing researchers highlight how these brands are perceived, by country, by type of respondent, they seem to ignore the brands' roots, their inner value and what makes them so unique. This is especially true for corporate brands for the two reasons previously discussed. First, executives have not given serious consideration to corporate brands until recently. Second, they have been trained for the most part with image or reputation concepts, not brand identity.

It would be interesting at this point in the chapter to give some examples of the link between brand identity (i.e., *projected* identity) and organizational identity (both *manifested* and *experienced*). We will first compare Renault and Peugeot, two generalist automakers originating from the same country, France. We shall then consider two cases in the service industry.

Renault

At the roots of Renault (the commercial brand) one finds such symbolic automobiles as the small 4CV or the mythical 4L, the Dauphine (the spearhead of Renault's first launch in the US), the Twingo, etc. Interestingly, although Renault has always produced large automobiles, which often outsold Citroën's or Peugeot's, they were not "marking." The Renault brand is very much associated with small, excellent, practical, and reliable autos with a lot of personality. Certainly, in mere quantitative terms, the company has sold many more small autos than larger ones.

In the years following World War II, as Europe was being rebuilt, people bought smaller automobiles because they were all they could afford. Like Volkswagen (whose name means literally "the automobile of the people"), Renault, once nationalized, became a prominent actor in the rebuilding of the nation by providing to the masses an auto they could afford. In fact, Renault's social dimension – being not only state-owned but also state-managed – had become well-known and even became a part of its product brand identity. Renault autos have never been show-off. Even the larger ones at the top of range, albeit their quality is excellent, remained very discrete in design, as if they purposely did not want to revive the dormant class struggle that was always on the verge of rising to the surface again. Once a wholly publicly-owned company, Renault was, for forty years, an ideal testing ground for trade unions' social experiments. These trade unions have historically held power in the company and they still do today. Interestingly, the social motives behind the historical nationalization of Renault had permeated into its product range up until the 1990s, that is, into the design of its automobiles. As a consequence, the corporate brand is still influenced by the memory of its productions, of the overwhelming power of the trade unions, and of the frequent strikes, most politically motivated. The brand is what remains imprinted in people's minds as a result of purposeful actions, but also because of unintentional behavior and direct experience.

The nature of Renault's CEOs, typically top-notch civil servants parachuted from their government seats to be executives of the state-owned company, has also strongly marked the corporate brand. Louis Schweitzer, the present CEO, is a paragon of such a destiny. It is also interesting to notice that the decision to be strongly present in the challenging and very costly Formula 1 motorsport competition was mostly geared toward building the corporate brand in order to reveal the true nature of the modern Renault. Renault's own market research has indicated that its participation, although extremely successful, produced no effect on the product brand image itself. However, it has had a definite impact on the perception of the corporation itself among many circles worldwide. Renault's successes in Formula 1 have resulted in a new corporate identity trait, dynamism, being attributed to the corporate brand by key audiences. Sponsorship of Formula 1 somehow indicated that the Renault organization had itself changed.

It is very interesting to speculate on the likely effect of Renault's prospective future CEO (i.e., official candidate), Carlos Ghosn. This exceptional international executive has made his reputation by worshipping exclusively the production of value, and by being indifferent to eventually laying off thousands of employees (as he did in Brazil and Japan as co-CEO of Nissan) or hiring thousands of them back again when the tide is up. Such behavior deviates so markedly from Renault's *manifested* identity that the nomination of Carlos Ghosn, notwithstanding the quality of his contribution, would mean that Renault would no longer be Renault. Or, to be more precise, it would signify that a new Renault had been born. It would be a Renault much more international in orientation, not so much in its commercial scope, but in its managerial culture. In short, Ghosn would probably manage Renault as would Jack Welch or Jack Nasser. What, then, would be left of Renault's organizational identity? Can Carlos Ghosn integrate with Renault's identity? The second question is tied to that of the Renault–Nissan corporate brand. In the future, the real living and producing body, the manufacturer, will be Renault–Nissan. Renault and Nissan themselves may become mere commercial brands. This will create the need to specify what the Renault–Nissan corporate brand should represent for its future collaborators, investors, suppliers, social analysts, and buyers. This requires that the Renault–Nissan identity be explored.

Peugeot

The story of Peugeot is completely different (Kapferer and Gaston-Breton, 2001). Like the Toyota family in Japan, the Peugeot family has always held the reins of the company, even if it has traditionally delegated the role of CEO to an external person hired for his exceptional qualities and his timely arrival. The family's values are well known. Originating in the eastern part of France, close to Germany, Peugeot values hard work, quality, rigor, effort, discipline, respect for order and hierarchy. The Peugeot family has always been very discrete and prefers to hide from the media spotlight. Interestingly, the Peugeot automobile brand has always reflected the family's personality. This is a clear case of identity transfer. Historically, Peugeot autos, unlike Renault's, have been praised for their quality, largely due to the company's unique know-how and its exclusive focus on mechanics and structure as key elements of an auto's performance. As a result, Peugeot's automobiles have gained a mythical reputation for durability, becoming renowned as the manufacturer of the best vehicles for those living in the Sahara desert (that was before the fashion for the 4WD). Peugeot's mechanical know-how also endowed their autos with an exceptional capacity to stay on the road almost indefinitely. On the other hand, until recently, their design, external appearance, and equipment were below par and inferior to those of their competitors. It was a sign that the organizational identity – both at the manifestation and representation levels – rewarded certain qualities (e.g., those linked to the very essence of automobile manufacturing), but not others (e.g., those associated with all that makes life in an automobile more pleasant and its look more fashionable). This is why Peugeot regularly hired an external agency, the classic Italian designer, Pininfarina, to design its convertibles. One cannot survive in the modern competitive arena, though, without listening to the markets. In 1995, at a time when sales were leveling off and employee morale was low, the company undertook with the author a major project on brand identity. The intention was not to exhume the brand's past deeds nor to celebrate its former glory, for example, the famous 205 auto-mobile. Rather, the project sought to define what the new brand identity would need to be to make Peugeot successful, at least on a European scale. What were the three or four key values the brand should now represent that would influence the future nature of its autos: the type and level of services, the design, etc.?

Naturally, the concept of identity reminds us that truth resides in oneself. A brand cannot borrow or import values. It must change while at the same time respecting some key facets of its former identity, those that are part of its kernel, without which the brand would not be itself, but instead, a homonym brand. Interestingly, insofar as the corporate brand is concerned, hiring an external CEO can strongly affect the brand's profile. Jacques Calvet was hired at a time when Peugeot was facing financial difficulties. A financier was needed. Coming from the BNP bank, Jacques Calvet was the executive the company was expecting. He recreated the conditions necessary for sound finance and success. A man of character, J. Calvet did not hesitate to voice overt criticism of automotive issues, which in fact were virtually political issues, for they concerned French state policies, or even European policies. For instance, he denounced the opening of the European market to Japanese automobiles without any reciprocal agreements in Japan. Consequently, he was perceived, mistakenly, as a conservative manager, promoting rather old-fashioned views (however justified they were). At a time when the Peugeot automobile brand had not yet undergone its internal mutation, and was there-fore still viewed as being not very innovative, the frequently broadcasted presence of the PSA (Peugeot Citroen Group) CEO expressing strong views on what the government should or should not be doing reinforced the impression many people had of the corporation's conservatism. This conservatism was exemplified by the very dull nature of the automobiles that PSA manufact-ured, despite their undisputed mechanical qualities.

The service industry

The service industry is another good example of the relationship between organizational identity, both *manifested* and *experienced*, and brand identity. Let us examine briefly two cases: a multiple retailer and a bank.

France's distribution system is characterized by the overwhelming – some would say exaggerated – power of its hypermarkets and supermarkets. Intermarché is one of the leaders in food and drug distribution. In organiza-tional terms, it is a voluntary associative chain of independent store owners, typically, self-made people having created their own businesses in the distri-bution of FMCG brands and products. They are all successful and have become rich as a result of their efforts made under the collective brand and organi-zation called Intermarché. Intermarché's differentiating attribute, as far as its structure and organization are concerned, is its associative status, unlike Carrefour, one of its competitors, which owns its stores. Interestingly, on the consumer side, Intermarché has, for a long time, adopted a nickname in all its communications: the "musketeers of distribution." The basic brand value is fighting in consumers' interests through the reduction of store prices, con-fronting manufacturers, and using vertical integration to itself produce at low cost those items for which no top quality manufacturer can be found at a specific price level. For instance, Intermarché has its own fishermen and fisheries. The musketeers, the brand's symbolic character, are intimately linked to Intermarché's very specific organizational identity. Historically, musketeers were a group of warriors with etiquette and panache, who voluntarily joined forces to serve their king, who at that time was the symbol of the nation. In like manner, the independent owners of each Intermarché supermarket have joined forces in the interests of the nation's buying power and the people's standard of living. That this symbolism has lasted for more than twenty years reveals that it is a deep source of identification internally. Externally, it encapsulates a number of values that indefectibly attract, seduce, and involve consumers who feel their interests to be defended by Intermarché. Most importantly, these values are true, for Intermarché is indeed a discount store. We can see, then, that for Intermarché, strong similarities exist between the brand identity and the organization's inner identity.

Another example of this relationship between organization and brand identity can be found in the case of Credit Mutuel. This bank is an actor in the segment of co-operative banks, characterized by the very specific nature of their organizational links and internal functioning. Unlike classic banks, the co-operative system allows, in theory at least, clients to participate in the bank's life, and eventually, to be elected to executive posts. In a way, a co-operative is a bank by the people for the people. Of course, the need to provide professional services to clients and the technical aspects of modern finance preclude the possibility of this kind of participation from becoming reality. However, the spirit remains. In such banks, there reigns a different atmosphere, even if in terms of services, they are on a par with the so-called "big ones." A project undertaken with the author on The Credit Mutuel's identity as a banking brand led to a recognition that the company's organizational specificity was the real differentiating source for the brand identity. To summarize, "nomen est omen" says the proverb: a company that calls itself "mutual credit" must live up to the expectations this name creates, both internally and externally. Not only is this name unique and specific, but it also evokes a set of benefits for customers, benefits that are highly praised by those refusing the classic banks. The identity's pivot was indeed in the brand name itself: "mutuel" is a very involving proposition, a relationship statement of a very specific nature. One recalls that "relationship" is one of the six facets of the identity prism of any brand, a facet particularly important for service brands. As a result, a new footline for all the advertisements and commercial documents was added: "A bank to whom you can speak." Clearly, it stressed the very open nature of this organization, its essence being the collaboration between people, as indicated by its name, Credit Mutuel. The word "credit," too, carries with it strong connotations. It has two meanings. The first, explicit, refers to lending money. The second meaning, implicit, refers to the underlying trust, a trust which, in this case, is reciprocal, mutual.

Conclusion

A study of the development of concepts and methods in brand management, and especially in corporate branding, leads to a major discovery: one cannot help but notice a convergence of tools between strategy and branding. The classical corporate strategy concepts of vision, mission, ambition, goal, values, etc., have been used for more than fifteen years to establish a sound platform for regular brands, even noncorporate ones. Brands need energy to compete. The key source of energy is knowing why they compete and for what cause. Reciprocally, organizations have understood that they have a symbolic dimension even for audiences who will never interact directly with either the organization or its representatives. The brand is the loudspeaker to herald what the company wants to stand for. As a result, the concept of identity has become of the utmost importance and has made the notion of image and its modern wording (reputation) seem less important.

Our exploration of identity issues in corporate branding leads us to reflect on the five-facet model presented in the introductory chapter of this volume. We have seen that the concept of brand identity is closely related to the *projected* facet of an organization's identity, notably in the case of corporate brands. The fact that both the brand identity and the *projected* identity stem from the same source, the organization itself, raises a challenging question. We have argued that features constitutive of a corporate brand identity are related to, but not identical with, those constitutive of the corporation's internal identity, that is, what Soenen and Moingeon (2002) refer to as the *manifested* identity. A corporate brand exists essentially in relation to external audiences, whereas an organization's *manifested* identity encompasses the results of all the corporation's interactions with all its constituencies and all its audiences over time. On the other hand, the five-facet model posits a systemic relationship between the different facets of an organization's identity. We have provided several examples of identity transfers (Renault, Peugeot, Intermarché, Credit Mutuel), between, on the one hand, the *manifested* and *experienced* identity, and on the other hand, the corporate brand identity/ *projected* identity. These examples actually reveal something more: that the existence of such a close connection between the organization's *manifested* identity and the identity it projects through its corporate brand is a sign of good health, a source of strength.

Divergence between identity facets can result in the often cited "mirror effect" (Dutton and Dukerich, 1991; Moingeon and Ramanantsoa, 1997). Our contribution reinforces the idea that the different facets of an organization's identity should be in harmony, but that the introduction of corporate brand identity complicates the issue of harmony. It is likely that the more open, networked, and decentralized an organization is, the greater the tensions, and hence, the threats to the harmony between the various facets of identity. The challenge for corporate branding is therefore as follows: corporate brands should be grounded in the brand's identity, which symbolizes the contract that ties the brand to its clients. This brand identity should be allowed to somehow differ from the organization's internal identity, that is, from the central and distinctive features both manifested historically in the organization's structure and processes and those *experienced* by organizational members. However, the corporate brand identity should not differ too much otherwise two negative consequences would ensue. First, a negative mirror effect may kick in and create internal tensions within the company. For instance, at the present time, too large a gap exists between the values attached to the Citroën name and the current internal identity. This internal identity is too constrained to liberate employees' and executives' creative energies – energy that is needed to help Citroën re-become the creative brand it once was in the not-so-distant past. Second, the brand may actually be promising things it cannot keep. For a corporate brand, upholding the contract with the client necessitates staying roughly in line with the *manifested* organizational identity. Between these two extremes, a balance must be found. This balance can only be discovered by looking within oneself. Brand management certainly remains much of an art.

References

Aaker, D. (1991) *Managing brand equity*, New York: Free Press.

Aaker, D. and Biel, A. L. (1993) *Brand equity and advertising*, Mahwah, NJ: Lawrence Erlbaum Associates.

Dutton, J. E. and Dukerich, J. M. (1991) "Keeping an eye on the mirror: image and identity in organizational adaptation," *Academy of Management Journal*, 34: 517–54.

Fombrun, C. (1996) *Reputation: realizing value from the corporate image*, Cambridge, MA: Harvard Business School Press.

Kapferer, J.-N. (1991) *Strategic brand management,* 1st edition, London and New York: Kogan Page.

Kapferer, J.-N. (1998) *Strategic brand management*, 2nd edition, London and New York: Kogan Page.

Kapferer, J.-N. (2001) *Re-inventing the brand*, London: Kogan Page.

Kapferer, P. and Gaston-Breton, T. (2001) *Peugeot: une griffe automobile*, Paris: Le Cherche Midi.

Kapferer, P. and Gaston-Breton, T. (2002) *The Peugeot saga*, Paris: Le Cherche Midi.

Larçon, L. and Reitter, R. (1979) *Structure de pouvoir et identité de l'entreprise*, Paris: Nathan.

Larçon, L. and Reitter, R. (1984) "Corporate imagery and corporate identity," in M. Kets de Vries (ed.) *The irrational executive*, Madison, CT: International Universities Press.

Macrae, C. (1996) *The brand chartering handbook*, London: Addison Wesley.

Moingeon, B. and Ramanantsoa, B. (1997), "Understanding corporate identity: the French school of thought," *European Journal of Marketing*, 31(5/6): 383–95.

Olins, W. (1978) *The corporate personality: an inquiry into the nature of corporate identity*, London: Thames & Hudson.

Olins, W. (1989) *Corporate identity: making business strategy visible through design*, London: Thames & Hudson.

Rosch, E. and Lloyd, B. (1978) *Cognition and categorization*, New Jersey: LEA.

Seguela, J. (1982) *Hollywood lave plus blanc*, Paris: Flammarion.

Soenen, G. and Moingeon, B. (2002) "The five facets of collective identities: integrating corporate and organizational identity," in B. Moingeon and G. Soenen (eds) *Corporate and organizational identities – integrating strategy, marketing, communication, and organizational perspectives*, London: Routledge.

Upshaw, L. P. (1995) *Building brand identity*, New York: John Wiley & Sons.

Index

Note: "n." after a page reference indicates the number of a note on that page.

DATE DUE

FEB 0 8 2004

BRODART Cat. No. 23-221